CONTENTS

INTRODUCTION   1

Chapter 1: What is Science?   13

Consider how you define science as a discipline. You may find that it is easier to describe than to define. Science is not simply the "study of the world," but is an endeavor consisting of three interrelated aspects, a body of knowledge, a set of methods and processes through which this knowledge is produced, and a way of knowing or understanding reality.

PART 1: OBSERVATION, INFERENCE AND THE NATURE OF SCIENCE

Chapter 2: Observation in Science – More Than Just Seeing Things!   22

Students participate in several activities designed to emphasize the critical role that observation and empirical evidence play in the development of scientific knowledge. In addition to defining observations and practicing their observation skills, students are challenged to consider how science ultimately depends on evidence to support its claims.

Chapter 3: Observation or Inference: A "Burning" Question   36

In this discrepant event activity, students record observations of a burning "candle," many of which turn out to be inferences. Then the teacher eats the candle, revealing it to be something other than what it appeared! The point of this lesson is to emphasize the role inferences play in constructing knowledge, in general, and scientific knowledge, in particular.

Chapter 4: Humor Is in the Mind of the Beholder   45

In this activity students construct lists of observations and inferences from comic strips. In the process, they hone their skills in distinguishing observations from inferences. Additionally, they further refine their understanding of the role of observation and inference in the construction of scientific knowledge. Next, students apply their understanding of observation and inference to the development of scientific knowledge as they explore the question "How do we know . . . ?" for a set of key science concepts and discoveries.

Chapter 5: The "Proof" Is in the Cookie   63

Everyone likes to eat, so this activity will appeal to both elementary and middle school students. The teacher presents students with spherical "mystery cookies" and challenges them to determine what secret ingredient lies at the center of each one. Students are given "probes" (toothpicks) to explore the shape, hardness, and other physical characteristics of the cookies and of the mystery objects contained within. Later, they are permitted to eat the cookies and can add taste and texture to their observations. At no time are they allowed to "open up" the cookie to see directly what's inside. The activity gives students excellent opportunities to practice making observations and inferences and can be used to teach that observations may be based on senses other than sight.

history of
structure of atom

Chapter 6: Trailing Fossil Tracks   72

Students develop a story to explain patterns of fossil footprints revealed on an overhead projector. Their stories change as the teacher reveals more of the footprint-containing strata. This inquiry activity provides further practice making observations and inferences and helps students distinguish between the two process skills. The nature of science is addressed as students relate the changes they make to their inferences and the way scientists change their explanations as new data become available.

Chapter 7: Fragmented Fossil Tales   81

In this activity, students are challenged to reconsider "the scientific method" after they complete an inquiry activity involving pieces of fossils. In the process, they practice their observation and inference skills as they attempt to reconstruct prehistoric organisms from fossil fragments. In regard to the nature of science, the lesson focuses on the roles of creativity and background knowledge in the development of scientific knowledge. Additionally, students revisit the concept that scientific knowledge is never absolute as they consider whether they (or scientists) can ever know that the organisms they reconstruct are 100% accurate.

Chapter 8: Of Cannon Balls and Tissue Paper   99

This Web-based, black-box activity focuses on the roles of observation and inference in the development of our understanding of the internal structure of the atom. As part of the lesson, students attempt to discern hidden shapes within a box by observing the flight pattern of projectiles that rebound off the hidden object. After completing the activity, students will discuss how observation and inference permitted them to develop a model of the internal structure of the black box, the characteristics of this model, and the way it relates to the work of scientists and the models they develop.

*Chapter 9: Laying Down the Law   113

In this activity, students learn about scientific laws, in general, and the Law of Superposition, in particular. They examine books placed on a desk and are challenged to devise an inferred chronological list of when the books were read by the teacher, who placed them there one at a time after reading them. After students list the books in terms of when they were probably read, the teacher announces that earlier someone disrupted the pile, thus changing the order. This activity reinforces the idea that scientific laws are not absolute.

Chapter 10: Scientific Theories and the Mystery Tube   124

In this activity, students observe the behavior of strings that are pulled through holes in a tube and infer the internal arrangement of the strings that best explains their behavior. In addition to providing another engaging way to practice observing and inferring, students learn the differences between facts, hypotheses, theories, and laws by creating their own "string theory" and "law of strings."

PART 2: CLASSIFICATION AND THE NATURE OF SCIENCE

*Chapter 11: Patterns, Patterns, Everywhere   142

The activities in this chapter use engaging pattern-seeking games to help students improve their skills at recognizing patterns, while they come to see that pattern-seeking is a goal of science. Students will be challenged to consider the issue of whether patterns in nature are invented or discovered by scientists. This chapter

* with Chris Schnittka

will serve as an introduction to the process skill of classification, since recognizing and applying patterns is at the heart of classification in science.

Chapter 12: Creativity and Constellations   153

Students will create their own constellations from star maps and compare their creations with the patterns created by diverse peoples throughout history. They will see how cultural perspective influences the star patterns people have seen in the sky. This activity will lead to the understanding that creativity and culture, as well as our perspective in time and space, all affect the patterns we see in the sky.

Chapter 13: Classified Information   166

Students will use their observation skills to develop classification schemes for sets of common household objects. Next, they will discuss whether these schemes are based primarily on physical characteristics of the objects (known in taxonomy circles as "artificial" classification), or whether they reflect functional relationships between objects (known as "natural" classification). This discussion will lead to the concepts that inferences (in this case, implied relationships in a classification system) may tell us more about the classifier than the classified.

PART 3: INQUIRY AND THE NATURE OF SCIENCE

*Chapter 14: Experiencing Experiments   180

In this activity, students develop deeper understandings of experiments and scientific inquiry. Not all science activities are inquiry-based, and not all inquiry is experimental, but each type has value in science. In completing the activities in this chapter, students will participate in scientific inquiry by designing and conducting a real experiment on an event that is as easy to do as it is spectacular. In so doing, they will gain a greater appreciation of the role of experimentation in science.

*Chapter 15: Subjectivity and the Boiling Point of Water   188

Working in small groups, students are challenged to determine the boiling point of water as accurately as possible. Students will wind up producing a variety of results, typically ranging from about 95°C to 105°C. The teacher then leads a discussion challenging students to explain the wide range of boiling points, given that these results were all based on careful observational data. Finally, students are asked to consider how scientists arrive at a single accepted value for the boiling point of water, despite having to deal with similarly disparate results.

PART 4: INTERPRETIVE FRAMEWORKS AND THE NATURE OF SCIENCE

Chapter 16: Perception and Conception: Two Sides of the Same Coin   202

Students observe confusing pictures of familiar objects and read ambiguous descriptions of familiar experiences. Students can make little sense of these objects and descriptions until the teacher provides some key hints. These hints provide interpretive frameworks (paradigms) that make the identification of the images and meaning of the passages clear. Students then learn that theories play a similar role in interpreting scientific data—there is seldom a direct line from observation to scientific concept—and that theories provide the context in which much of science is done.

* with Chris Schnittka

Chapter 17: Of Mice, Men, and Scientists   221

In this activity, students learn that observations can be influenced by the context in which they are made. Students in separate classes are asked to observe one of two series of line drawings and then are asked to identify a final, somewhat ambiguous image that could be seen as a man or a mouse. Students will find that the theme of the prior images strongly influences their perception of the final image. This effect is known among psychologists as "perceptual set" and refers to the predisposition to perceive a thing in relation to prior perceptual experiences. When broadly applied to science, students learn that scientists' educational background, training, and prior experience can influence their observations and interpretations of the results of investigations.

Chapter 18: Science as a Way of Knowing   234

Students continue to explore the meaning of science by taking a closer look at what is meant by "science as a way of knowing." Additionally, they compare science to other ways of understanding reality and the human condition. In completing the activity, students learn that we all view the world through a variety of perspectives and that each perspective contributes something unique to our perception of reality. Thus, while science has proven to be one of the most powerful ways we have of understanding the world and learning to manipulate the world for our own purposes, it is not the only lens available for making sense of reality. In fact, there are many critical questions in life that science alone cannot address.

PART 5: WRAPPING UP

Chapter 19: Assessment and the Nature of Science   250

This chapter describes several approaches to assessing student understandings of the nature of science, including formative, summative, informal, and formal. Traditional multiple-choice tests, open-ended questionnaires, and alternative assessments are also addressed. The chapter provides a wide variety of examples of previously developed nature of science assessments to serve as guides for developing your own assessment tools specifically tailored to the needs of your students.

Chapter 20: Conclusion   263

The concluding chapter summarizes what the activities described in this book teach about process skills and the nature of science and discusses a variety of strategies for addressing process skills and the nature of science throughout the school year. It concludes with two cautionary notes. The first concerns the developmental appropriateness of teaching abstract ideas to school-aged children, and the second deals with the consequences of choosing to avoid instruction about the nature of science.

Suggested Readings   272

An annotated bibliography of nature of science-related books, manuscripts, and Web sites is provided as a resource for teachers who wish to expand on their nature of science understandings and instructional activities.

References   275

Index   277

ACTIVITIES

Chapter 2

Magnifying Water Droplets   27
Jelly Belly Tasting Game   27
Blind Meet-a-Tree   28
Texture Scavenger Hunt   29
Smelly Cans   29
Grasshopper Gazing   30
One of a Collection   30
Fascinating Feathers   32
When Is a Worm Not a Worm?   32

Chapter 3

The Burning Candle   37
Crazy Ketchup   40

Chapter 4

Comic Strip Observation and Inference   47
Observing and Inferring Children's Picture
   Books   49

Chapter 5

Mystery Cookies   64
Probing Film Canisters   68

Chapter 6

Fossil Tracks   73

Chapter 7

Fossil Fragments   84

Chapter 8

Mystery Shapes Game   106

Chapter 9

Book Stacking   119

Chapter 10

The Mystery Tube   127
Mystery Cans   136

Chapter 11

Petals Around the Rose   143
Inquiry Cubes   146
Tricky Cards   147

Chapter 12

Creative Constellations   154

Chapter 13

Classifying Everyday Objects   171

Chapter 14

Candy and Soda   183

Chapter 15

Boiling Point of Water Lab   190
Finding the Freezing Point Depression   193

Chapter 16

Ambiguous Images   204
Reading is Fundamental (or Is It)?   207
The Morphing Man   209
Seeing Saturn   211

Chapter 17

Bugelski and Alampay Images   225

Chapter 18

Ways of Knowing   237

[handwritten note] good intro to inquiry labs + designing procedure *[arrow pointing to Chapter 15]*

PREFACE

This book is unlike a typical science activity book. It's not about *what* we know in science, it's about *how* we know in science. It doesn't focus so much on science content, but on the characteristics of scientific knowledge. Science educators would call this a book about the *nature of science*. Philosophers would call this a book about science *epistemology*. Don't fret—that's the last time you will see that word in this book. This book is intended to be accessible to all who teach science, *particularly* those who have never had a philosophy course. I wanted to make the text entertaining, easy to follow, and free of technical jargon and complex arguments.

Second, although the book features descriptions of more than 40 engaging activities designed to help you teach the characteristics, or nature, of science, it is more than a simple collection of activities. Each activity is preceded by a teacher-friendly discussion of background information to help you become comfortable and familiar with the target concepts of the activity. The activities themselves have been designed, selected, and modified to be highly engaging and applicable across a wide range of grade levels and science content. Some of the activities involve stories, some include laboratory exercises, some are hands-on, and others involve technology. Many of the activities may seem familiar at first glance, but on closer scrutiny you'll see that all involve additional material that makes them different (and more useful for teaching the nature of science) than what you have seen before. Every activity is designed to get students to think—not only about what they are doing in class but, more importantly, about how what they do in class relates to the work of scientists.

Organization of This Book

Take a moment to look at the table of contents so that you can familiarize yourself with the book's organization. Following this introduction is a chapter designed to help you organize your instruction so that your students gain a more complete picture of science as a discipline. This chapter differs from the ones that follow in that the activities it describes are more for you, the teacher, than for your students. Consider it an orientation.

Next comes Part 1 of the book, which is divided into ten chapters, each using lessons about the process skills of observation and inference as a springboard into instruction about the nature of science. This section of the book has the most chapters because, as you will see when you read through this section, there is a lot you can teach about the nature of science by starting with observation and inference. Second, observing and inferring are basic process skills that are appropriate for students of all ages. I think you will find the activities in this section to be particularly enjoyable to teach, as well as fun for your students.

The chapters in Part 2 address the process skill of classification through a variety of engaging activities ranging from simple pattern-finding to having students create their own classification schemes. As students explore in-depth lessons about classification, they will learn that there is no single "correct" classification scheme and that all such schemes are created, not discovered, by scientists. Thus classification is a process skill that truly reflects the human element of science.

The two chapters in Part 3 deal with experimentation and measurement. They seek to address the question, "Exactly what is a hypothesis?" and help students understand that scientists often reach different conclusions from the same investigation. Thus, scientific conclusions are often reached through argumentation and consensus, rather than a single "right" answer emerging from a definitive experiment.

Part 4 deals with the process skill of reaching conclusions from experimental data, but with a twist. The activities in this section encourage students to recognize and reflect on the necessity of interpretive frameworks in making sense of data. The activities are designed to (1) introduce the concept that interpretive frameworks are necessary in everyday life and in science investigations, (2) consider some of the strengths and limitations of using interpretive frameworks, and (3) help students view science itself as one of many interpretive frameworks for making sense of the world around us.

The fifth and final section of the book ends with a chapter on assessment and a final recap of the principle ideas the book has addressed. This is followed by Suggested Readings which will serve as a guide in your future explorations of the nature of science.

You will note that no suggested grade levels are given for activities. The main reason for this omission is that the activities in this book are designed to be engaging and appropriate for a wide range of student ages and abilities. For example, although the book is targeted for elementary and middle school students, I have used to good effect the majority of the book's activities, with only slight modifications, in both high school and university settings. Students of all ages love to think outside the box, and that is what good nature of science lessons are designed to encourage students to do.

Although there is no worry that the activities described here are too elementary for older students, you should be aware that students in the early elementary grades may not be developmentally ready for a few of the activities as written. Chapters 9 and 10, which deal with details about scientific theories and laws, may best be reserved for upper elementary and middle school students. The same is true for the activities in Part 4, which address the abstract notion of perceptual frameworks. Even so, these activities can easily be modified to be appropriate for younger children. For example, you could use the activities in chapters 9 and 10 simply to address the relationships among observation, inference, and tentativeness in science, rather than going deeper into the differences between scientific theories and laws. Ultimately, you will be the best judge of whether your students are ready for a particular activity and how best to modify an activity for the needs of your students.

There is no way to cover every facet of the core ideas of the nature of science in one book. I hope, though, that by reading through this book and employing the activities and strategies it illustrates, you will expand your own knowledge of science while making your class more interesting and relevant to your students. This book can serve as a map to guide you and your students' exploration of what science is and what scientific knowledge can (and cannot) do. By using these activities to explore the realm of science, you and your students can begin to see science in a new light—one that is both more interesting and accessible. In so doing, you and your students will gain a more accurate perspective on this exciting endeavor we call science.

ACKNOWLEDGMENTS

Few books are a solo effort and this book is no exception. Although the lessons presented in this book reflect my own approach to nature of science instruction, the root of many of the activities began with others. I am grateful to the science educators whose work I've drawn upon in the development of the lessons in the book. I have tried to acknowledge the original sources of ideas whenever these are known. I apologize in advance for any omissions or mistakes in these efforts.

Thanks to graduate students Doug Toti, Ian Binns, Lara Smetana, and Heather Farquahar, who worked diligently to help me flesh out ideas, proof the text, and complete many of the tedious tasks that go with preparing a manuscript for publication. Special thanks to Chris Schnittka, not only for the artwork that graces these pages, but also for contributing significant portions of text to chapters 9, 11, 14, and 15.

Comments and suggestions from a number of teachers and science educators have helped me make the book more accurate, readable, and practical. I thank Cassi Weathersbee, David Ridenour, Juanita Jo Matkins, Pablo Zatz, and Steve Metz, for their thoughtful contributions and insights that have helped make the book better and reviewers Teresa F. Wilson, Myrtle H. Stevens Elementary School, Jacquelyn Herst, Los Angeles Unified School District/Local District 3, Julie Alexander, Columbia Public Schools, Alyce Surmann, Sembach Middle School, Suzanne Lull, Washington Elementary School, Andrew Gatt, Ravenscroft School, Andrea S. Martine, Warrior Run School District and Carol J. Skousen, Twin Peaks Elementary School.

Thanks to Norm Lederman, whose excellent instruction and guidance started me on the path of exploring the nature of science. I appreciate the hard work of my editor, Kelly Villella Canton, her assistant, Angela Pickard, and the production team at Allyn and Bacon. Their efforts helped transform the ideas for the book into reality.

Thanks to Lynn Bell, whose editing, writing, organizational skills, and encouragement were beyond compare. When the writing is done for the day, it's finding Lynn, Jessi, and Adrianne there for me that makes it all worthwhile. Thanks for the love, smiles, and joy that you give my life.

ABOUT THE AUTHOR

Randy Bell is an Associate Professor of Science Education in the Curry School of Education at the University of Virginia, where he teaches courses in science teaching methods, educational technology, and science education research methods. His educational background includes degrees in Botany, Forest Ecology, and Science Education. Randy taught middle and high school science for six years in Oregon, where he was presented with the Tandy Technology Scholars Outstanding Teacher Award, and was recognized as the Oregon Science Teachers Association's "New Science Teacher of the Year."

Randy's primary research and curriculum development interests center on teaching and learning about the nature of science and scientific inquiry. Additionally, Randy is developing materials that facilitate the integration of technology into science teaching and learning. In addition to dozens of journal articles, Randy has co-authored an elementary science teaching methods textbook, and has co-edited a book on integrating technology in science instruction.

Introduction

WHY TEACH ABOUT THE NATURE OF SCIENCE?

You may be wondering why you should bother with nature of science instruction in the first place. The short answer is that research supports it and standards require it. But the short answer doesn't begin to do justice to the rationale for teaching about the nature of science, so permit me to elaborate.

Much of what makes modern living better (including longer lifespans, an increased standard of living, and technological devices from MP3 players to cell phones) is the direct result of scientific knowledge. Therefore, helping students appreciate the critical role of science in modern society as they learn the crowning achievements of science should be an important goal of science instruction (Driver et al., 1996).

Many decisions (from the personal to the local, state, or national policy levels) involve scientific knowledge. Which, if any, vitamin supplements should I take? Does the lower environmental impact of a hybrid automobile justify its increased cost? Should I vote for a local green space ordinance? Should the U.S. government encourage the use of stem cells in research? Informed decisions on such socioscientific issues require individuals to understand what particular scientific knowledge is relevant, the degree to which this knowledge is reliable, and the limitations of such knowledge. Using scientific knowledge in decision-making involves understanding not only the products of science, but also the processes by which these products are generated and the grounds for confidence in them. In other words, using science in our everyday lives requires understanding of the nature of science (Bell & Lederman, 2003; Carey & Smith, 1993; Shamos, 1995).

Unfortunately, research into what students know about the nature of science clearly indicates that most have picked up inaccurate views of science very early in their educational careers (Lederman, 1992). Thus, students view science as a rather boring enterprise that focuses on careful observations and employs exacting rules of conduct to guard against overly creative approaches and subjective thinking. They think scientists strictly adhere to "*the* Scientific Method," and in so doing, produce knowledge that is untarnished by human limitations. In this absolute view of science, hypotheses are educated guesses, theories have yet to be proven, and laws are absolute and infallible. Science itself is seen as the simple accumulation of facts about the natural world. It's no wonder that such so many students fail to see any connection between what they learn in science class and the real world where science controversies abound and scientists often disagree about the results of investigations.

Why do students develop absolute views of science? The answer is complicated, but likely reflects too much emphasis in school science on *what* we know and too little emphasis on *how* we know it. Add to this a penchant for step-by-step "cookbook" approaches to science activities, and you have a recipe for developing absolute views of science.

Additionally, it is not uncommon for textbooks to promote erroneous views of such common topics as the scientific method. To make matters worse, the way scientists use scientific terminology such as *hypothesis, theory,* and *law,* differs markedly from the everyday common usage of these terms, and these differences add to the confusion of the future scientists, engineers, and voters that grace our classrooms.

Research Supports Teaching the Nature of Science

The nature of science has been the subject of science education research for more than 50 years. Over time, science educators have come up with a wide variety of reasons to include instruction about the nature of science in the science curriculum. For example, teaching about the nature of science has been shown to enhance students' understanding of science content. In one study, Songer and Linn (1991) demonstrated that students who viewed science as a dynamic process that produced new understandings developed richer understandings of physical science than those who saw science as static knowledge.

Teaching students about the nature of science has also been related to increased student interest (Lederman, 1999; Meyling, 1997; Tobias 1990). As you will see as you read through this book, many of the activities are highly engaging and provide students with opportunities to explore new perspectives and to think deeply about what they are learning.

Additionally, incorporating the nature of science in your instruction helps students see the human side of science and portrays science as an adventure, rather than the memorization of disconnected facts (McComas, Clough, & Almazroa, 1998). Along these lines, understanding the nature of science has been promoted as a prerequisite for teachers who wish to teach from an inquiry-oriented, constructivist perspective (Duschl, 1987).

Although the research and arguments presented in the previous paragraphs provide ample justification to teach students about the nature of science, I believe there is a more compelling reason to teach about this oft-neglected facet of science. Teaching students accurate views of the scientific enterprise is in itself a worthy goal of science instruction. Certainly, one aspect of developing our students into scientifically literate citizens involves helping them adopt accurate views of the scientific enterprise and the nature of the knowledge that it produces. Without these understandings, students are in danger of viewing science as irrelevant and ineffectual when confronted with the real-world messiness of the science surrounding issues in everyday life and in the news media (Bell & Lederman, 2003; Collins & Pinch, 1998). What good have we teachers accomplished if our students can regurgitate scientific facts and concepts but have no clue about how science works to generate and confirm these ideas?

If teachers are to help students develop more appropriate views of science, then a different kind of science instruction is called for. This instruction calls for less *telling* and more *doing* in science teaching. This assertion is supported in the

U.S. science education reform documents (American Association for the Advancement of Science, 1993; National Research Council [NRC], 1996) and the writings of a number of science educators (e.g., Duschl, 1990; Hodson, 1988; Lederman, 1992; Matthews, 1994).

Standards Documents Support Teaching the Nature of Science

A number of reasons for teaching the nature of science have been described. However, there's one more compelling reason that we have yet to explore—the nature of science in the national science standards documents.

The primary goal for science education at both the state and national levels is scientific literacy for all students (not just those pursuing science careers). The term *scientifically literate* has been defined in various ways, but the *National Science Education Standards* (NSES) offers a good description for our purposes:

> Scientific literacy means that a person can ask, find, or determine answers to questions derived from curiosity about everyday experiences. It means that a person has the ability to describe, explain, and predict natural phenomena. Scientific literacy entails being able to read with understanding articles about science in the popular press and to engage in social conversation about the validity of the conclusions. Scientific literacy implies that a person can identify scientific issues underlying national and local decisions and express positions that are scientifically and technologically informed. A literate citizen should be able to evaluate the quality of scientific information on the basis of its source and the methods used to generate it. Scientific literacy also implies the capacity to pose and evaluate arguments based on evidence and to apply conclusions from such arguments appropriately. (NRC, 1996, p. 22)

It is clear from this description that there is more to scientific literacy than understanding science content. According to the NSES, scientifically literate citizens must also understand how science is done and the nature and limitations of the knowledge that science produces.

Thus, current science education standards typically promote instruction about the nature of science as a principal component of scientific literacy. For example, consider *Benchmarks for Science Literacy*, the national science standards developed by the American Association for the Advancement of Science (1993), which devotes an entire chapter to the nature of science and provides specific standards for all grade levels, K–12 (see Table I.1). You may be more familiar with the NSES which includes the nature of science as a strand in all of its content standards from kindergarten through twelfth grade (see Table I.2).

Teaching about the nature of science is not just an issue in the national standards documents. Many state standards also promote instruction about the nature of science, which reflects the widespread recognition of the role that the nature of science plays in developing scientific literacy. Table I.3 provides a sampling of my home state's nature of science standards as an example. You'll want to check your own state standards to learn what your state specifically requires.

Table I.1

Nature of Science in the *Benchmarks for Science Literacy.*

Source: American Association for the Advancement of Science, 1993. *Benchmarks for Science Literacy.* New York: Oxford University Press. Reprinted with permission.

Grade Levels	Benchmark Examples
K–2	People can often learn about things around them by just observing those things carefully, but sometimes they can learn more by doing something to the things and noting what happens.
3–5	Results of similar scientific investigations seldom turn out exactly the same. Sometimes this is because of unexpected differences in the things being investigated, sometimes because of unrealized differences in the methods used or in the circumstances in which the investigation is carried out, and sometimes just because of uncertainties in observations. It is not always easy to tell which.
	Scientific investigations may take many different forms, including observing what things are like or what is happening somewhere, collecting specimens for analysis, and doing experiments. Investigations can focus on physical, biological, and social questions.
	Scientists' explanations about what happens in the world come partly from what they observe, partly from what they think. Sometimes scientists have different explanations for the same set of observations. That usually leads to their making more observations to resolve the differences.
	Scientists do not pay much attention to claims about how something they know about works unless the claims are backed up with evidence that can be confirmed and with a logical argument.
6–8	Scientific knowledge is subject to modification as new information challenges prevailing theories and as a new theory leads to looking at old observations in a new way.
	Scientists differ greatly in what phenomena they study and how they go about their work. Although there is no fixed set of steps that all scientists follow, scientific investigations usually involve the collection of relevant evidence, the use of logical reasoning, and the application of imagination in devising hypotheses and explanations to make sense of the collected evidence.
9–12	From time to time, major shifts occur in the scientific view of how the world works. More often, however, the changes that take place in the body of scientific knowledge are small modifications of prior knowledge. Change and continuity are persistent features of science.
	No matter how well one theory fits observations, a new theory might fit them just as well or better, or might fit a wider range of observations. In science, the testing, revising, and occasional discarding of theories, new and old, never ends. This ongoing process leads to an increasingly better understanding of how things work in the world but not to absolute truth. Evidence for the value of this approach is given by the improving ability of scientists to offer reliable explanations and make accurate predictions.

Continued

Table I.1
Continued

Grade Levels	Benchmark Examples
9–12	In the short run, new ideas that do not mesh well with mainstream ideas in science often encounter vigorous criticism. In the long run, theories are judged by how they fit with other theories, the range of observations they explain, how well they explain observations, and how effective they are in predicting new findings.

Grade Levels	Standards
K–4	Although men and women using scientific inquiry have learned much about the objects, events, and phenomena in nature, much more remains to be understood. Science will never be finished.
5–8	Scientists formulate and test their explanations of nature using observation, experiments, and theoretical and mathematical models. Although all scientific ideas are tentative and subject to change and improvement in principle, for most major ideas in science, there is much experimental and observational confirmation. Those ideas are not likely to change greatly in the future. Scientists do and have changed their ideas about nature when they encounter new experimental evidence that does not match their existing explanations. Tracing the history of science can show how difficult it was for scientific innovators to break through the accepted ideas of their time to reach the conclusions that we currently take for granted.
9–12	Scientists are influenced by societal, cultural, and personal beliefs and ways of viewing the world. Science is not separate from society but rather science is a part of society. Science distinguishes itself from other ways of knowing and from other bodies of knowledge through the use of empirical standards, logical arguments, and skepticism, as scientists strive for the best possible explanations about the natural world. Scientific explanations must meet certain criteria. First and foremost, they must be consistent with experimental and observational evidence about nature, and must make accurate predictions, when appropriate, about systems being studied. They should also be logical, respect the rules of evidence, be open to criticism, report methods and procedures, and make knowledge public. Explanations on how the natural world changes based on myths, personal beliefs, religious values, mystical inspiration, superstition, or authority may be personally useful and socially relevant, but they are not scientific. *Continued*

Table I.2
National Science Education Standards Examples.
Source: Reprinted with permission from National Science Education Standards © 1996 by the National Academy of Sciences, Courtesy of the National Academies Press, Washington, D.C.

Table I.2
Continued

Grade Levels	Standards
9–12	Because all scientific ideas depend on experimental and observational confirmation, all scientific knowledge is, in principle, subject to change as new evidence becomes available. The core ideas of science such as the conservation of energy or the laws of motion have been subjected to a wide variety of confirmations and are therefore unlikely to change in the areas in which they have been tested. In areas where data or understanding are incomplete, such as the details of human evolution or questions surrounding global warming, new data may well lead to changes in current ideas or resolve current conflicts. In situations where information is still fragmentary, it is normal for scientific ideas to be incomplete, but this is also where the opportunity for making advances may be greatest.

The historical perspective of scientific explanations demonstrates how scientific knowledge changes by evolving over time, almost always building on earlier knowledge. |

Table I.3
Nature of Science in the *Virginia Standards of Learning.*
Source: Virginia Board of Education, 2003.

Grade Levels	*Virginia Standards of Learning* Examples
K–2	Observation is an important way to learn about the world. Through observation one can learn to compare, contrast, and note similarities and differences.

A *prediction* is a forecast about what *may* happen in some future situation. It is based on information and evidence. A prediction is different from a guess.

In order to communicate accurately, it is necessary to provide a clear description of exactly what is observed. There is a difference between what one can observe and what can be interpreted from an observation. |
| 3–5 | Questions frequently arise from observations. Hypotheses can be developed from those questions. Data gathered from an investigation may support a hypothesis.

An *inference* is a conclusion based on evidence about events that have already occurred. Accurate observations and evidence are necessary to draw realistic and plausible conclusions.

Scientific conclusions are based both on verifiable observations (science is empirical) and on inferences.

A scientific *prediction* is a forecast about what *may* happen in some future situation. It is based on the application of factual information and principles and recognition of trends and patterns. |
| 6–8 | Patterns discerned from direct observations can be the basis for predictions or hypotheses that attempt to explain the mechanism responsible for the pattern. |

Continued

Table 1.3
Continued

Grade Levels	*Virginia Standards of Learning* Examples
6–8	A scientific *prediction* is a forecast about what may happen in some future situation. It is based on the application of scientific principle and factual information. An *inference* is a conclusion based on evidence about events that have already occurred.
	Mental and physical models can be helpful in explaining events or sequences of events that occur. They can be used as part of scientific explanations to support data or represent phenomena, especially those that are not easily seen directly or must be inferred from data.
	Experimental studies sometimes follow a sequence of steps known as the Scientific Method: stating the problem, forming a hypothesis, testing the hypothesis, recording and analyzing data, stating a conclusion. However, there is no single scientific method. Science requires different abilities and procedures depending on such factors as the field of study and type of investigation.
	Investigations can be classified as *observational* (descriptive) *studies* (intended to generate hypotheses), or *experimental studies* (intended to test hypotheses).
	Scientists rely on creativity and imagination during all stages of their investigations.
9–12	*Scientific laws* are generalizations of observational data that describe patterns and relationships. Laws may change as new data become available.
	Scientific theories are systematic sets of concepts that offer explanations for observed patterns in nature. Theories provide frameworks for relating data and guiding future research. Theories may change as new data become available.
	It is typical for scientists to disagree with one another about the interpretation of evidence or a theory being considered. This is partly a result of the unique background (social, educational, etc.) that individual scientists bring to their research.
	A hypothesis can be supported, modified, or rejected based on collected data. A *hypothesis* is a tentative explanation that accounts for a set of facts and that can be tested by further investigation. A *theory* is an explanation of a large body of information, experimental and inferential, and serves as an overarching framework for numerous concepts. It is subject to change as new evidence becomes available.
	Constant reevaluation in the light of new data is essential to keeping scientific knowledge current. In this fashion, all forms of scientific knowledge remain flexible and may be revised as new data and new ways of looking at existing data become available.
	Science is a human endeavor relying on human qualities, such as reasoning, insight, energy, skill, and creativity as well as intellectual honesty, tolerance of ambiguity, skepticism, and openness to new ideas.

THE NSTA AND THE NATURE OF SCIENCE

However, even if your state has yet to adopt the nature of science in its standards documents, it's important to realize that the nation's premier organization for science instruction strongly recommends teaching about the nature of science. Before getting into the specifics, a little background information should prove helpful.

The mission of the National Science Teachers Association (NSTA) is "to promote excellence and innovation in science teaching and learning for all." In addition to a great Web site (www.nsta.org), NSTA provides a variety of resources and opportunities for professional development. These include regional and annual conferences, and three journals available to members:

- *Science & Children* (elementary teachers)
- *Science Scope* (middle school science teachers)
- *The Science Teacher* (high school science teachers)

By the way, if you have yet to join NSTA, I suggest that you do so soon. You will not regret your decision to do so.

In addition to journals and conferences, the NSTA has developed a number of position statements to guide science instruction and science education policy. Germane to this book is NSTA's policy statement on teaching about the nature of science. The statement builds on the nature of science standards and benchmarks discussed earlier and thus can be seen as a comprehensive compilation of what should be taught about the nature of science in public schools (see sidebar). These concepts comprise the view of the nature of science addressed by the activities in this book.

SIDEBAR 1.1

The National Science Teachers Association Position Statement on the Nature of Science

Preamble

All those involved with science teaching and learning should have a common, accurate view of the nature of science. Science is characterized by the systematic gathering of information through various forms of direct and indirect observations and the testing of this information by methods including, but not limited to, experimentation. The principal product of science is knowledge in the form of naturalistic concepts and the laws and theories related to those concepts.

Declaration

The National Science Teachers Association endorses the proposition that science, along with its methods, explanations and generalizations, must be the sole focus of instruction in science classes to the exclusion of all non-scientific or pseudoscientific methods, explanations, generalizations and products.

The following premises are important to understanding the nature of science.

- Scientific knowledge is simultaneously reliable and tentative. Having confidence in scientific knowledge is reasonable while realizing that such knowledge may be

Continued

abandoned or modified in light of new evidence or reconceptualization of prior evidence and knowledge.

- Although no single universal step-by-step scientific method captures the complexity of doing science, a number of shared values and perspectives characterize a scientific approach to understanding nature. Among these are a demand for naturalistic explanations supported by empirical evidence that are, at least in principle, testable against the natural world. Other shared elements include observations, rational argument, inference, skepticism, peer review and replicability of work.
- Creativity is a vital, yet personal, ingredient in the production of scientific knowledge.
- Science, by definition, is limited to naturalistic methods and explanations and, as such, is precluded from using supernatural elements in the production of scientific knowledge.
- A primary goal of science is the formation of theories and laws, which are terms with very specific meanings.

1. *Laws* are generalizations or universal relationships related to the way that some aspect of the natural world behaves under certain conditions.
2. *Theories* are inferred explanations of some aspect of the natural world. Theories do not become laws even with additional evidence; they explain laws. However, not all scientific laws have accompanying explanatory theories.
3. Well-established laws and theories must:
   - be internally consistent and compatible with the best available evidence;
   - be successfully tested against a wide range of applicable phenomena and evidence;
   - possess appropriately broad and demonstrable effectiveness in further research.

- Contributions to science can be made and have been made by people the world over.
- The scientific questions asked, the observations made, and the conclusions in science are to some extent influenced by the existing state of scientific knowledge, the social and cultural context of the researcher and the observer's experiences and expectations.
- The history of science reveals both evolutionary and revolutionary changes. With new evidence and interpretation, old ideas are replaced or supplemented by newer ones.
- While science and technology do impact each other, basic scientific research is not directly concerned with practical outcomes, but rather with gaining an understanding of the natural world for its own sake.

Position statement reprinted courtesy of the National Science Teachers Association, Arlington, VA, www.nsta.org/position.

The point is that there is widespread agreement exists among science educators and policy makers that science instruction at all grade levels should address accurate views of the nature of science. Therefore, in today's world, it is encumbent on teachers to find ways to include the nature of science in their instruction.

HOW TO TEACH ABOUT THE NATURE OF SCIENCE

Perhaps now you are convinced that the nature of science should be a part of your science instruction. Now how do you go about teaching this rather esoteric subject? After all, teaching about the characteristics of scientific knowledge and the scientific enterprise seems pretty dry, at least on the surface. It turns out that decades of research on teaching and learning about the nature of science has accumulated, and this research points to some specific approaches that can make instruction about the nature of science more effective and engaging.

First, it is important to realize that doing hands-on activities is not the same as teaching about the nature of science. This is true even if these activities involve students in various aspects of investigations and experiments.

Consider a recent investigation I conducted with several colleagues concerning this very issue (Bell, Blair, Crawford, & Lederman, 2003). We followed a group of high-achieving secondary students as they completed full-time, eight-week summer internships with scientists and engineers. These students were involved in helping out with all aspects of science investigations alongside their science mentors (not simply doing grunt work and washing glassware). If anyone ever had an opportunity to learn about the nature of science by doing science, it was these students.

In fact, they developed an incredible depth of knowledge and understanding about the particular topics they were investigating and the skills needed to use laboratory equipment and conduct fieldwork. Yet, in our interviews of these students before and after the internship, we found that they had gained very little understanding of the nature of science!

Learning about the nature of science requires explicit discussion and reflection on the characteristics of scientific knowledge and the scientific enterprise—activities students are not apt to engage in on their own, even when conducting experiments. Students need someone to guide them through the process of learning *about* science as they *do* science, and that's where you come in.

Of course, hands-on activities and science lab exercises are absolutely important. Such experiences are critical to effective science teaching and learning. However, students will learn what we want them to learn about the nature of science only when we teach about it purposively. In this sense, teaching about the nature of science is really no different than teaching any other instructional goal. If we want students to learn the differences between solids, liquids, and gases, we must teach them these differences. If we want students to learn how to use a triple-beam balance to measure mass, we must teach them how to do it. If we want students to learn that one of the strengths of scientific knowledge is that it undergoes revision as new evidence becomes available, then we must teach them this concept.

Purposive instruction is *not* synonymous with direct instruction. Students are not likely to develop meaningful understandings of the nature of science simply by having someone tell them that scientific knowledge is based upon observation and inference, or that all scientific knowledge is subject to change. The nature of scientific knowledge is too removed from everyday life for most students to understand simply from being told. Instead, students need to experience specific activities designed to highlight particular aspects of the nature of science. It's even better if

Table I.4

The Relationship Between Sample Process Skills and the Nature of Scientific Knowledge.

Process Skill	Nature of Science Tenet
Observing	Scientific conclusions are based upon evidence. They can change as new evidence becomes available.
Inferencing	Scientific conclusions involve observation and inference (not just observation alone).
Classifying	There is often no single "right" answer in science.
Designing experiments	There are many ways to do good science. There is no single scientific method that all scientists follow.
Predicting/ Hypothesizing	Scientific theories provide the foundation on which predictions and hypotheses are built.
Concluding	Scientific conclusions can be influenced by scientists' background knowledge. Theories provide frameworks for data interpretation.

these activities are designed to build upon students' experiences and capture their imaginations, which is just what the activities in this book are designed to do.

What does effective nature of science instruction look like? There is no single "right" approach, but I have found that teachers experience the most success when they link nature of science instruction to science process skills instruction (see Table I.4). Science process skills are a familiar topic for most elementary teachers. At an early age, we teach students to observe, measure, infer, classify, and predict as part of normal science instruction. It turns out that lessons addressing these familiar process skills provide an excellent bridge to the less familiar aspects of the nature of science. By integrating some basic instruction about the nature of scientific knowledge into a lesson on process skills, students can learn *about* science as they learn the skills necessary to *do* science.

As you read through this book you will notice a consistent pattern. Each activity focuses on a specific science process skill (or set of skills). In fact, many of these activities will appear familiar at first, because they have been promoted as good activities to use to teach science process skills (note that I have tried to trace the original source of such activities). However, as you read through the lesson description, you will notice clear direction about how to use the activity as a springboard for teaching about the nature of science. Once again, the goal is to link the more familiar to the less familiar. Each activity presented in the book links specific science process skills to specific aspects of the nature of science. Thus, by teaching the activities in this book you will give your students opportunities to learn and practice process skills while they also develop understandings of the more abstract facets of the nature of science.

To help you through the process, each chapter begins with a general introduction to the concept it addresses, followed by an engaging description of how to teach both the process skills and nature of science portions of the lesson. Specific learning outcomes for both the process skills and nature of science are provided for each activity, as well as engaging ways to introduce, teach, and conclude the lesson. Chapters conclude with a notebooking assignment for students to complete as they work through the lesson with you. In most cases, additional activities that can serve as alternatives or extensions are provided. Fellow science educator, writer, and artist Christine Schnittka has added her special touch by illustrating many of the concepts discussed in the book and by providing drawings that can serve as transparencies.

A Word About Science Notebooks

Each chapter of this book concludes with a Notebook Assignment. While these assignments can be photocopied and passed out to your students, it is recommended that you use them as prompts for student notebook entries. Science notebooks (either bound composition books or spiral notebooks) are an ideal way for students to record their work and thinking, and a great way for you to monitor and assess their learning as the year goes by. Your students can keep page-numbered notebooks of their ideas, research, and experimental activities just as scientists do.

There are many ways to organize and use science notebooks—there is no one "right" way. From personal experience I've found that having students put a title and date on every entry helps keep things straight, but from there the possibilities are vast. If you type "science notebooks" (in quotation marks) into an Internet search engine, you'll find many sources for guidance. Brian Campbell and Lori Fulton (2003) have written a book called, *Science Notebooks: Writing About Inquiry.* It is a well-written beginner's guide to using science notebooks with students in the elementary and middle grades.

It is ideal for students to use science notebooks with the activities in this book because the activities build on each other, and students may make better connections between them if ideas are all recorded in one place. Also, as you integrate activities about the nature of science with the rest of your science instruction, students will be able to make better connections among the three aspects of science (see Chapter 1).

The goal of this book is to provide you with everything you need to begin teaching exciting lessons about the nature of science. Let the journey begin!

1

What Is Science?

Consider how you define science as a discipline. You may find that it is easier to describe than to define. Science is not simply the "study of the world," but an endeavor consisting of three interrelated aspects, a body of knowledge, a set of methods and processes through which this knowledge is produced, and a way of knowing or understanding reality.

LAYING THE GROUNDWORK

I love books—all books. Give me a good book and (if I have enough time to myself) I'm likely to read it cover to cover. My love affair with books began at an early age. I remember in first grade discovering the Book Club. For a couple of dollars, I could buy three or four paperback books that I could take home and keep for my very own!

One of the very first books I bought was about science. I can still picture the section of the book on how snowflakes form and what they look like under a microscope. I read that book in one sitting and reread it often afterwards. I was hooked, and I couldn't wait to learn more about this cool thing called science.

In third grade I learned that the Bookmobile came to my community. Every two weeks I would trek a half mile down to the Bookmobile stop and check out my limit of eight books. Before long I had gone through all of the science books available on the Bookmobile. In fact, I had to start reading identification guides to get my science fix. I read these guides cover to cover and learned to identify reptiles, mammals, animal tracks, flowers, mushrooms, constellations—you name it.

A Naïve View of Science

With all this reading I accumulated a lot of scientific knowledge for my age. At the same time, and without actually being aware of it, I was developing a naïve view of science. I began to see science as consisting primarily of knowledge and the progression of science as a straightforward process of accumulating knowledge through application of the scientific method. If science did not have the answer to a question, then the answer likely didn't exist (or the question was not worth asking). I believed scientific knowledge itself was conclusive and unquestionable, at least once it had been proven by repeated experimentation. Certainly the laws of science were fixed laws of nature and would never be altered.

In short, by focusing on the knowledge of science to the exclusion of the processes of science and the nature of science, I developed an absolute view of science as the ultimate kind of knowledge. In science education circles today, this view is known as *Scientism*.

When I began teaching science in my mid-20s, I found that the majority of my students held this same naïve view of science. Most of my students had learned their science primarily through books, too—in this case their science textbooks. Like the books of my youth, science textbooks tend to emphasize science as a body of knowledge at the expense of any discussion about how this knowledge was developed. By presenting scientific concepts and principles largely as fact without any discussion of the history of their development, and by avoiding discussion of science controversies, science textbooks send the unintended message that science is all about facts.

Most students recognize that scientific knowledge can change over time, but they think this change happens primarily as a consequence of accumulating facts. Worse still, students develop the notion that science will eventually come up with a correct answer for every question about the natural world. This view is further exacerbated by the cookbook-style lab exercises found in most textbooks, which can easily lead students to view doing science as a process of seeking the "right answer," rather than as a process of conjecture, exploration, and discovery.

A More Complete View of Science

One of the many problems with this naïve view of science is that it is far too limiting. Science is much more than a body of knowledge. A complete view of science includes an array of processes, assumptions, and values. However, few science textbooks give any attention to these critical aspects of science. In my view, these are what make teaching and learning science so much richer and more interesting.

To explore this topic further, consider the personal view of science that you bring to teaching. Complete the "Science is . . ." statement written on the chalkboard in Figure 1.1.

What do you think your students might write? Over the years when I have asked students this question, they usually respond in fairly typical ways:

"Science is my favorite subject."
"Science is boring."
"Science is the study of the earth and everything in it."
"Science is the study of everything."
"Science is a way to learn the truth about the world."

You'll notice some commonalities in these responses. Naturally, students often see science as a classroom subject, as reflected in the first two sample responses. When thinking of science as a discipline, however, for most students, science is knowledge. As discussed earlier, this view reflects the classroom and textbook emphasis on the scientific body of knowledge. And while some students will suggest that science is "the study of . . .," you can bet that they're thinking of "study" in

Figure 1.1
Write in this space what you believe science is.

the academic rather than experiential sense. Thus, even these responses focus on science as a body of knowledge.

Few students will consider how this knowledge is produced, that is, the processes of science. I'll even predict that none of your students would offer a response related to the characteristics of scientific knowledge, unless they say something like "science is truth" or "science is sure knowledge." Students usually have a rather narrow, absolute view of science.

Dictionary Definition of Science

If you try this definition challenge yourself, you'll see that articulating an adequate definition of science can be difficult. In fact, precisely defining science poses problems for even the most persistent philosophers! If you look up the word *science* in a dictionary, you'll find something like the following.

> The observation, identification, description, experimental investigation, and theoretical explanation of phenomena.
> (*American Heritage Dictionary*, 4th ed., 2004)

Such definitions tell us something about science, but not nearly enough for our purposes. Science is such a complex and rich endeavor that it defies concise definition. So rather than trying to present a precisely worded definition that tells us little, the activities in this book seek to illustrate science in all of its richness—at least those aspects of science most relevant to school-aged children.

Exploring Further

Consider this quotation by the distinguished American physicist, award-winning teacher, and Nobel Laureate Richard Feynman (1968):

> Science is the belief in the ignorance of experts.

What does this rather curious definition of science mean to you? What would it mean to your students? When I ask my students to comment on this definition, the conversation usually turns toward the idea that questioning is important in science; that nothing in science should be taken for granted. It's not enough to accept an idea because someone says so, even if that someone is an eminent scientist. Experts can be wrong. A beloved bird species deemed extinct may actually not be! (See Sidebar The Debate Over the Ivory-Billed Woodpecker, page 17.)

SIDEBAR 1.1

Was Einstein Wrong?

Consider the fact that Albert Einstein's general theory of relativity, published in 1916, proposed a theory of gravity that predicted either an expanding or contracting universe. Unfortunately, data available at the time indicated that it was doing neither, but instead was stationary. To account for this, Einstein added a fudge factor to his equations ("the cosmological constant") that offset gravitational attraction, allowing for a static universe. A few years later, Edwin Hubble's work convincingly demonstrated the expansion of the universe and, thus, refuted the static universe perspective. Einstein later referred to the cosmological constant as his "greatest blunder."

Fast forward to the present. Current research indicates that the expansion of the universe may not be constant over time. If that is the case, then there may actually be a need for the cosmological constant, and Einstein's greatest blunder may yet be viewed as one of his great accomplishments. Thus, Einstein, the eminent physicist, may have not only been wrong, but he may have been wrong about being wrong!

Skepticism is at the heart of science, and the value of a scientific idea lies not in the credentials of who says it's "true," but in how the idea stacks up against the data. In other words, science is based on evidence (but not wholly on evidence, as we shall see in subsequent chapters).

Now, consider this second quotation attributed to Richard Feynman, a man known not only for his work in quantum electrodynamics, quark theory, and superfluidity, but for his masterful skill in teaching and in clearly explaining the most complex scientific concepts:

> Science is a way of trying not to fool yourself.
> From lecture "What Is and What Should Be the Role of Scientific Culture in Modern Society," given at the Galileo Symposium, in Italy, 1964.

What do you think Feynman meant by this statement about science? The most obvious message is that doing science involves trying to limit personal bias. We know from personal experience that it is human nature to emphasize the importance of our own accomplishments and ideas; hence, the proverbial tendency of fishermen (and fisherwomen) to overestimate the size of their catch.

Scientists face similar temptations as they investigate and test the validity of their ideas. Where the fisherman's ego lures him into exaggerating the size of fish he catches, the scientist's desire for an important discovery tempts her to emphasize data that support her conclusions over those that do not. While such personal bias can never be eliminated, science seeks to limit the effects of bias through formal procedures, checking and re-checking findings, and full disclosure to experts in the field (who are less likely to share the same biases of the scientist).

Considering these quotations by Feynman can lead you to understand some important characteristics of science. The first Feynman quotation emphasizes the point that, ultimately, science is not based upon authority, but on evidence. "Experts say . . ." is not good enough. What matters in the end is how the evidence backs up an idea, not who said it. Feynman's second quotation recognizes the danger of personal bias and stresses the importance of limiting bias in the construction of scientific knowledge. While personal bias can never be totally eliminated (as we shall see in subsequent chapters of this book), scientists often seek to limit personal biases as they conduct their work.

SIDEBAR 1.2

The Debate Over the Ivory-Billed Woodpecker

Even though the ivory-billed woodpecker (*Campephilus principalis*), had been considered extinct for the past 60 years, Tim Gallagher, editor-in-chief of Cornell Lab of Ornithology's *Living Bird* magazine, refused to believe it. When he heard that a kayaker and outdoorsman named Gene Sparling was startled by a large red, black, and white woodpecker in an Arkansas swamp, he had to go and have a look for himself. Gallagher and a friend named Bobby Harrison, a long-time ivory-bill searcher, traveled to Arkansas' Cache River National Wildlife Refuge in February 2004 and waited in the cypress swamp until they saw what they had come to find—a living, breathing ivory-billed woodpecker—or so they thought.

In April 2004, there were three additional reported sightings of an ivory-billed woodpecker by ornithologists. Later, David Luneau, Jr., an engineering professor at the University of Arkansas at Little Rock, captured a four-second video of a bird some believe is the ivory-billed woodpecker. Other searchers have since captured audio recordings of noises similar to the ivory-bill's double knocking and distinctive nasal sound.

However, as Carl Sagan noted, extraordinary claims require extraordinary evidence. There are plenty of scientists, birders, and conservationists who are eager to believe that the ivory-billed woodpecker is not extinct, and they are thrilled by these findings. Thus, the possibility exists that they are "fooling themselves," as Feynman would say.

On the other hand, some ornithology experts disagree with their interpretation of the data, believing that the bird in the grainy video is more likely a common pileated woodpecker (*Dryocopus pileatus*). Others remain skeptical that the current evidence is intriguing but not compelling.

Until there is more reliable evidence—evidence that not even the skeptics can deny—the scientific community is not likely to come to a consensus about the ivory-bill's existence in Arkansas.

A FRAMEWORK

This chapter is designed to help you, the teacher, think about what science is and to set the stage for the activities described in the rest of the book. However, I provide a notebook assignment at the end of the chapter in case you would like to explore some of these ideas with your students. I like to provide students with a framework for the scientific understandings and activities that we will explore together in my science course. Therefore, I present them with Figure 1.2, which graphically represents a view of science based on ideas presented in Spector and Lederman (1990). I ask them to write specific examples in the spaces below each of the major aspects of science shown in the graphic. What examples can you list for each of these three aspects of science?

"A body of knowledge" refers to the products of science—the kinds of information you find in textbooks and scientific reports. Typical kinds of information falling into this category include all of the facts, concepts, and explanations that come to mind when we think of science. It's what we know about the natural world.

"A set of methods/processes" refers to the methods by which the body of knowledge is produced. Though more complex, these are akin to the process skills we teach in science classrooms, including observing, predicting, measuring, and experimenting. It's how we have come to learn what we know about the natural world.

"A way of knowing" is a bit more abstract and less familiar. In fact, I'd be willing to wager that most people reading this book have scarcely considered this

Figure 1.2
Three major aspects of science.

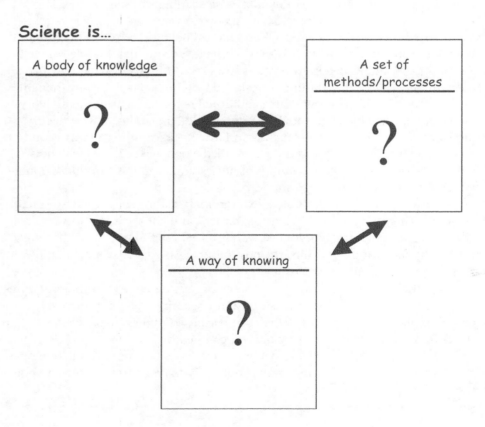

aspect of science. Nevertheless, it is worth a try to see if you can come up with examples. In general, you can think of "science as a way of knowing" as dealing with such things as what science values and the characteristics of scientific knowledge. More specifically, "science as a way of knowing" includes concepts about scientific knowledge such as the fact that it is based upon evidence (empirical), that it can change over time (tentative/revisionary), and that it is produced by a wide variety of creative approaches. It's how science is a unique way of knowing about the natural world—one of several ways of knowing.

LESSON WRAP-UP

With every topic you explore in science class you might try to address the three aspects of science: A body of knowledge, a set of methods/processes, and a way of knowing. In doing so, your students will gain a much more complete view of science and be able to answer the question, "How do we know?" in addition to the more typical question, "What do we know?"

Of course, we've only begun to explore what we call the *nature of science*, or "science as a way of knowing." Rather than providing you with a complete "right" answer at this point, I'll close this chapter with the thought that "science as a way of knowing" deserves a bit more attention than the other two aspects of science, precisely because of its unfamiliarity. Thus, the focus of this book is to explore this aspect of science in greater depth and to provide activities that engage students in talking and thinking about the scientific endeavor. Meanwhile, I hope that the present chapter has piqued your curiosity about science and that you are ready to learn more about the nature of science and how you can portray science more accurately in your own classroom.

You may find that the information presented in this chapter would make a useful lecture or discussion for upper elementary and middle school students. The questions in Notebook Assignment 1.1 at the end of the chapter are designed to elicit student feedback if you decide to teach the lesson to your students. Science notebooks are highly recommended in conjunction with all the activities in this book, but if your students do not use science notebooks, the assignment questions can be used as photocopied worksheets. If you teach younger students, you can adapt this assignment by providing the phrases from Figure 1.3 and letting students put the phrases in the appropriate boxes. The following is a suggested lesson overview.

LESSON AT A GLANCE

1. Students share ideas about what science is.
2. Teacher provides dictionary definition of science.
3. Students discuss statements about science by Richard Feynman.
4. Teacher discusses science as a
   - Body of knowledge
   - Set of methods/processes
   - Way of knowing

Figure 1.3
Three major aspects of
science with some
examples.

Science is...

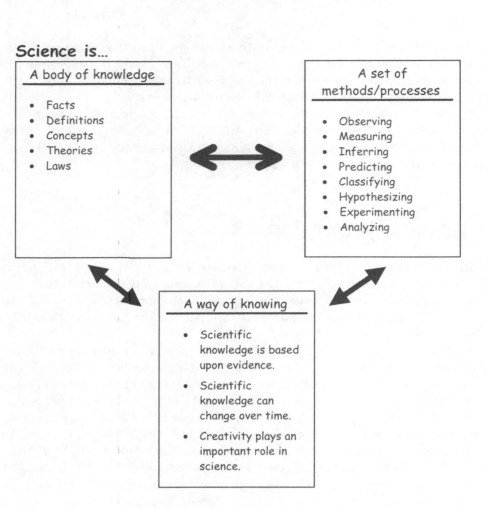

A body of knowledge

- Facts
- Definitions
- Concepts
- Theories
- Laws

A set of
methods/processes

- Observing
- Measuring
- Inferring
- Predicting
- Classifying
- Hypothesizing
- Experimenting
- Analyzing

A way of knowing

- Scientific knowledge is based upon evidence.
- Scientific knowledge can change over time.
- Creativity plays an important role in science.

What Is Science?

Name: _____ Date: _____

1. Science is . . .

   _____

   _____

2. What did Richard Feynman mean by saying that "Science is the belief in the ignorance of experts"?

   _____

   _____

3. What did Feynman mean by saying that "Science is a way of trying not to fool yourself"?

   _____

   _____

4. Describe a time when you really wanted to believe something even though the evidence wasn't there to support your belief.

   _____

   _____

5. Complete the following chart with examples that fall under each of the three main aspects of science discussed in class.

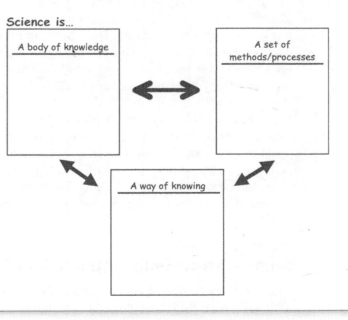

2

Observation in Science – More Than Just Seeing Things!

Students participate in several activities designed to emphasize the critical role that observation and empirical evidence play in the development of scientific knowledge. In addition to defining observations and practicing their observation skills, students are challenged to consider how science ultimately depends on evidence to support its claims.

LAYING THE GROUNDWORK

I have at least one characteristic that my wife finds endearing—I have an uncanny ability to notice things. Some people say that noticing small details is not a common trait among male humans, and I have no doubt that Lynn appreciates my unusual observation skills. I never fail to notice the littlest things, such as when she rearranges the furniture, builds a new bookcase, or changes the locks to the doors of our house. So maybe my ability to notice and observe things is not so impressive after all. At least I don't miss the obvious (most of the time). And one concept that has become obvious to me as I learn more about observation is that, as used in science, observation is so much more than just *seeing* things. In science, observation refers to a whole set of skills, some that are based upon our senses and others that use technology to extend our senses; all of these skills are used as the measuring stick to test scientific ideas.

Students do not automatically understand the nuances of observation as it is used in science. So it is up to you, the teacher, to help them develop more complete conceptions—exactly what this chapter is designed to help you do. The stories and activities described here are but a few of the many you can use to help your students improve their skills in making observations and drawing conclusions about the world around them as they come to know and appreciate the role of observation in science.

Some Observations About Scientific Observation

One good way to start any lesson about observation is to find out how your students define the term. For most, the first idea that comes to mind when they hear the word *observation* is to see something. As the Greek philosopher Aristotle recognized, so much of what we know is centered on our ability to see:

> We value our sight above almost everything else. The reason for this is that of all the senses sight makes knowledge most possible for us and shows us the many differences between things.
>
> Aristotle, *Metaphysics, Book I*

Certainly, our sense of sight plays a major role in the way we talk about what we know. Consider the following common phrases:

- Seeing is believing!
- Let me see.
- It's good to see you.
- I see . . .
- I'll believe it when I see it with my own eyes.
- We don't see eye to eye.
- It was love at first sight.
- What does she see in him?
- See what I mean?

Yet, it is important to realize that in science, observing does not refer simply to the act of *seeing*. Instead, observation is defined more broadly to include the use of all the senses. Thus, in science, we refer to observation as:

- using your five senses to collect information about natural phenomena,

or

- using what you see, feel, taste, hear, or smell to gather information about the world around you.

In addition to using all five senses, making scientific observations also implies a sense of purpose and care. Scientists strive to pay attention to minute details when making and recording observations. After all, our observations ultimately determine which scientific ideas are worthy of acceptance. It is not going too far to say that scientific conclusions are only as strong as the observations upon which they are built.

Even so, no matter how careful we are in making observations, a degree of fallibility always exists. Illusions, hallucinations, and simple perceptual errors can undermine the reliability of what we observe and result in our being deceived by our senses. Scientists work to limit such errors through experimental design, sophisticated instrumentation, and repetition of observations and measurements to increase reliability. None of these measures can completely eliminate the human element, however, so the potential for being deceived by our senses remains.

In addition to human nature, fallibility also extends from the very training and background knowledge scientists bring to the table. A trained observer can observe things that an untrained person cannot hope to ascertain. One only has to discuss the results of an X-ray with a physician to know that this is true. What appears to most patients as a blurry image with no useful detail can reveal a hairline fracture or a mass of scar tissue to the physician's trained eye. Further, scientists' individual background knowledge and training can influence which aspects of a phenomenon they pay particular attention to, or even whether they ascertain a particular aspect at all!

Despite these potential differences, a primary assumption of science is that observation provides the best benchmark to test whether scientific claims correspond with reality. Thus, scientists rely heavily upon empirical evidence to test their ideas, and agreement with observational data largely determines whether scientific claims are to be accepted, rejected, or modified. Science writer and skeptic, Michael Shermer (2002), describes dependence upon empirical evidence as one of the key characteristics that separates science and pseudoscience (as well as history and pseudohistory) and the primary mechanism by which scientific knowledge changes over time.

Science is different from pseudoscience, and history is different from pseudohistory, not only in evidence and plausibility, but in how they change. Science and history are cumulative and progressive in that they continue to improve and refine knowledge of our world and our past based on new observations and interpretations. Pseudohistory and pseudoscience, if they change at all, change primarily for personal, political, or ideological reasons (p. 38).

Observation in science is so much more than simply seeing. It is using all of our senses to collect and carefully record information about our world. Scientific observation includes the use of technology to collect information beyond the reach of our senses, and, most relevant to the topic of the nature of science, observation

SIDEBAR 2.1

Tycho Brahe: Observer of the Sky

Tycho Brahe (pronounced tee'-koh brah'-uh) was born in 1546 to a noble Danish family. While he was a teenager away at school, he began his life's work, observing the planets and the stars. At first, he used very simple tools to help him; he would measure the distance between stars with a string held taught at arms' length. Later, he got a better tool, a cross staff to measure the distance between stars, and he recorded all his measurements, comparing them to measurements published in books. He found that the books were wrong, and he set out to correct them. Eventually, he had a large piece of equipment made for him called a *Quadrans maximus*. It was used to measure the distance from the horizon to a star or planet.

When Brahe moved to an island in the sound between Denmark and Sweden, he built an observatory complete with huge pieces of equipment for making precise observations, and he hired workers who were willing to stay up through the night to help him observe. Brahe and his helpers would make hundreds of measurements of the same observations just to average out the errors. He wanted all of his observational records to be within one degree of accuracy.

Over his lifetime, he compiled an incredibly large, very accurate, and complete set of data about the planets and stars. He used this data to form his own theory about how the universe was structured. Later, astronomers used Brahe's data and formed new theories about the universe, including the heliocentric (sun-centered) theory we use today. And just think, Brahe did all this work before the telescope was invented. He used his eyes alone to look and special equipment to help him measure with precision.

Jane Goodall: Observer of Chimpanzees

Jane Goodall was born in 1934 in London, England. As a child she was fascinated by animals, and by the time she was 11 she'd decided she wanted to go to Africa. At the age of 26 she was in Africa, studying chimpanzees with her mentor, Louis Leakey, a famous anthropologist. At first she watched the chimpanzees from a distance with binoculars, but eventually she was able to get closer to them. She was the first person to observe that chimpanzees use tools. She would sit and watch them peel grass blades into shapes, then poke the blades into termite mounds, pull the blades out (covered with termites) and gobble the termites up. Until this time, scientists thought that only humans created and used tools. Since then, many other animals have been seen using tools. In 2005, female dolphins off the coast of Australia were observed using sea sponges to help them forage for food. Goodall also observed that chimpanzees kiss each other, tickle each other, hug each other, and hold hands. They have lasting family relationships, and they even pat each other on the back!

A surprising thing that Goodall observed was that chimpanzees are not strict vegetarians. Scientists had always thought that chimps ate only fruits and vegetables with the occasional termite snack thrown in. But Goodall observed something disturbingly different. She saw packs of chimpanzees hunt and kill red colobus monkeys. Another disturbing observation was that chimpanzee groups engage in "warfare" with other chimpanzee groups. She observed a four-year-long brutal battle in which one group of chimps actually killed off another group.

Jane Goodall spent nearly 40 years observing chimpanzees in Tanzania, Africa.

provides the standard for testing scientific claims and the means by which scientific ideas are modified. Change is at the heart of science—nothing is proven to the extent that there is no possibility for future modification as new data and interpretations become available. Even scientific "facts," should be viewed as *confirmed* rather than *proven*. As Shermer (2002) aptly concluded,

> Science is not the affirmation of a set of beliefs but a process of inquiry aimed at building a testable body of knowledge constantly open to rejection or confirmation. In science, knowledge is fluid and certainty fleeting. That is at the heart of its limitations. It is also its greatest strength (p. 124).

Teaching About Observation and the Nature of Science

Once your students have shared their ideas about what observation means, the time has come to begin teaching them a more complete view of what observation and empirical evidence mean to science. As discussed previously, you'll ultimately want your students to understand the following aspects of scientific observation:

- *Observation* may be defined as using what you see, feel, taste, hear, or smell to gather information about the world around you.
- Scientists (and students of science) use observations to describe what they experience.
- Scientists (and students of science) make and record observations with care.
- Scientists (and students of science) often use tools to extend or enhance their observations.
- Scientists (and students of science) test their ideas against observations.

Of course, not all of these ideas are appropriate for every student—you'll want to adjust what you teach to the maturity level of your students. Also, be aware that this list represents an appropriate order in which to introduce these ideas, ranging from the concrete to the more abstract. Now all we need are some creative and engaging ways of addressing these aspects of observation.

THE ACTIVITIES

The nine activities described in this chapter follow the same general pattern, so the Lesson at a Glance box applies to all. The overall plan is to first get students to discuss their ideas about the term *observation*; then work with the class to define/describe what the term *observation* means to scientists. Next, give students opportunities to make their own observations through one of the creative activities described in this chapter. Finally, end the lesson with a discussion about how your students used their observations to construct knowledge about what they observed, and how this is similar to the way that scientists use observations to develop knowledge.

The first five activities in this chapter can be used to emphasize that observations are not just about seeing, but can involve any or all of our senses. Additionally, these activities can be used to emphasize that students (and scientists) use observations to describe what they experience.

LESSONS AT A GLANCE

1. Teacher elicits students' ideas about *observation*.
2. Teacher works with students to define/describe *observation* as used in science, emphasizing one or more of the following points:
   - An observation is what you see, feel, hear, taste, or touch.
   - Scientists use observations to describe what they experience.
   - Scientists make and record observations with care.
   - Scientists often use tools to enhance their observations.
   - Scientists test their ideas against their observations.
3. Students complete one or more of the observation activities described in this chapter.
4. Students discuss observation activity results and the relationship between the work of scientists and the ways that they made and used their observations.

Activity 1: Magnifying Water Droplets

Place newspaper print on students' desks, and provide each student with a square of waxed paper, a small cup of water, and a pipette (eyedropper) for placing drops of water on the waxed paper. Have students observe what they see when they look at the newsprint through the drops of water that they place on the waxed paper. Do students observe different views through smaller or larger drops? What shape do students describe the drops to be? Challenge students to drag the drops around on the waxed paper with the tip of the pipette and describe what happens when one drop meets another drop. Does the view through the drop change then?

Extension. After students have had plenty of time to make observations with the beads of water drops, provide them with a small amount of dishwashing liquid or liquid hand soap. This can simply be squirted onto a juice can lid or another shallow dish. Give each student a flat toothpick and tell them to dip it into the liquid soap, just enough to pick up the tiniest bit of soap. Have students carefully observe what happens when they touch the surface of the water drops with the soap-covered toothpick. Students will be amazed that the water drops appear to be "popping"! Challenge them to drag their drops of water around on the waxed paper once they have popped the drops and observe the changes.

Note that you will have to supply new pieces of waxed paper several times, as students become very engaged in this activity and after one piece of waxed paper becomes covered with water droplets, students will want to start over.

At the end of the activity, discuss students' observations with the goal of describing how the water droplets affected what the students observed in the newsprint. Encourage students to consider how the ways they used their observations compare to the way scientists use observations when describing something new.

Activity 2: Jelly Belly Tasting Game

The Jelly Belly Candy Company is famous for its wide variety of flavored jelly beans. They make jelly beans with names like root beer, cantaloupe, cinnamon, popcorn, peanut butter, and even toasted marshmallow. Your students will have a fun time using their powers of observation with these delightful jelly beans.

Since the color of the jelly bean can be a big hint, you might want to have students close their eyes and put out a freshly washed hand to receive the bean. Alternatively, let them see the bean and make observations about the way it looks and smells. Some of the beans have a solid color, but some have unique speckled patterns. You can give every student in your class the same flavor, or each work group can receive a separate flavor. That way, the work group can discuss their observations and debate about the flavors they taste in the bean. Emphasize to students that their job is to make observations about the taste, not necessarily to guess what the official company name of the bean is.

Once all the tasting and observations are completed, close the activity with a discussion about how we can use senses other than sight (such as taste) to make observations and that this is true for scientists as well. Although scientists don't usually taste their experiments, those involved in food science certainly do. These scientific specialists are known for their expert abilities in discerning subtle flavors as they develop and refine food products. Be sure to remind students never to taste anything in your class unless it's food specifically given to them by their teacher. Also, note the National Science Teachers Association (NSTA) Position Statement on Safety and School Science Instruction in the Safety Considerations box.

STRATEGY 2.1

Safety Considerations

Teachers should be aware of food safety concerns associated with eating in the classroom and take necessary precautions. For example, the National Science Teachers Association (NSTA) Position Statement on Safety and School Science Instruction states:

> *"Materials intended for human consumption shall not be permitted in any space used for hazardous chemicals and/or materials."*

If hazardous chemicals and/or materials are not stored or used in your classroom (which is the case for many elementary and middle school classrooms), then food safety is probably not an issue.

For those classrooms in which chemicals are present and this precaution does apply, you should consider conducting the activity at an alternate location, such as the school cafeteria or outdoor courtyard.

The entire NSTA Position Statement on Safety and School Science Instruction can be found on the Web at http://www.nsta.org/positionstatement&psid=32.

Activity 3: Blind Meet-a-Tree

This is an outdoor activity you should conduct where there are plenty of trees. Pair students, and give them a central starting place in the park or woods. Have one blindfold the other with a soft cloth and guide the blindfolded student to a tree. Blindfolded students should explore their trees with their hands, hug them, smell them, and listen to them, making as many observations as possible without looking. Now, still blindfolded, the sighted partners should guide the blinded ones back to the starting place. After the first round of students have returned to the central starting place and taken off their blindfolds, challenge these students to find their trees in the forest based on the observations they recall making with their senses. This will be a difficult activity if all the trees are similar, and you may find that the sighted partners need to be extra helpful. Next, have students switch roles.

Before the trip, be sure to check out the location and make sure the trees do not have poison ivy vines growing on or around them. Also, you'll want to make sure that you choose a site on level ground with few obstacles. Note that this activity works best when there are a variety of trees with different bark textures and diameters.

Close the activity with a discussion about how observation can mean using senses other than sight. To get a complete description of the tree, the students must use touch and smell.

Activity 4: Texture Scavenger Hunt

This activity also emphasizes the sense of touch as an observational tool. Find an area around your school grounds that has an abundance of plants, trees, or grass. If in an urban setting, you could create an environment to investigate in your classroom by bringing in plants, seeds, flowers, rocks, and leaves. Hand individuals or small groups of students index cards with one of the following words on them. The number of words you hand out can depend on the age level of the students.

hairy	spongy	bumpy	slimy	smooth
silky	sticky	prickly	fuzzy	waxy
rough	dry	sandy	moist	soft

Once students have their texture cards, bring them to an area where they can touch all of the living and nonliving things around them. Be sure to check out the area beforehand to make sure an abundance of textural items are available and to avoid dangerous items like broken glass and poison ivy. Encourage students to touch as much as they can, which is the exact opposite of what their parents want them to do when they're out in the world. Here is their big chance!

When students find an item that fits one of their texture words, they may either take the item with them or write a description of it. Remind students to be respectful of living organisms, suggesting they remove a leaf or a flower from a plant, instead of taking the entire plant out of the ground. Provide time for students to sit in a circle and share the texture cards they had and the item(s) they found to match them. You might also display all the cards and have student groups try to guess which texture card matches the items that they discovered by passing the items around the circle of students. Facilitate a discussion of the multitude of textures found in nature and the possible reasons for them. With older students, you might discuss how these textures may be adaptations for plant survival (waxy—water retention, prickly/sticky—seed dispersal, etc.).

Close the activity with a discussion about how observation in science is not just about seeing—it can refer to using other senses as well, in this case, touch.

Activity 5: Smelly Cans

In addition to emphasizing the sense of smell, this activity illustrates the importance of making and recording observations with care.

Before class, prepare film canisters or other containers that seal well. Each container should contain a cotton ball with several drops of a different scented oil or essence added to each one. Make sure that each container is easy to seal and easy to open. Make sure that none of the scent liquids can drip out and that the cotton ball has absorbed all of the liquid. Film canisters or other small containers are ideal because the cotton ball will be wedged inside and it won't fall out. Choose scents that students will be able to describe as floral, fruity, or like specific foods they know. Choose natural products. Do not choose any scents that have vapors that might irritate the eyes or nose. Test them out on yourself first! Suggestions include extracts for baking such as vanilla, orange, and almond extract and essential oils, such as lavender, rose, and spearmint oil.

Label each container with a number. Be sure to teach your students the proper way to smell unknown substances by "wafting" the odor toward their noses with the other hand. Demonstrate this for the class and have them practice on empty containers before beginning the activity.

Depending on how many scented containers you have prepared, you can set up stations around the classroom or merely pass them around the room. Since the canisters will be labeled with a number, students will be able to describe their observations and compare them. Younger students can draw what they "observe" with each smell. For example, they may draw a rose when they smell rose oil, or they may draw a stick of chewing gum when they smell spearmint oil. Older students can create a table and fill it in with as many written observations as possible about each numbered scent.

Be sure to include in your closure to the lesson a discussion about how observation in science uses senses other than sight, in this case, smell.

In the next four activities, students use tools to enhance their observation skills.

Activity 6: Grasshopper Gazing

It is easy to overlook the interesting features of the smaller organisms all around us. Young scientists need opportunities to observe these creatures to facilitate understanding and appreciation of the frequently overlooked wonders of science that abound in our everyday environment.

Provide pairs of students with a hand lens and a grasshopper. It may be possible for your young scientists to collect grasshoppers from the field. Alternatively, crickets can be purchased from a pet store or bait shop to substitute for grasshoppers. In order to slow down the normal movement of the insects, store them in a refrigerator prior to observing them. Glass mason jars, aquarium tanks, or wire kitchen strainers can be used to keep the insects from hopping around the room (although this does add to the excitement!). A discussion about the proper handling of live organisms is critical before starting the investigation (see the Use of Live Animals box).

Have students get out their science notebooks and make careful observations of the characteristics of grasshoppers, including movement, communication, color, antennae, mouth, head, wings, legs, and any other interesting features. You may need to prompt younger students about which aspects to observe, or you can ask questions aloud during the observations. Older students can record written observations next to each characteristic.

To close the activity, lead students in a discussion about what they learned from observing the grasshoppers and how the observations of their classmates compare to their own. You should also encourage students to compare what they've learned about observing grasshoppers to what scientists learn from observing other animals (see, for example, the Jane Goodall box presented earlier in this chapter). You'll also want to emphasize the role of technology, in this case, the hand lens, in extending our senses and thus improving our abilities to observe.

Activity 7: One of a Collection

This activity is modified from one involving whole peanuts. With the severity and prevalence of peanut allergies, starting off with a collection of seashells, rocks, or pinecones is preferable (see Figure 2.1). Any type of natural object you have on hand that has inherent slight variations will do.

Use of Live Animals

When using live animals in the classroom, teachers should ensure that the animals are treated responsibly. Before bringing an animal into the classroom, learn its proper living environment and nutrition requirements. Plan for its care during weekends and school breaks. Protect animals from any harmful chemicals being used in the room. Model safe handling of animals, and do not allow students to hurt animals in any way. Make sure you have a plan for disposition of any animals after activities, and do not release them to a nonindigenous environment.

The NSTA has developed a Position Statement on Responsible Use of Live Animals and Dissection in the Science Classroom with a complete list of issues of concern. It can be found on the Web at http://www.nsta.org/ positionstatement&psid=44.

Pass out one object each to students, along with an index card, and have them observe the object carefully, taking good qualitative and quantitative notes about the object on the index card (students should put their names on the cards). Provide students with hand lenses, metric rulers, and scales or balances to enhance their observations. Tell the students that after they make careful observations, the objects will be retrieved, placed in a bowl, and mixed up. Then, another student in the class will have to find their object based on their clear and precise notes and careful observations.

At the conclusion of the activity, emphasize the need for making and recording precise observations, and how the measuring and observing tools assisted the process. Compare what students did to complete this activity to the work of scientists, who also use tools to assist them in making and recording accurate observations.

Figure 2.1
Box of rocks and shells.

Figure 2.2
Feather as seen with a
microscope.

Activity 8: Fascinating Feathers

A feather is a fascinating object to observe on many levels. Feathers can have beautiful colors and shapes, they can be soft and delicate to the touch, and their barbs pull apart and stick back together with remarkable precision. Students of all ages enjoy picking up a feather and observing it, and if you add a hand lens or low-power microscope to the mix, they're sure to enjoy observing it even more (see Figure 2.2).

Pass out an assortment of feathers. Stick with natural feathers rather than the artificially dyed ones. An arts and crafts or fabric store may be a good source for finding natural feathers (like peacock and pheasant tail feathers) since they will be sterilized and safe for handling.

Initially, have students make general observations about the color, texture, size, and shape of the feathers. You might even have them sketch portions of the feather on paper. Then, pass out hand lenses, or better yet, set up microscope stations if you have dissecting microscopes or digital microscopes available for viewing opaque objects. If you have a computer projector in your classroom and a digital microscope (like the Digital Blue QX5), you can project the magnified feather on a large screen. Have students make observations about the individual barbs sticking out from the rachis (the center spine) that they can't see with their eyes alone. Each barb looks like its very own feather! Tell your students that scientists use tools like microscopes, telescopes, and hand lenses to help them make better observations. Have them add to their original observations, now that technology has allowed them to see more. Encourage them to come up with a list of other tools that scientists use to make better observations.

Activity 9: When Is a Worm Not a Worm?

In this activity, students use their observations as evidence for their conclusions and for testing their ideas.

Teaching students the significance of making detailed observations can be challenging. This observation activity explicitly challenges students' perceptions and fosters detailed observation skills. Start off by showing students a container and telling them that there is a worm inside it. Ask students to share what they think is inside the container. Tell them that they are going to be making some detailed observations to determine the characteristics of a worm. Provide student groups with hand lenses and a small container of live earthworms. A brief discussion concerning proper treatment of animal subjects is recommended (see the previous Use of Animals box). Have students get out their science notebooks and encourage them to use all of their senses (except taste) to make qualitative observations of the worms at their tables.

After students have had ample time, tell them that what they just observed was actually not the worm hidden in your container. Remove the containers of earthworms and place plastic worms in front of the students to record observations. Ask them to share any observations that they made of the real worms that do not apply to this new worm. Once again, inform students that you are sorry to disappoint them, but this is still not the same worm that is hidden in your container. Remove the plastic worms and replace them with gummi worms. For this section of the observation lab, they can use their sense of taste if you allow them.

While students are recording observations for their new worms, ask them to be thinking about how their observations have changed. Next replace the gummy worms with a picture of a worm and have students record their limited observations. Finally, reveal to them that this is still not the worm in your container. With added suspense, slowly open the container and reveal the worm inside, which will be a piece of paper with the word *worm* written on it.

Lead the class through a discussion of the following questions:

1. At what point does the worm stop being a worm? Encourage students to justify their answers by using their observations as evidence.
2. Which of the samples is *not* a worm at all? Discuss why or why not.
3. What does a worm mean to you? Be very specific and defend your answer.
4. Why is it important to be specific when describing something to another person or recording information?

LESSON WRAP-UP

In Chapter 1 we presented a framework identifying the three aspects of science. You can practice using this framework by thinking about the observation activities presented in this chapter and how what you've learned about observation fits in the three boxes of the diagram.

1. *Science is a body of knowledge.* The definition of observation and specific examples of scientific observations are part of the scientific body of knowledge.

2. *Science is a set of methods/processes.* Making and recording observations, using tools to improve observations, and using observations to develop and test conclusions are part of the processes of science.

3. *Science is a way of knowing.* Discussing that scientific knowledge is based (in part) upon observation, as well as the seminal role that observation plays in developing and testing scientific knowledge provides insight into the nature of science.

Figure 2.3 shows the "Science is . . ." diagram with the major points of the observation activities placed appropriately in the three boxes. We'll refer to this framework again in other lessons to help you understand and become more familiar with applying the framework. Distinguishing between these three aspects in a lesson is a first step in being able to teach a complete view of science that includes the nature of science.

Figure 2.3
Connection among the
three aspects of science
for the observation
activities.

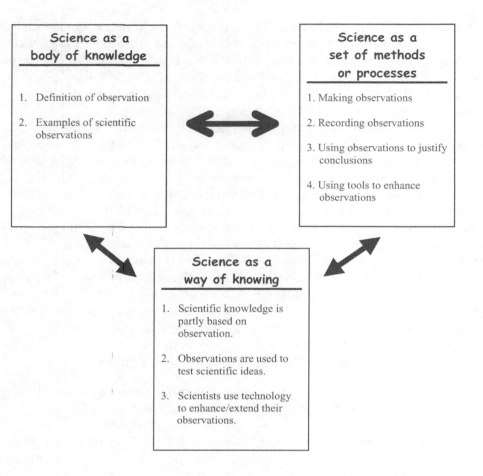

**Science as a
body of knowledge**

1. Definition of observation

2. Examples of scientific
   observations

**Science as a
set of methods
or processes**

1. Making observations

2. Recording observations

3. Using observations to justify
   conclusions

4. Using tools to enhance
   observations

**Science as a
way of knowing**

1. Scientific knowledge is
   partly based on
   observation.

2. Observations are used to
   test scientific ideas.

3. Scientists use technology
   to enhance/extend their
   observations.

ASSESSMENT

The final section of each activity chapter in this book provides assessment ideas related to the process skills and nature of science concepts addressed in the chapter.
There are too many activities in this chapter to provide a specific assessment for
each one. Instead, I'll provide a general template that you can modify for the specific activity you choose. The key is to assess students' understandings of both the
process skills and nature of science aspects of the lesson. You can use these assessments as handout worksheets or as science notebook prompts.

Observation Activity

Name: _____ Date: _____

1. Define *observation*.

   _____

   _____

   _____

2. List three examples of observations that involve senses other than sight.

   _____

   _____

   _____

3. List your observations about the _____ provided by your teacher in the space below.

   _____

   _____

   _____

4. Describe an example of how scientists use observation to better understand some aspect of the natural world.

   _____

   _____

   _____

5. Explain why scientists take such care in making their observations.

   _____

   _____

   _____

3

Observation or Inference: A "Burning" Question

I n this discrepant event activity, students record observations of a burning "candle," many of which turn out to be inferences. When the teacher eats the candle, it is revealed to be something other than what it appeared! The point of this lesson is to emphasize the role inferences play in constructing knowledge, in general, and scientific knowledge, in particular.

LAYING THE GROUNDWORK

I remember the first lesson of my eleventh-grade chemistry class almost as if it were yesterday. Our teacher, Mrs. Ferree, had a reputation for being a caring teacher who really knew her stuff. She was definitely not a teacher to disappoint. Therefore, when she placed a burning candle on the demonstration table and asked the class to make as many observations about the candle as we could, my classmates and I took the task quite seriously. We soon found, however, that making observations was not as easy as we first thought.

I remember how the class's collective ego was deflated a bit after we shared our observations with Mrs. Ferree. After commending us for our observational prowess, she went on to make observation after observation that none of us had considered. The take-home message was clear. To succeed in chemistry, we must pay closer attention to detail, because, just as in the real world of science, the knowledge we gained in Mrs. Ferree's class would be built upon evidence.

This was a great lesson for us to learn. Scientific knowledge does have an empirical base, and this empirical base serves as an important distinction between science and other ways of knowing, as we saw in the previous chapter. However, there is a danger in emphasizing observation as the only source of knowledge in science, for scientific knowledge is not built upon the accumulation of careful observations alone. Rather, the concepts, theories, and laws of science are products of both human observation and *thinking*. To be more precise, scientific knowledge is based upon observation and inference.

If your students are like mine, this straightforward concept will likely be difficult for them to understand and accept. Most students hold the oversimplified view that scientific knowledge is solely based upon the accumulation of careful observations.

For them, the mantra of the scientist is much like that of Sergeant Joe Friday on the old television show *Dragnet*: "Just the facts, Ma'am." In this view, the reliance on careful observation coupled with the avoidance of subjective thought and speculation distinguishes science from other disciplines. In actuality, the practice of science is much more complex (and interesting) than simply making careful observations.

THE ACTIVITY[1]: THE BURNING CANDLE

This activity is designed to help students recognize the role inference plays in perception, and in so doing, help them to understand that scientific knowledge is a synthesis of observation *and* inference.

LESSON AT A GLANCE

1. Students define *observation.*
2. Teacher lights "candle" (or shows ketchup bottle) and students record observations.
3. Composition of "candle" (or contents of ketchup bottle) is revealed.
4. Students define *inference.*
5. Students identify the inferences in their original list of "observations."
6. Students discuss how observations and inferences are used in everyday situations.
7. Students discuss how observations and inferences are used in science.
8. Conclusion: Scientific knowledge is based on observation and inference.

Preassessment

The lesson begins with a brief discussion of the definition of observation. First ask students to define observation. Common responses include:

> "Looking at something."
> "Using any of your five senses to collect information."
> "Making measurements."

Each of these statements is accurate and presents a different perspective of the way the term *observation* is used in science (see Chapter 2 for an elaboration on the definition of *observation*). It is particularly important to remind students that observing in science can mean using any of your five senses—not just sight.

Making Observations

Challenge students to make some observations of a scientific phenomenon—in this case, a burning candle. The lesson continues much in the same way as

---

[1] This lesson is a highly modified version of the "potato candle" activity that has been floating around science education circles for years. An earlier description of a similar activity can be found in Chapter 5 of Erik Elkins' (1999) book, *School Tools: Structures for Learning* (Fulcrum Publishing).

Figure 3.1
"Burning candle" set-up for students to observe.

Mrs. Ferree's observation lesson. The difference is, though, that this candle is not what it seems.

Light what looks like a candle and hold it for the class to see (Figure 3.1). Students can complete a list of observations individually, or if time is an issue, you can solicit observations verbally and record the resulting list of student observations on the board. Typical observations include:

"The candle is about 10 cm tall."
"The candle is burning."
"The wax is white."
"The wick is black at the top and white where it enters the wax."
"The wick is about 1cm tall."
"The flame is yellow."
"The flame is about an 3 cm high."
"The flame flickers at times."

The Teachable Moment

About the time students have exhausted their ideas for observations (or if the you notice the candle is about to go out), draw the class's attention to the candle by stating, "You have a good list of observations, but I think that it's important for you to observe one more thing before we conclude the lesson." At this point, dramatically open your mouth, take a big bite of the candle and chew it with relish (flame, wick, and all)! The impact on the students will be great—how is it possible to eat a burning candle? Well, it turns out that the "candle" is not really a candle. Rather, it is a piece of string cheese with an almond sliver for a "wick" (see the boxes for a materials list

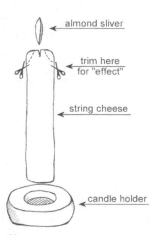

Figure 3.2
Construction of the
string-cheese candle.

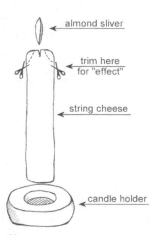 almond sliver
trim here for "effect"
string cheese
candle holder

Materials Required for the Activity

- String cheese (alternatively, you can make a convincing "candle" from the core of a raw potato using an apple corer.
- Almond slivers (it is the oil in the sliver that burns, so be sure to get your sliver from a freshly opened bag. After a bag has been opened for a few weeks, much of the oil evaporates, which greatly reduces burn time).
- A candle holder (optional—this makes the illusion that much more convincing).
- Matches or a lighter

and demonstration tips and Figure 3.2 for a diagram of the "candle" setup). When lit, the setup appears very much like a candle, and it is easy for students to make the perceptual leap to assume that they are seeing the familiar candle they have seen many times in the past.

This, of course, provides an excellent teachable moment for you to introduce the concept of inference.

STRATEGY 3.2

Hints for a Better Burning Candle Demonstration

1. The almond sliver "wick" will only burn for a few minutes. Once the oil in the sliver is exhausted, it goes out. If you allow this to happen during the demonstration, it will cue your students into the fact that something is amiss. To avoid this, use fresh almond slivers and pay close attention to the strength of the flame as you solicit student observations. When it begins to weaken, you need to decide whether enough observations have been made. If so, go ahead and take a bite out of the candle. If not, tell students that you are going to blow out the flame so that they can make additional observations. This will lead to a new set of observations such as "smoke appears," "there is a red tip on the wick," etc. After you have exhausted your students' observations, go ahead and take a bite out of the candle.

2. There is a potential for burning your tongue when you bite the candle, so be careful! It is safest to wait a couple of seconds after blowing out the candle before biting it. However, you will get a bigger response from your students if you eat the candle while it is burning. This requires a bit of practice. First, be sure to start with a moist mouth. Then, give a puff of air as you place the candle into your mouth to extinguish the flame and cool the almond sliver. Extra saliva on your tongue will serve to further extinguish and cool the sliver. Finally, chew quickly to distribute the hot and cool parts of the candle evenly. (By the way, I'll also warn you that the burnt almond tastes pretty bad.)

If you are concerned that this activity might cultivate your students' culinary inquisitiveness in inappropriate ways, you may want to try the alternative version of the activity described in the Crazy Ketchup Alternate Activity. It illustrates the same points without requiring you to eat anything.

ALTERNATIVE ACTIVITY: CRAZY KETCHUP

1. Prepare a clean ketchup squeeze bottle by threading a length of red yarn (about 75 cm works nicely) through the spout. Tie a small knot on both ends of the yarn to prevent the yarn from slipping through the spout. Finally, coil a length of yarn into the bottle and screw on the cap. You are now ready for the observation/inference lesson.

2. The lesson proceeds in exactly the same manner as the string cheese candle, except this time you are asking students to make observations about the bottle you have prepared. (Be careful not to refer to it as a "ketchup bottle".) If you have chosen the yarn color carefully, the little knot barely protruding out the end of the bottle will look just like that little glob of ketchup that you always find stuck to the spout.

   a. Students define *observation*.

   b. Teacher presents prepared bottle and encourages students to make observations.

   c. After students' observations have been exhausted, teacher points bottle toward class and squeezes hard. The red yarn will fly out of the bottle, looking exactly like a spurt of ketchup.

   d. After students have recovered from the "shock" of this discrepant event, teacher guides class in defining *inference*.

   e. Students identify the inferences in their original list of "observations." Teacher helps students realize that many of their "observations" were actually inferences, reflecting their incorrect assumption that there was ketchup in the bottle.

   f. Students discuss how observations and inferences are used in everyday situations.

   g. Students discuss how observations and inferences are used in science.

Comparing definitions can help students understand better, so it is a good idea to contrast the meaning of inference with the meaning of *observation*. Remind students that observation is:

"Using your five senses to collect information about natural phenomena."

Defining Inference

Many students will already have a reasonable understanding of the concept of inference, so you may ask older students to define the term and then build a formal definition from their responses. For younger students, you may want to use a more deductive approach by offering the formal definition yourself. Either way, the goal of this segment of the lesson is for students to understand the meaning of *inference*. Acceptable definitions would be something like the following:

"To reach a conclusion based on evidence."
"Using observations to reach a logical conclusion."

Figure 3.3
List of example initial "observations" by students.

Original "Observations"

"The candle is about 10 cm tall."

"The candle is burning."

"The wax is white."

"The wick is black at the top and white where it enters the wax."

> These statements include inferences

"The wick is about 1 cm tall."

"The flame is yellow."

"The flame is about an inch high."

"The flame flickers at times."

Or, to simplify matters without sacrificing too much of the meaning, say:

> "An observation is what you see, feel, taste, hear or smell. An inference is what you *think*."

Now is the time to refer back to the list of student observations about the "burning candle" and to assess which statements are observations and which, if any, are inferences. Typically, students will include many inferences in their list of observations, as is true in our original list (see Figure 3.3).

LESSON WRAP-UP

As you draw this lesson to a close, talk with students about just how readily people make inferences. In fact, it is so natural for people to draw conclusions, that we often make inferences when we think we are making observations. Recognizing this natural tendency is the first step toward making more accurate observations, an important process skill. It is also a bridge to understanding many key aspects of the nature of science, as we shall see in subsequent chapters.

Emphasize to students that inference is a critical component of much of what we know. Your students will likely come to class believing that in science "seeing is believing." Certainly, science relies heavily on empirical evidence. However, all of us, scientists included, rely not only on what we see but also on what we infer to make sense of the world. Scientists construct knowledge from observation and inference, not observation alone. At this point, it's enough simply to introduce this idea. Subsequent chapters will elaborate on and provide examples of the roles of observation and inference in science. Chapter 4 provides some specific examples of how scientific inferences are made from observations.

Finally, you'll want to caution your students about the dangers of tasting objects indiscriminately. Emphasize that while it appeared to them that you were eating a candlestick, in fact, you were eating something quite common and harmless—string cheese. Tell students this demonstration is not something that they should try at home. Remind your students (especially the younger ones) that they should seek guidance from an adult before tasting or eating anything out of the ordinary.

A FINAL NOTE

In Chapter 1 we presented a framework identifying the three aspects of science. You can practice using this framework by thinking about this lesson and how what we've learned about observation and inference fits with the three boxes of the diagram. This lesson includes instruction on all three aspects of the framework:

1. *Science is a body of knowledge*. The definitions of *observation* and *inference* are part of the scientific body of knowledge.
2. *Science is a set of methods/processes*. Making observations of the candle, identifying students' inferences, and distinguishing between the two are all processes of science.
3. *Science is a way of knowing*. Discussing that scientific knowledge is constructed of observation and inference gives students insight into the nature of science.

Figure 3.4 shows the "Science is . . ." diagram with the points of this lesson placed appropriately in the three boxes.

ASSESSMENT

Students may be assessed on their understanding of the terms *observation* and *inference* and on their ability to distinguish between the two. It is also important to help them relate what they have learned from the "burning candle" activity to the nature of science. The following Notebook Assignment is an example of how you might assess what students have learned from this activity.

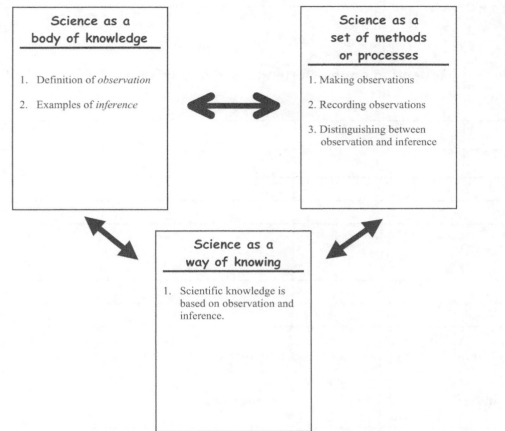

Figure 3.4
Connection among the three aspects of science for the "burning candle" lesson.

Science as a body of knowledge

1. Definition of *observation*
2. Examples of *inference*

Science as a set of methods or processes

1. Making observations
2. Recording observations
3. Distinguishing between observation and inference

Science as a way of knowing

1. Scientific knowledge is based on observation and inference.

Reflection on the Burning Candle Activity

Name: _____ Date: _____

1. Define *observation*.

   _____

   _____

   _____

2. Define *inference*.

   _____

   _____

   _____

3. List below some of your class's observations and inferences about the "candle" you saw in class.

Observations	**Inferences**
_____	_____
_____	_____
_____	_____

4. Why are most people easily fooled by the "burning candle" activity?

   _____

   _____

   _____

5. How does being fooled by what you *think* is real affect what you *think* you observe?

   _____

   _____

   _____

6. Describe an example of how scientists use observation and inference to understand some aspect of the natural world.

   _____

   _____

   _____

4

Humor Is in the Mind of the Beholder

I n this activity students construct lists of observations and inferences from comic strips. In the process, they hone their skills in distinguishing observations from inferences. Additionally, they further refine their understanding of the role of observation and inference in the construction of scientific knowledge. Next, students apply their understanding of observation and inference to the development of scientific knowledge as they explore the question, "How do we know . . . ?" for a set of key science concepts and discoveries.

LAYING THE GROUNDWORK

If you're like me, one of the first sections you turn to when you get the newspaper is the comics. I usually need some mood adjustment after reading the headlines and world news, so the comics section is where I go.

We love comic strips because we love to laugh. But that raises an interesting question—what is it about comic strips that make them humorous? As we explore this question, it becomes apparent that there are different types of humor. For instance, slapstick humor relies heavily on physical action—think pie-in-the-face or the hapless slip on a banana peel. A lot of comic strips feature this type of humor (see, for example, Figure 4.1).

However, there is another, more subtle type of humor in comic strips. For example, look at Figure 4.2. As in the previous example, absurdity is at the heart of the humor in this comic. In this case it's not so much what you *see* that makes it funny, but what you *think*. Does this sound familiar? Yes, it's our new friend "inference" making another appearance. Comics that are funny due to inference are much more sophisticated and, for many, more humorous than their slapstick counterparts.

Gary Larson's *The Far Side* is a classic comic strip that often features inferential humor. Larson also knows science and has incorporated many scientific principles into his comics. This combination of science and inferential humor makes *The Far Side* a perfect tool for science students to practice making observations and inferences. (Note, however, that any use of *The Far Side* comics requires express written permission from Creators Syndicate. Teachers wishing to use any of these comics may request permission by writing to: FarSide@creators.com.)

Figure 4.1
Comic strip illustrating slapstick humor.

Figure 4.2
Illustration of a *The Far Side* comic requiring the reader to use inference.

THE FAR SIDE® BY GARY LARSON

"Shhhh, Zog! ... Here come one now!"

You are certainly not limited to *The Far Side* comics; any of your favorite comic strips will regularly use inferential humor. With a little searching you're likely to find comic strips that will work. Just remember that cartoons and comic strips, like any other published works, are copyrighted materials. You must always obtain written permission from the appropriate copyright holder in order to reprint and/or use such materials in your classroom lessons and presentations (or any other use). Photocopying or reprinting cartoons and comics without obtaining proper permission is an infringement and a violation of copyright law.

THE ACTIVITY: COMIC STRIP OBSERVATION AND INFERENCE

LESSON AT A GLANCE

Part 1

1. Students practice listing observations and inferences about a comic strip (or picture book).

2. Students discuss the importance of making appropriate inferences from the observations.

Part 2

1. Students find information about a scientific concept by doing an Internet search or visiting the library, then write a brief summary about the topic, answering the question "How do we know . . . ?"

2. Students try to determine which of the information comes from observations and which comes from inferences.

3. Conclusion: Scientific knowledge is based on observation and inference.

Part 1: Observation and Inference in the Comics

Have students turn to a clean sheet of paper in their science notebooks and draw a line down the middle to create two columns, labeling one column "Observations" and the other "Inferences."

Next, ask students to look carefully at Figure 4.2 and make five observations from the comic strip panel and record them in the "Observation" column. Remind them that observations are based on what can be detected with the five senses (sight only in this case). With some attention to detail, they are likely to come up with a list similar to the following:

1. There is a volcano in the background.
2. There is a stick supporting a box.
3. There is a rope tied to the stick.
4. An animal is approaching the box.
5. There are four feet under the box.

When you do this activity with your students, it's a good idea to have them share observations with the class after they've completed their lists. This will give you a chance to assess the quality of their observations, the class will have the opportunity to check that no one has included inferences by mistake, and students will be reinforcing their observation skills as well as their understanding of the distinction between observations and inferences.

Once students have completed their lists of observations and checked to make sure that they've included only observations, it's time to move on to inferences. Under the column "Inferences" ask students to briefly describe five inferences they can make from the comic strip panel. While inferences will vary, the list may look something like the following:

1. Two people are trying to capture an animal.
2. The people are using meat as bait.
3. The people will be trapped in the box with the animal.
4. The people will be eaten by the animal.
5. The people aren't very intelligent.

Again, while teaching this activity to your students, have them share their inferences. They will enjoy hearing what other students come up with, and you will be able to assess the quality of their inferences and offer help as needed.

In addition to practicing their observing and inferring skills, your students can learn much about knowledge, in general, and scientific knowledge, in particular, in this activity. For instance, note that inferences by nature are less certain than observations. In fact, inferences are typically used to "fill in the gaps" created by our limited abilities to observe.

In the case of comic strips, this need to infer is often accentuated, in that our observations are somewhat limited by the nature of the simplified drawings. We have to infer the missing pieces. Although the ability to make such inferences is necessary for understanding the world (as well as comic strips), at the heart of every inference is an assumption and, often, a set of assumptions. Since the possibility always exists that our assumptions are incorrect, the inferences dependent on these assumptions can never be considered absolute or proven.

Inferences differ from observations in that there is less chance of widespread agreement. In the comic strip activity, your students are likely to agree on the observations they make. Even if there is a dispute about a particular detail, they will generally be able to resolve it by looking again at the comic strip. On the other hand, students may not be able to agree as readily on their inferences. Since inferences are interpretations built on assumptions, they will find that not everyone will readily agree on the same set.

Still, not all inferences are created equal. Inferences can be assessed for how well they reflect, and account for, the observations on which they are based. It can be enlightening for students to consider which of their inferences from the cartoon strip fit their observations best. For instance, an inference that the people will be trapped inside the box with the animal is supported by the observation that four feet can be seen under the box.

You may find that at least one student in every class will come up with some pretty wild inferences. This presents a teachable moment when you can have students analyze why this particular inference appears absurd. The answer lies in the fit of the inference to the data and in the appropriateness of the assumptions underlying the inference. For example, a student could infer from this panel that the line, "Shhhh, Zog! . . . Here come one now!" was actually being spoken by a second saber-toothed tiger that is off-screen to the right of the one that can be seen, and that the two tigers are actually talking about traps being set by inept prehistoric people. However, since we have no experience of talking tigers, your students may judge this inference to be less compelling than the some of the others.

Clearly, inferences are critical to making sense of comic strips, picture books, and everyday knowledge, but are they as critical to science? For younger students, it may be enough to simply tell them that scientists use observations and inferences to make sense of the world in much the same way that they used observations and inferences to make sense of comic strips and picture books. For older students, you may want to go further by applying this concept to specific ideas in science, as described in the next activity.

ALTERNATIVE ACTIVITY: OBSERVING AND INFERRING CHILDREN'S PICTURE BOOKS

If you prefer children's picture books to comic strips, you might want to have your students complete the observation/inference activity using well-written and illustrated children's picture books. Even older children can enjoy and learn from these picture books when they are used for this purpose.

Imagine all of the observations a young child can make as you read that book *Goodnight Moon* aloud and show the pictures. Think of the balloon, the mush, the comb and brush, the two clocks, the telephone, the moon and stars out the window, the restless bunny, the kittens, the mittens, the little mouse, and of course, the little old lady in the rocking chair. There are so many different things to observe, children love pointing out and looking for new observations each time they read the book. What about inferences? The slowly darkening images evoke a passage of time. The rising moon can prompt students to infer a scientific explanation if they know of one, or it can provide an opportunity to share all sorts of explanations. Why is the bunny getting out of the covers? Why are the kittens on the chair? Why does the balloon stay up at the ceiling? Children can infer all sorts of explanations for what they see in the gentle progression of images in this delightful classic bedtime story.

What Do You Do with a Tail Like This? by Steve Jenkins and

Goodnight Moon by Margaret Wise Brown. HarperCollins Children's Books, New York.

Cover from *What Do You Do With a Tail Like This?* by Robin Page and Steve Jenkins. Houghton Mifflin Company, New York. Used with permission.

Robin Page seems like it has been specifically designed for an observation and inference activity. In this cleverly illustrated, award-winning book, children examine the unusual body parts of different animals. They are asked, "What do you do with ears like this?" or ". . . noses like this?" or ". . . tails like this?" When they see the star-shaped nose of a mole or the pincer-like tail of a scorpion, they are asked, without knowing it, to infer the practical use of the animal's special adaptation. This is an ideal book to help reinforce the differences between observations and inferences and tie in some science content as well.

Here are some other books that could be used for this activity.

- *Seven Blind Mice* by Ed Young
- *Insectigations* by Cindy Blobaum
- *Snowflake Bentley* by Jacqueline Briggs Martin
- *I Took a Walk* by Henry Cole
- *Animals: Black and White* by Phyllis Limbacher Tildes

Part 2: Observation and Inference in Science

Having students make observations and inferences in class can make for a fun and engaging lesson, whether you use comic strips or children's literature as your source. However, in order to address the nature of science, you must show students that scientists use observation and inference to construct knowledge in much the same ways that they did in the comic strips activity. One way to do this is to have students collect information on scientific concepts, with the goal of answering the question, "How do we know _____?" By perusing books, popular articles, or Internet sites, students can begin to see how observation and inference are used to support scientific knowledge.

To begin, you should start with a list of relevant questions. These questions should address common knowledge from the science curriculum. It's certainly appropriate to have your students brainstorm a list of questions in class, or you can provide questions for your students, if you prefer. We've provided a list of examples in the box to get you started.

My students have found success in searching for answers to their questions by typing the question (with quotes) in a search engine such as Google.

"how do we know" (type topic here)

If a student wanted to search for evidence on how we know that the Earth is round, she would type:

"how do we know" the Earth is round

in Google or another search engine. From the resulting list of "hits" the search engine provides, she would then write a short summary (one or two paragraphs) explaining how we know that the Earth is round. Finally, she would list all of the observations and the inferences to which these observations lead. [Note: Be sure you provide appropriate supervision, and configure classroom Internet browsers and search engines to filter out undesirable material.]

Example Topics to Explore

How do we know that the Earth is round?
How do we know the structure of DNA?
How do we know the distance to the stars?
How do we know what dinosaurs looked like?
How do we know that cigarette smoking can cause cancer in humans?
How do we know the internal structure of the Earth?
How do we know what's inside of an atom?
How do we know that the Big Bang actually happened?
How do we know that evolution happens?
How do we know how old the Earth is?

The following summaries provide examples of answers for select topic questions. You can have students search for the answers to these questions, or if time is limited, you can present one or more of these summaries to your students at the conclusion of the Part 1 activity to relate observation and inference to science.

1. HOW DO WE KNOW THE EARTH IS ROUND?

Step outside and look in any direction with an unobstructed view and you get the distinct impression that the Earth stretches on forever toward the horizon. There is no end or curve in sight—no wonder early scholars who considered the shape of the Earth thought it was flat. However, today we know that the Earth is a sphere, and we decided this long before we had the technology to go into space and look back at Earth.

So how do we know the Earth is round? It turns out that there are several lines of evidence that support the conclusion of a spherical Earth.

1. The mast of a ship is the last thing we see as departing ships gradually sink from sight below the horizon.
2. During lunar eclipses the shadow of the Earth is projected onto the moon. This shadow is clearly circular, which implies a spherical Earth, a fact recognized by Aristotle more than 2,300 years

ago: "The sphericity of the Earth is proved by the evidence of our senses, for otherwise lunar eclipses would not take such forms . . . in eclipses the dividing line is always rounded . . . if the eclipse is due to the interposition of the Earth, the rounded line results from its spherical shape."

3. As you travel north or south along the Earth, the constellations that are visible above the horizon change with your change in latitude. This would not be true on a flat Earth.

4. People commonly fly and sail around the world. This would not be possible on a flat Earth.

5. Our understanding of gravity indicates that for large bodies round is a more stable shape than any other. Thus, a flat Earth would tend to collapse toward the center, and the force of gravity would decrease significantly as you traveled along the surface away from the center.

6. We now have pictures of the Earth taken by spacecraft. These images clearly show that our planet is round.

How Do We Know the Earth is Round?

Observations	Inferences
Masts are the last thing we see of departing ships.	The departing ship is sinking below the curved horizon.
The Earth casts a circular shadow on the moon during a lunar eclipse.	The spherical Earth casts a circular shadow.
Visible constellations change depending on latitude.	We are looking out into space from the surface of a sphere. Changing our position on the sphere changes the region of space that we can see.
Airplanes fly around the world.	The Earth is a sphere.
Large objects in space are generally spherical.	The Earth is a large object in space, so it should be a sphere as well.
The Earth appears round in images from space.	A spherical Earth would look round in photographs.

References

Bad Astronomy http://www.badastronomy.com/bitesize/flatearth.html

A Brief History of Time (Stephen Hawking), "Chapter 1: Our Picture of the Universe" http://www.scribd.com/doc/3511/ Stephen-Hawking-A-Brief-History-of-Time

Critical Thinking, Science, and "Proof" http://mmcconeghy.com/ students/supcriticalthinking.html

2. HOW DO WE KNOW WHAT IS INSIDE THE EARTH?

The deepest hole ever drilled in the Earth was only about 12 km deep, yet scientists are confident that they understand the internal structure of the Earth thousands of kilometers below the surface. How is this possible? This is another example of the importance of observation and inference for developing scientific knowledge. Scientists rely on several factors for determining the internal structure of the Earth. This includes Earthquake waves, volcanic activity, and meteorites and asteroids. There are two types of Earthquake, or seismic, waves that occur underground. P-waves, or compressional waves, are the first and fastest type of seismic wave. They are followed by S-waves, or shearing waves. P-waves travel through both solids and liquids, but are slower in liquids. S-waves travel only through solids. With this information, scientists can observe the seismic waves and infer solid and liquid layers within the Earth.

Volcanic activity transports material from deeper in the Earth to the surface, which allows scientists to study the material's composition and structure. Unfortunately, the deepest material comes from the upper mantle, but the physical properties of these materials can be compared to what they have learned from seismic waves. This helps solidify the current theory of the Earth's interior.

A third piece of evidence used to infer the interior of the Earth comes from meteorites. Currently, the leading theory for the formation of the Earth suggests that the Earth is similar in composition to meteorites and asteroids. Scientists can study meteorites and asteroids that have impacted the Earth's surface and compare their findings to rocks from the Earth's surface. Since rocks from the Earth's surface do not have the same composition as meteorites and asteroids, scientists infer that the composition of the interior of the Earth is similar to the composition of meteorites and asteroids.

How Do We Know What Is Inside the Earth?

Observations	Inferences
Seismic waves	Solid or liquid parts of the Earth's interior
Volcanic activity	Composition of the mantle
Asteroids and meteorites	Composition of the core

References

Chapter 3: The Earth: Differentiation & Plate Tectonics http://www.indiana.edu/~geol105/1425chap3.htm

MadSci Network: Earth Sciences http://www.madsci.org/posts/archives/oct98/909513628.Es.r.html

Simulation of P and S waves moving through the Earth's interior http://sunshine.chpc.utah.edu/labs/seismic/seismic.swf

3. HOW DO WE KNOW THAT GERMS CAUSE DISEASE?

Since the time of the ancient Greeks, *miasma*, or bad smelling air, was thought to be the cause of illness, and many foul-smelling observations were used to substantiate this inference. Not until the mid-1800s were new discoveries made that led to the development of a new theory, the germ theory of disease.

In the early 1800s, the Italian farmer, Agostino Bassi, observed the devastation affecting the local silkworm industry. The worms were dying after being covered by a fine, white powder. Bassi studied this powder and determined that it was a living, contagious organism. In 1835 he published his findings, and recommended sanitation practices that saved the silkworm industry. Eventually this organism was identified as a fungus and named *Beauveria bassiana* in his honor. Bassi had developed a new theory, the germ theory of disease.

In 1848 a severe outbreak of cholera killed 7,000 Londoners in one month. A local physician, John Snow, analyzed where people were getting sick and inferred that the water from one particular well was tainted with the cholera germ. When he removed the handle from the Broad Street water pump, it ended an epidemic in that area.

Louis Pasteur, a French chemist, later did some experiments that reinforced the germ theory. In 1862 he demonstrated that if a beverage like milk is gently heated, the mold and bacteria that normally spoil it would be destroyed. Pasteur concluded that if germs could infect food, then they could infect the human body too.

Pasteur's ideas spread across the scientific community and were noticed by the English surgeon, Joseph Lister. At that time, surgeons still believed in the miasma theory of disease. Surgeons aired out their hospitals and operating rooms to make them smell better, but didn't bother with washing their hands, or even washing their patients' wounds. Terrible infections were killing nearly half of Lister's patients, and he decided to use Pasteur's ideas to try and save them. He used a chemical, carbolic acid, to kill germs on his patients' wounds, on his hands, in the air, and on his surgical equipment. In 1867 he announced that he hadn't lost a single patient to infection in nine months.

Today, the germ theory of disease is widely accepted. Scientists have the technology to magnify and see all sorts of germs, from bacteria to viruses. Controlled experiments directly show the causal link between germs and diseases such as chicken pox and influenza. Many breakthroughs in medicine, like antibiotics and immunizations, have been developed because of our knowledge about how germs spread and replicate inside plants and animals.

How Do We Know That Germs Cause Disease?

Observations	Inferences
When the white powder on a dead silkworm is injected into a healthy one, it too gets covered in powder and dies.	The white powder is made of the spores of a living fungus that causes a disease in silkworms.
People living near a particular water source in London got sick and died of cholera more often than people living elsewhere.	The water was tainted with a certain type of bacterium that causes disease. The water was contaminated by raw sewage.
Fresh milk from a cow will spoil much faster than milk that has been pasteurized (heated to 72°C for 15 seconds).	Pasteurization kills the mold spores and bacteria that would otherwise reproduce and spoil the milk.
Without proper sterilization methods, many surgical patients die with infected wounds.	Sterile surgical methods prevent bacteria from invading and infecting the body.

References

Agostino Bassi Bicentennial (1773-1973) by J.R. Porter, in
    Bacteriological Reviews, Sept. 1973. http://www.pubmedcentral.nih
    .gov/picrender.fcgi?artid=413819&blobtype=pdf
Germ Theory of Disease, Wikipedia, The Free Encyclopedia http://en
    .wikipedia.org/wiki/Germ_theory
LIFE Online: Top 100 Events of the Millennium http://www.life.com/
    Life/millennium/events/06.html
Polio: Kids Health http://kidshealth.org/parent/infections/
    bacterial_viral/polio.html

4. HOW DO WE KNOW THE STRUCTURE OF DNA?

James Watson and Francis Crick made their famous discovery of the hel-
ical nature of the deoxyribonucleic acid (DNA) molecule without being
able to observe the structure directly. DNA is simply too small. Instead, they inferred the structure using evidence from previous studies (such as data on the chemical composition of DNA, how the con-
stituents of DNA bonded together, and the symmetry of DNA crystals) in
combination with an X-ray diffraction photograph of DNA taken by
Rosalind Franklin in 1952.

Franklin created the image by shooting a beam of X-rays onto a
photographic plate containing a sample of DNA.

How Do We Know the Structure of DNA?

Observation	Inference

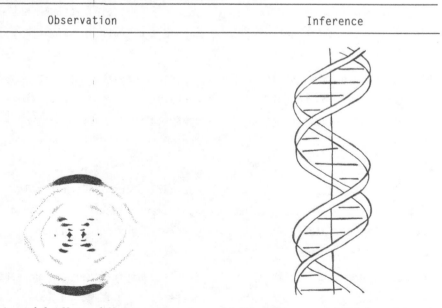

A drawing of the X-ray diffraction image
photographed by Rosalind Franklin . . .

which led Watson and Crick to this inferred
structure for DNA.

References

Biology: DNA (BA Magazine) http://www.ba-education.demon.co.uk/for/
     science/dnamain.html

Watson L. D. and Crick F. H. C. (1953) "Molecular Structure of Nucleic
     Acids: A Structure for Deoxyribose Nucleic Acid" *Nature*, 171,
     737-738.

An annotated version of Watson and Crick's article: http://www
     .exploratorium.edu/origins/coldspring/printit.html

5. HOW DO WE KNOW THAT CIGARETTE SMOKING CAN CAUSE CANCER IN HUMANS?

It is speculated that half of all smokers will die because of a
smoking-related illness such as cancer, emphysema, stroke, or heart
disease. But how do we know that these illnesses are indeed smoking-
related? Certainly no one has performed a controlled study, randomly
assigning individuals to smoke or not smoke and then waiting to see
what diseases they eventually acquire. That would be unethical, based
on what we know from epidemiological studies and other inferential
statistics. While we have no "proof" that cigarette smoking causes
these diseases in humans, there is an extremely strong, consistent
body of evidence that smoking can cause many types of cancer in humans. The Surgeon General's 1990 Report on the Health Benefits of
Smoking Cessation states that "tens of thousands of studies have documented the associations between cigarette smoking and a large number
of serious diseases. It is safe to say that smoking represents the
most extensively documented cause of disease ever investigated in the
history of biomedical research."

Scientists have even gone so far as to study particular chemical
compounds in cigarette smoke and found strong etiological links to genetic mutations in the P53 tumor suppressor gene, the gene that is
supposed to protect our cells from cancer. Subjecting human bronchial
epithelial cells in a laboratory to these particular chemicals, scientists see the same mutations in the P53 gene that they see in actual
lung cancer tumors.

This is just one piece of the evidence that points toward the
smoking-cancer link. Smokers have twice the risk of dying of heart
disease and twice the risk of dying of stroke. However, people who
quit smoking eventually have the same risk of dying of these diseases
as nonsmokers. That's called "reversibility," and along with consistency, it's just one of the many criteria used for determining the
causation of a disease.

How Do We Know that Cigarette Smoking Causes Cancer in Humans?

Observations	Inferences
The longer a person smokes, the higher his or her chances of getting cancer.	The cancer risk increases due to cigarette smoking.
The more cigarettes a person smokes on a regular basis, the higher the chances are for getting cancer.	The cancer risk increases due to cigarette smoking.
In controlled studies with rats, exposure to tobacco smoke increased the likelihood of lung tumors.	Similar results would be obtained if we could conduct the same type of experiments on humans.
Smoking causes the same gene mutations in humans that have been linked to cancer in laboratory experiments.	Smoking causes the gene mutations that lead to cancer in humans.

References

The BBC News report on cancer and second-hand smoke. http://news.bbc .co.uk/1/hi/health/2053840.stm

The Centers for Disease Control (CDC) tobacco information Web site. http://www.cdc.gov/mmwr/preview/mmwrhtml/00001800.htm

Pao, A., Tang, M., & Pfeifer, G.P. (1996). Preferential Formation of Benzo[a]pyrene Adducts at Lung Cancer Mutational Hotspots in P53. *Science*, *274*(5286), 430-432.

The Surgeon General's 1990 Report on the Health Benefits of Smoking Cessation http://www.cdc.gov/mmwr/preview/mmwrhtml/00001800.htm

LESSON WRAP-UP

As you draw these lessons to a close, remind students that making observations and inferences is commonplace in everyone's life. In fact, we make observations and inferences so readily that we seldom notice when we are doing so. Yet, in your class students must learn to move beyond the casual observations and inferences of everyday life to the more accurate and formal observations useful in science. Analyzing the comic strip panels is a fun way to begin this process. But don't let the fun get in the way of learning! Review the definitions of, and differences between, observation and inference. And remind your students that accurately describing observations is an important process skill in science, as is making appropriate inferences that are supported by accurate observations.

You'll also want to remind students that inference is an important aspect of much of what we know. Inferences not only help make comics funny, but they also help us make sense of the world around us. Scientists, too, use both observations and inferences to make sense of what they study. This is a good time to review the roles that both observation and inference play in the development of important scientific knowledge, using some of the specific examples listed in Part 2 of this chapter (and the discoveries that your students make in their Internet searches).

Figure 4.3 shows the "Science is . . ." diagram completed for the comic panel and "How do we know?" activities. You'll notice that this diagram is similar to the one presented in the previous chapter. That's because the activities in the present chapter are designed to reinforce what students have already learned about observation and inference. A key point for you to remember is that teaching the nature of science requires more than just having students make observations and inferences. You need to help them connect these process skills to the work of scientists and the development of scientific knowledge. Understanding the difference between teaching process skills and teaching the nature of science is a critical skill for you to learn as you help your students develop more complete conceptions of science.

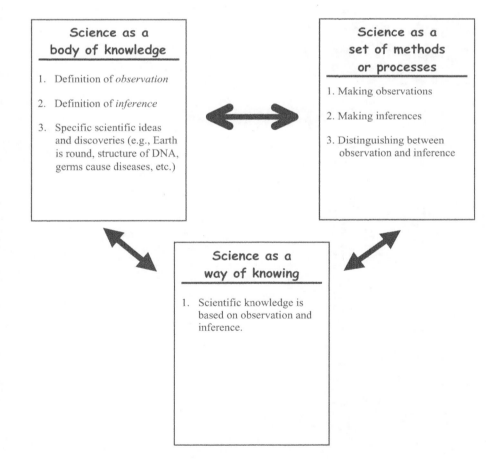

Figure 4.3
The three aspects of science.

ASSESSMENT

The following Notebook Assignments provide examples of assessments that go along with the activities presented in this chapter. The first is designed to be used in conjunction with a comic strip or panel of your choosing. Notebook Assignment 4.1 closely parallels the comic strip activity described in this chapter and, in so doing, assesses students' abilities to make and distinguish between observations and inferences. The last question of the assignment encourages students to apply what they've learned about observation and inference to the development of scientific knowledge.

Notebook Assignment 4.2 expands on this concept by having students search for "How we know . . ." answers on the Internet. This is a more open-ended activity, as students are asked to write a short summary of how we know about specific science concepts. After they've completed their summaries, the second part of the assignment tasks students with listing some of the important observations and inferences that support scientists' understanding of the concept. Student responses should be similar to the examples given in this chapter.

Observations and inferences in the comics

Name: _____ Date: _____

1. Take a good look at the comic strip your teacher has provided. You use your five senses while making observations in science, but just *look* at this comic. Look closely! List five observations.

   Observations

   _____

   _____

   _____

   _____

   _____

2. Now using your observations, what can you infer from the comic strip panel? What do you think will happen next? Can you make any inferences about the past? List five inferences.

   Inferences

   _____

   _____

   _____

   _____

   _____

3. Describe how your observations were used to support your inferences.

   _____

   _____

   _____

4. Do you think scientists ever make observations and inferences like you just did? Explain, giving at least one example of how scientists use observation and inference in your answer.

   _____

   _____

   _____

NOTEBOOK ASSIGNMENT 4.2

How Do We Know . . . ?

Name: _____ Date: _____

1. Using the Internet or other information resources, answer the question "How do we know?" for a concept selected from the list of scientific topics provided by your teacher. Your summary should include the primary evidence supporting scientists' views, including both observations and the inferences that scientists draw from these observations.

   _____

   _____

   _____

   _____

   _____

   _____

   _____

   _____

   _____

   _____

2. On the lines below, list as many observations and inferences as you can from your summary in part 1 of this assignment.

   Observations   **Inferences**

   _____   _____

   _____   _____

   _____   _____

   _____   _____

   _____   _____

   _____   _____

   _____   _____

   _____   _____

5

The "Proof" Is in the Cookie

Everyone likes to eat, so this activity will appeal to both elementary and middle school students. The teacher presents students with spherical "mystery cookies" and challenges them to determine what secret ingredient lies at the center of each one. Students are given "probes" (toothpicks) to explore the shape, hardness, and other physical characteristics of the cookies and of the mystery objects contained within. Later, they are permitted to eat the cookies and can add taste and texture to their observations. At no time are they allowed to "open up" the cookie to see directly what's inside. The activity gives students excellent opportunities to practice making observations and inferences and can be used to teach that observations may be based on senses other than sight.

LAYING THE GROUNDWORK

My Aunt Winney was an excellent cook. Whether the dish was wild game, fresh vegetables, potato salad, or baked beans, she knew how to give each dish that special "something" that set it apart from standard fare.

Unfortunately, Winney was not the kind of cook who was eager to share her expertise with others. She was quick enough to tell you how she prepared a particular dish when asked, but she always left out at least one key ingredient. That way, no one could duplicate her mouth-watering recipes, and she was able to maintain her culinary superiority at Bell family gatherings. Thus, when Aunt Winney passed away, she took her cooking secrets to the grave with her.

Since that time, several of my relatives have made something of a project of recreating Winney's gastronomic delights. For example, the first Thanksgiving after Winney's death, my sister-in-law, Orphah Rae, claimed that she had duplicated Aunt Winney's famous pumpkin pie, my childhood favorite. I was a bit skeptical of this claim at first because Orphah Rae had a reputation for unsuccessful attempts at reproducing Winney's dishes. This time I was pleasantly surprised, though. The pumpkin filling was just the right consistency; it was sweet, but not too sweet, and the pecan topping had the perfect blend of crunch and chewiness. Even the spices were perfect, a balanced blend of nutmeg and cinnamon.

After complementing Orphah Rae on her accomplishment, I asked her what Aunt Winney's secret ingredient was. "Glory™ brand canned sweet potatoes" was her reply. "Sweet potatoes in a pumpkin pie!" I exclaimed. "Are you out of your gourd?" (pun intended).

"Well, yes, actually," replied Orphah Rae. "I waited too long to purchase the pie filling from the local store and they were all out. So I tried sweet potatoes instead."

Of course, even though Orphah Rae's pie was entirely consistent with my memories of Aunt Winney's, this in itself does not *prove* in any absolute sense that Orphah Rae had duplicated Winney's recipe. The best we can conclude is that Orphah Rae had stumbled upon a combination of ingredients that *worked* (i.e., the pie looked, smelled, and tasted just like Aunt Winney's recipe). Whether it really was Aunt Winney's recipe is a moot point, since there is no way to prove it without consulting Aunt Winney. In the following activity, students learn a similar lesson about science as they attempt to discover the "secret ingredient" at the center of special "mystery cookies." If you are unable to prepare the cookies or find a suitable space for serving them, an alternate non-food activity is described in the strategy box on probing film canisters later in this chapter.

By the way, in case you were wondering, this was a fictional story. Such stories can be a fun way to engage students' attention as you introduce an activity. Feel free to make up your own set of relatives if you choose to introduce this activity with a story similar to mine.

THE ACTIVITY: MYSTERY COOKIES

LESSON AT A GLANCE

1. Students collect data on a cookie with an unknown object inside.
2. Students make inferences about the identity of the unknown object based on their data.
3. Students collect additional data by eating the cookie; then they revise their inferences.
4. Students discuss the work of scientists and the role of consensus in the scientific community.
5. Conclusions
   - Scientific knowledge can change with new observations and inferences.
   - Sometimes scientists can't directly observe what they want to know.
   - Good inferences allow scientists to be very sure of things they can't directly observe.

The Setup

This lesson can begin with a brief review of the terms *observation* and *inference*. If you have completed the candle activity (Chapter 3), students should remember that in science, *observation* refers to using your senses (sometimes with the help of specialized tools) to collect information about natural phenomena, while *inference* refers to using your observations to reach a logical conclusion. Next, you can set the context for the activity by telling a story similar to the one used to introduce this chapter.

Explain to your students that your friend has given you some very interesting cookies. They are sweet and chewy on the outside, and they have a surprise center. You have asked her to share the recipe, which she has—to a degree—but you know that she failed to tell you what is at the center of each cookie. Their job is to discover what lies at the cookie center, without alerting your friend to their mission. Therefore, they cannot break open the cookies, cut them in half, or in any way directly observe what lies in the center.

STRATEGY 5.1

Mystery Cookies Recipe

(*Makes 21 cookies*)

   1 box vanilla wafers (approximately 81 wafers)
   3 tablespoons corn syrup
   $1^1/_2$ teaspoons almond extract
   3 tablespoons softened butter
   3 tablespoons water
   6 tablespoons powdered sugar

Shhhh!!! 2 dozen gummi bears for hiding inside the cookies (other possibilities include M & Ms, Reeses Pieces, Red Hots, peppermint LifeSavers, etc.)

Extra powdered sugar for rolling the cookies in

1. Put the vanilla wafers in a plastic zip bag, push out most of the air, and close the bag.
2. Use a rolling pin (or whatever's handy) to smash the wafers into a powder without breaking the plastic bag.
3. Add the next five ingredients to the bag and mix thoroughly until you have pliable dough.
4. Pinch off 1 tablespoon of dough and hide the secret ingredient inside. Form the cookie into a sphere, then roll the cookie in the extra powdered sugar.
5. Make the rest of the cookies. Store the cookies in a sealed container with a dusting of powdered sugar to keep them from sticking together.
6. Eat the leftover gummi bears!

Observation Tools

At this point you can have the class brainstorm how they might explore what lies at the center of the cookies without breaking them open or altering their shape. While other possibilities exist, the most practical solution is to use some sort of probe to examine the interior of the cookie. You may want to point out to students that in a similar way, scientists make good use of probes when they wish to investigate objects or phenomena they cannot directly observe. For example, astronomers have learned much about other planets from probes they have sent into space. Oceanographers have used probes to explore what lies at the bottom of the ocean. And even doctors use probes to help them diagnose and fix problems within their patients' bodies.

Toothpicks make excellent probes for the activity. Using a toothpick as a probe, each student (or pair of students) is to record observations of what they "feel" with the toothpick. Before having students begin their exploration with the cookie probes, you will want to remind them of a few basic rules (see the Rules for Cookie Investigation box).

STRATEGY 5.2

Rules for Cookie Investigation

1. All students must wash their hands thoroughly before beginning the investigation.
2. Students may "drill" with their toothpick probes, but they may not tear open the cookie or dig a hole to see what is inside.
3. Students should take care to alter the appearance of the cookie as little as possible (we don't want the teacher's friend to know what we're up to).
4. Toothpicks are sharp, so be careful not to poke yourself or other students while completing the activity. If an accident occurs, notify the teacher at once.

Exploring the Cookies

Once students understand the basic rules, they can begin their explorations. Your job at this point in the lesson is to circulate around the room, making certain that students follow the rules and offering any help needed. Be careful not to give any hints about what lies at the center of the cookie. Encourage students to make observations about both the outside and inside of the cookie. Also, have them record as many observations as possible before trying to infer what lies at the center of the cookie. (See Notebook Assignment 5.1.) Student observations are likely to include such things as:

1. The cookie is round.
2. The cookie smells nutty.
3. The cookie is brown in color.
4. The cookie does not crumble easily.
5. There is something firm in the center of the cookie.
6. I can push the toothpick into the object in the middle of the cookie.

Making an Inference

After students have recorded their observations, have them infer what lies at the cookie's center. They should do this individually at first, but then have them share their inferences in small groups. Challenge them with the goal of reaching group consensus about what lies at the center. Have them record this group inference.

Getting More Data

Once you have discussed the inferences with students, they are ready for the final part of the activity. Tell students that although you promised your friend that no one would open up a cookie you didn't say anything about *eating* the cookies. Tell them to go ahead and eat their cookies, but so that you can be true to your word with your friend, they must pop the entire cookie in their mouths at once. Say, "Just pop the cookie in your mouth, chew it up, and swallow." Tell them *not* to bite off a piece to view what is inside and *not* to open their mouths and show their friends what lies inside the cookie. Once everyone has agreed to these rules, have them eat their cookies.

Of course, this step provides students with additional information about what is inside the cookie. By tasting the cookie and experiencing its texture as they chew, students will be able to add to their observation lists. These additional observations will support or refute their inferences about what secret ingredient lies at the center of the cookies.

Again, have students discuss the results of this investigation in small groups, and try to reach consensus on the identity of the secret ingredient. Make sure students record their modified inferences in their notebooks.

STRATEGY 5.3

Safety Considerations

Teachers should be aware of food safety concerns associated with eating in the classroom and take necessary precautions. For example, the NSTA Position Statement on Safety and School Science Instruction states:

> *Materials intended for human consumption shall not be permitted in any space used for hazardous chemicals and/or materials."*

If hazardous chemicals and/or materials are not stored or used in your classroom (which is the case for many elementary and middle school classrooms), then food safety is probably not an issue.

For those classrooms for which food safety is a concern, consider conducting the activity at an alternate location, such as the school cafeteria or outdoor courtyard.

To read the entire NSTA Position Statement on Safety and School Science Instruction, see http://www.nsta.org/positionstatement&psid=32.

ALTERNATIVE ACTIVITY: PROBING FILM CANISTERS

As an alternative to probing and eating cookies, you can have your students probe and then feel (with eyes closed) the contents of little plastic film canisters (you can still get these from your local film developer). To prepare for this activity, you'll want to find a film canister with a lid for every student in your class and then drill some holes in the lid and base with a small drill bit. Fill each canister with a mystery object such as a bolt, cotton ball, small pebble, marble or other small object. Glue the lid shut on each canister with plastic model cement or super glue.

When you pass out the filled and drilled canisters, give students a toothpick too. They can probe the canister, shake it, listen to it, and do anything they wish to make observations and inferences—they just can't open the lid! Your students may want to use the questions in Notebook Assignment 5.2 as a guide.

Be sure to remind them that scientists often do not have access to all the data, and that our powers of observation are limited in most cases, which is why they must not *look* into the canister.

LESSON WRAP-UP

Finally, have each group share their consensus inferences with the entire class. Again, the goal is to reach group consensus; however, you will likely find that the different groups come up with more than one inference that fits the data, making consensus difficult to reach.

Take advantage of this opportunity to compare the activity to the work of scientists. You can compare the difficulty your students experience in reaching consensus to what scientists experience at a scientific conference where they share their findings with other scientists from around the world. Also, you can point out that even in real science, sometimes there is not enough data to definitively decide between competing ideas.

Additionally, you can emphasize the tentative nature of scientific knowledge by asking students if it is possible to *prove* the identity of the secret ingredient. To any who believe that it is possible, ask them how they can go about proving this now that all of the data has been consumed. This question can lead to a discussion about how it is more accurate to state that the data lead to or support a particular inference rather than *prove* it absolutely.

As in the previous activities, it is not possible to prove unobservable entities and phenomena. Instead, scientists work to build strong cases for particular conclusions and explanations. Such conclusions that withstand the scrutiny of other scientists are accepted into the body of knowledge of a particular scientific field. Conclusions that do not withstand scrutiny are generally revised or eliminated from further consideration.

Scientists have theories that explain what lies at the center of our Earth, how our sun was formed, and what makes up an atom. Although we are unable to look directly at the center of the Earth, or watch for billions of years as stars are born and die, or even look inside an atom, we have enough data from various types of observations to form well-supported conclusions. Your students will be interested to know that scientists probe the inner workings of many types of "mystery cookies," just as they did in this activity.

Figure 5.1 illustrates the connections among the three aspects of science for the activity in this chapter.

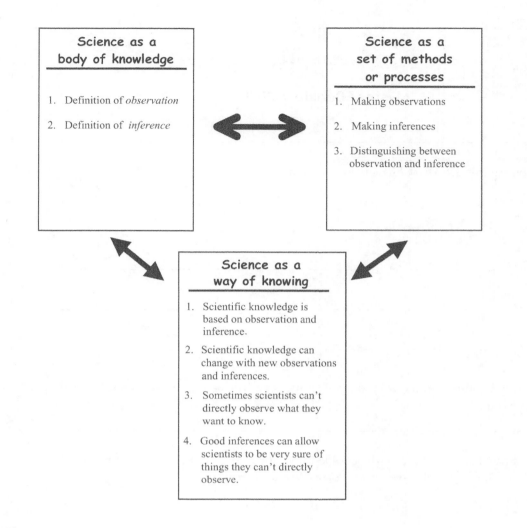

Figure 5.1

Connection among the three aspects of science for the "Mystery Cookie" lesson.

Science as a body of knowledge

1. Definition of *observation*
2. Definition of *inference*

Science as a set of methods or processes

1. Making observations
2. Making inferences
3. Distinguishing between observation and inference

Science as a way of knowing

1. Scientific knowledge is based on observation and inference.
2. Scientific knowledge can change with new observations and inferences.
3. Sometimes scientists can't directly observe what they want to know.
4. Good inferences can allow scientists to be very sure of things they can't directly observe.

ASSESSMENT

Notebook Assignment 5.1 may be helpful in guiding students' steps in this investigation. It closely follows the mystery cookie activity and provides a means for further assessing students' ability to distinguish between observation and inference but adds an opportunity for students to use senses other than sight for observation.

Notebook Assignment 5.2 is designed to go along with the alternative activity on probing film canisters.

Mystery Cookie Activity

Name: _____ Date: _____

1. Using your senses, list *your observations* about the cookie.

   What do
   you see? _____

   What do
   you smell? _____

   What do
   you feel? _____

   What do
   you hear? _____

2. Based on these observations, what do you think lies at the center of the cookie? (This is *your inference*.)

   _____

3. When your teacher says to, pop the cookie into your mouth and chew. Don't bite off a piece! No peeking inside! Write down *your observations.*

   What do you
   taste? _____

   What do you
   feel with your
   mouth? _____

4. Has your inference about what lies at the center of the cookie changed? If so, how?

   _____

   _____

5. Scientists often make inferences about things they can't actually see. Describe an example of when this has happened, when a scientist has had to make an inference about something without actually *seeing* it.

   _____

   _____

Film Canister Activity

Name: _____ Date: _____

1. Using your senses, list *your observations* about the object in the film canister.

What do you
see? _____

What do you
smell? _____

What do you
feel with the
toothpick? _____

What do you
hear? _____

2. Based on these observations, what do you think lies inside the film canister? (This is *your inference*.)

_____

_____

3. Scientists often make inferences about things they can't see. Describe an example of when this has happened, when a scientist has had to make an inference about something without actually *seeing* it.

_____

_____

_____

_____

6

Trailing Fossil Tracks

Students develop a story to explain patterns of fossil footprints revealed on an overhead projector. Their stories change as the teacher reveals more of the footprint-containing strata. This inquiry activity provides further practice making observations and inferences and helps students distinguish between the two process skills. The nature of science is addressed as students relate the changes they make to their inferences and the way scientists change their explanations as new data become available.

Laying the Groundwork

When I was a child, I loved exploring the creek that ran through our property in rural West Virginia. You never knew what you might find in the cool, fast-flowing waters of Witcher Creek. Of course, there were the ubiquitous crayfish (or "crawdads" as we called them). Minnows ("minners") were common enough, as were various larvae ("grubs") and worms. If I was lucky, I might uncover a salamander from underneath a rock, always one of my favorite finds.

There were also many interesting rocks to be found in the creek bed, with sedimentary rocks making up the vast majority of my finds. The shale and sandstone could take on a variety of colors, and I always kept a sharp lookout for any rock that looked particularly interesting.

I can still remember the excitement I experienced when I found my first fossil in the creek bed. I lifted up a palm-sized piece of gray shale and was thrilled to see a clear imprint of a fern frond on the underside of it. I remember wondering just how the fern imprint got in the rock and where it had come from.

Later, I learned that the fossil was a frond from a type of plant known as a tree fern from the Carboniferous Period, about 300 million years ago. During that time, scientists believe, the hollows and ridges I called home did not exist. Instead, the area was part of a shallow coastal swamp that extended for hundreds of miles, featuring vast tropical forests of ferns and primitive trees. Also known as the "Age of Plants," the Carboniferous Period was a time of ferns and fernlike trees, giant horsetails, and club mosses. Some of the land animals common during the Carboniferous

Period were primitive amphibians, reptiles, enormous dragonflies, and hundreds of varieties of cockroaches. Certainly, my home state was a very different place in the distant past!

Although it is exciting to discover fossils and think about the way the Earth looked in ancient times, it is also interesting to consider how we know what the Earth was like long before there was anyone around to describe it. It turns out that much of science deals with phenomena and entities that cannot be described through direct observation, so this question can be asked more generally: How do scientists know so much about things they cannot directly observe? As you may have guessed, the answer is found in the interplay of observation and inference, and the following classroom activity allows you to emphasize this point as students play the role of paleontologists.

THE ACTIVITY: FOSSIL TRACKS[1]

LESSON AT A GLANCE

1 Students consider a portion of a fossil showing animal tracks, making observations and inferences.

2 Students gain more data as additional sections of the fossil are made available.

3 Students revise observations and inferences.

4 Students discuss the work of real paleontologists and the role of inference in science.

5 Conclusions:
   - Scientific knowledge can change with new observations and inferences.
   - Scientists produce explanations that fit the evidence, even if they can't absolutely prove that such explanations are "true."

The Setup

Tell your students to imagine the class has gone on a fossil-hunting field trip somewhere in the wilds of Alberta, Canada. While exploring a dry creek bed someone turns up an interesting specimen—a large slab of rock containing numerous interesting impressions. Realizing immediately that this is an important find, you quickly gather to perform an initial field analysis of the fossil (see Figure 6.1). You can make a transparency of this fossil image and place it on the overhead projector for students to view.

---

[1] The activity described here is adapted from *Investigating the Earth* by William H. Matthew, III, Chalmer J. Roy, Robert E. Stevenson, Miles F. Harris, Dale T. Hesser, and William A. Dexter. Copyright © 1973 by Houghton Mifflin Company. All rights reserved. Reprinted by permission of McDougal Littell, a division of Houghton Mifflin Company.

Figure 6.1

The first piece of exposed fossil (transparency image 1).

Figure adapted from an activity in *Investigating the Earth* by William H. Matthew, III, Chalmer J. Roy, Robert E. Stevenson, Miles F. Harris, Dale T. Hesser, and William A. Dexter. Copyright © 1973 by Houghton Mifflin Company. All rights reserved. Reprinted by permission of McDougal Littell, a division of Houghton Mifflin Company.

1 meter

Making Initial Observations

In keeping with your emphasis on the role of observation in the development of scientific knowledge, ask students to record as many observations about the impressions in the fossil as they can in their science notebooks (see Notebook Assignment 6.1). Once students have completed their lists, ask them to share their results. At first, your students may tend to embellish their observations with inferences like the following:

- There are two different kinds of dinosaur tracks here!
- One dinosaur was bigger than the other.
- The big dinosaur was chasing the little one.

Point out to students that these "observations" include quite a bit of interpretation and, in fact, are actually inferences. After reminding students that observations should be limited to what you can directly observe, ask students to try again. Over the next few minutes, with a little guidance from you, students may come up with observations like the following:

- There are 14 impressions on the rock.
- The impressions have three distinct appendages on one side.
- There are two sets of impressions, one larger than the other.
- The two sets of tracks appear to converge on a common point.

Making Initial Inferences

Once you and your students agree on a list of observations, ask them to come up with a list of good inferences to go along with the observations. Remind them that to make good inferences, they should use their observations to draw reasonable conclusions. Of course, your students were ready to do this from the very beginning. They may come up with something like the following:

- The impressions in the rock are fossilized dinosaur footprints.
- The large prints and small prints represent two different kinds of dinosaurs.

- The large dinosaur is a carnivore.
- The large dinosaur sees the smaller one and approaches it to attack.

You may also have students who offer a different interpretation:

- The smaller impressions were laid by an infant dinosaur of the same species as the large prints.
- The tracks converge, not because the large dinosaur is attacking the smaller one, but because the larger one has found her lost young.

The different inferences or interpretations among your students create a "teachable moment" for discussing the idea that often more than one inference can fit the available data. Then ask students, "How can we know what really happened?" At least two possible solutions should emerge: Either we go back in time to observe how the tracks were laid down (which is impossible), or we uncover more of the rock slab with the hope that additional observations will help clarify our inferences.

Obtaining More Data

In this scenario, it just so happens that you can uncover more of the rock slab, revealing more impressions (Figure 6.2). You can make a transparency of this fossil image and place it on the overhead projector for students to view.

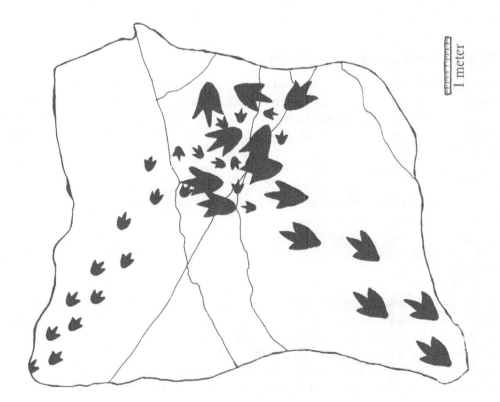

1 meter

Figure 6.2
More of the fossil is exposed (transparency image 2).

Figure adapted from an activity in *Investigating the Earth* by William H. Matthew, III, Chalmer J. Roy, Robert E. Stevenson, Miles F. Harris, Dale T. Hesser, and William A. Dexter. Copyright © 1973 by Houghton Mifflin Company. All rights reserved. Reprinted by permission of McDougal Littell, a division of Houghton Mifflin Company.

Once again, ask your students to carefully inspect the rock slab, this time concentrating their observations on the newly uncovered portion of rock. After a few minutes of rock inspection and note taking, have students begin to share their new observations. They may say something like the following:

- "In the middle of the new section of rock, the two sets of prints come together."
- "The large prints turned to converge upon the smaller ones."
- "The spacing of the smaller prints increases in this section of rock."
- "Here the large prints and small prints are all jumbled together."

This time your students will probably stick more to observations, without prematurely interjecting inferences. Next, have them make inferences about what the prints indicate. Consistent with their previous ideas, the students generally will interpret the prints as indicating a large carnivorous dinosaur attacked a smaller one. To encourage further creative thinking from your students, ask if there are any other plausible explanations for the pattern of prints.

I've had students suggest that perhaps the smaller prints are those of a baby dinosaur and the larger prints belong to its mother. The mother sees the baby, and approaches it, at which point they dance around a bit as the mother tries to feed the baby or perhaps pick it up. Another student may point out that there is no real evidence that the prints were laid down at the same time. The smaller dinosaur may have passed by first, followed by the larger dinosaur that was following its trail.

A student may even suggest that the larger dinosaur wasn't even tracking the smaller dinosaur to attack and eat it. Maybe the two sets of prints are from male and female dinosaurs of the same species. If that is the case, then perhaps they approached each other for a more romantic purpose.

The Entire Fossil Is Exposed

After hearing your students' creative, but plausible explanations, ask them what they might do to find out more. Maybe they could uncover more of the rock slab to see if there are any *more* markings. It just so happens that they can (see Figure 6.3). Make a transparency of this fossil image and place it on the overhead projector for students to view.

This time, students' observations may include the following:

- The small prints are missing from this portion of the rock.
- The large prints are present.
- The large prints are spaced closely and evenly.
- The three appendages are facing in the same general direction in all of the prints.

Ask students whether these additional observations reinforce their previous explanations or lead them to construct new ones. Most of my students usually insist that the new evidence provides confirmation of the carnivore/prey explanation and go on to infer that the absence of small tracks is proof that the large dinosaur ate the small one. However, sometimes a student or two has pointed out that the mother/baby explanation is just as plausible in that the absence of small tracks

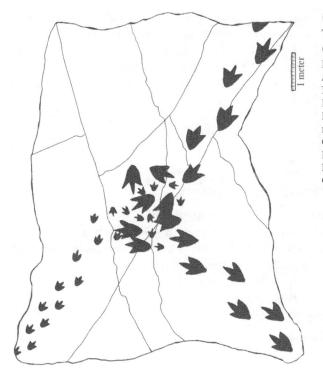

Figure 6.3
The entire fossil is exposed (transparency image 3).

Figure adapted from an activity in *Investigating the Earth* by William H. Matthew, III, Chalmer J. Roy, Robert E. Stevenson, Miles F. Harris, Dale T. Hesser, and William A. Dexter. Copyright © 1973 by Houghton Mifflin Company. All rights reserved. Reprinted by permission of McDougal Littell, a division of Houghton Mifflin Company.

could have resulted from her picking up her baby to carry it. Another scenario I've heard goes like this:

- A small dinosaur passes through a muddy area, leaving tracks in the mud.
- The small dinosaur discovers a number of worms in the mud, and excitedly darts about, eating its fill. Once full, the small dinosaur climbs a nearby tree for a safe place to nap.
- Sometime later, a large dinosaur smells the small one and follows the small dinosaur's trail.
- The large dinosaur follows the confused trail for a time, but eventually loses it in the place where the small dinosaur ate the worms.
- Disappointed, the large dinosaur wanders away.

LESSON WRAP-UP

Now it's time to discuss the similarities between students' work in this activity and the work of real paleontologists. Students made inferences about the origin of the fossil tracks based on careful observations of the available evidence. Additional data became available as more of the rock slab was "uncovered," resulting in modifications of the students' inferences. Eventually, several plausible explanations emerged. These explanations consisted of collections of individual inferences. The class analyzed the alternative explanations by comparing their logic and their abilities to account for the evidence.

In the end, students were not able to narrow down the possibilities to a single preferred explanation. The evidence was simply not conclusive. However, the process of observing, inferring, developing explanations, and weighing the explanations against the evidence is completely in line with the work of scientists. This process works in terms of producing explanations that fit the evidence, even if scientists can't prove that such explanations are "true."

ASSESSMENT

The following Notebook Assignment can be used in conjunction with the figures included in this chapter. It provides a means for you to assess students' understanding that scientists produce explanations that fit the evidence even when they cannot "prove" that their explanations are right.

Fossil Footprints Activity

Name: _____ Date: _____

Part of a large fossil is revealed, and you take a look. List three things that you observe.

1. _____

2. _____

3. _____

From these observations, you can make inferences about what might have happened. List three inferences.

1. _____

2. _____

3. _____

Ah! The second part of the fossil is revealed. Make three more observations.

1. _____

2. _____

3. _____

Have any of your inferences changed? If so, list your changed inferences below.

1. _____

2. _____

3. _____

Finally, the whole fossil is uncovered. You can now make even more observations.

1. _____

2. _____

3. _____

With the full picture, can you make different inferences from the ones you made before?

1. _____

2. _____

3. _____

Additional Questions

1. Did your inferences change as the activity proceeded? Why?

_____

_____

_____

2. How could you be absolutely sure about what happened on the rock slab more than 65 million years ago?

_____

_____

_____

3. In scientific cases like this, the evidence "supports" rather than "proves" an inference. Give an example of a different scientific case where this is true.

_____

_____

_____

7

Fragmented Fossil Tales

I n this activity, students are challenged to reconsider "the scientific method" after they complete an inquiry activity involving pieces of fossils. In the process, they practice their observation and inference skills as they attempt to reconstruct prehistoric organisms from fossil fragments. In regard to the nature of science, the lesson focuses on the roles of creativity and background knowledge in the development of scientific knowledge. Additionally, students revisit the concept that scientific knowledge is never absolute as they consider whether they (or scientists) can ever know that the organisms they reconstruct are 100% accurate.

LAYING THE GROUNDWORK

My tenth-grade biology teacher, Mrs. Smith, encouraged all of her students to put together a project for the school science fair; thus, I entered my very first science fair when I was 15. Since I had been reading about hydroponics, I decided to set up an investigation on growing plants without soil. My dad, an experienced gardener, encouraged my efforts to build a soil-less garden in the basement of our house in the middle of a snowy February.

First, I built a box and lined it with plastic to make it watertight. I filled the box with perlite (a material made from volcanic rock that looks like small Styrofoam beads), which served as the substrate for the plants by giving their roots something to grasp and by helping to hold moisture.

Next, I drilled a hole in one end of the box, just big enough to accept a small plastic hose. I glued the other end of the plastic hose inside a second hole I had drilled into a five-gallon bucket. Inside this bucket I prepared a special solution of plant fertilizer. By raising the bucket above the plant box, I could flood the box with the fertilizer solution. After soaking the box for a few hours, I would lower the bucket to the floor to allow the excess solution to drain back into the bucket. I repeated this process twice daily for the duration of the project. Finally, I used a bank of fluorescent light bulbs as a source of light for any plants that grew (Figure 7.1).

Figure 7.1
My hydroponic garden setup
when I was 15 years old.

In this box I planted a variety of garden vegetables, including leaf lettuce, radishes, onions, and tomatoes. For my research question I simply wanted to know how well these vegetables would grow without soil, in my basement, in the middle of winter. For the next several weeks I diligently raised and lowered the bucket of plant fertilizer solution, turned the light on and off at 12-hour intervals, and kept careful records of when the plants sprouted. As the plants grew to maturity, I measured the growth rate of each plant and calculated the average growth rate for each variety, which I recorded in my notebook.

When the day of the science fair finally came, my dad helped me pack up all of the materials and take them to school. My biology teacher was duly impressed with my efforts, and I was selected as one of a handful of students to represent our school at the regional science fair. By this time my hydroponics project had grown into a full-fledged garden, and I received many compliments from the other contestants who were impressed at what I had accomplished in my basement.

I still remember my trepidation as the team of judges came by to evaluate my work and my disappointment when they asked me hardly any questions and failed to look at the detailed notes I had so carefully recorded in my notebook. Instead, they simply wanted to know whether I had followed the scientific method. When they learned that I did not test a hypothesis and that I had not included a control group in my investigation, they quickly marked me off their list and moved on to the next project. Apparently, because I did not follow the scientific method I had failed to complete a "real" science project in their view. Were they right?

References to the scientific method are ubiquitous in science classrooms across America. Look in the first chapter of nearly any science textbook and you will find a description of the scientific method. Ask any student how scientists do their work and they're likely to describe the scientific method. Talk to most teachers and they will tell you that it is the scientific method that distinguishes science from pseudoscience. But ask scientists to describe the details of their work and they will not likely mention *any* of the steps of the scientific method.

How can this be? I believe this is a critical question, and we will work together to answer it in this chapter.

Let's take a look at the view of the scientific method presented in a recent-edition third-grade science textbook. In this book, the scientific method is organized in a chart that shows the steps that scientists use when solving a problem in science (Moyer et al., 2002). According to the authors, scientific investigations involve six primary steps (p. S6).

- Observation
- Question
- Hypothesis
- Experiment
- Conclusion
- Results support hypothesis/Results do not support hypothesis

Do these steps look familiar? This emphasis on the scientific method as *the* process that scientists use for problem solving is not unique to this particular textbook. Similar language may be found in the vast majority of science textbooks at all grade levels. For example, a modern physical science textbook introduces the scientific method as a "formal method for doing science and is based on rational thinking and experimentation." The authors state that the scientific method works as follows:

1. Recognize a question or a problem.
2. Make an educated guess, a hypothesis, to answer the question.
3. Predict consequences that can be observed if the hypothesis is correct. The consequences should be absent if the hypothesis is not correct.
4. Do experiments to see if predicted consequences are present.
5. Formulate the simplest general rule that organizes the three ingredients: hypothesis, predicted effects, and experimental findings.

Conceptual Physical Science: Explorations, 2003, p. 4.

And in *Science Explorer: Life Science* (Coolidge-Stolz, Cronkite, Jenner, Jones, & Lisowski, 2005), the authors list the following steps of the scientific method:

- Posing questions
- Developing a hypothesis
- Designing an experiment
- Collecting and interpreting data
- Drawing conclusions
- Communicating

They subsequently state, "There is no set path that a scientific inquiry must follow. Observations at each stage of the process may lead you to modify your hypothesis or experiment" (p. 17).

Although both of these textbooks include text asserting that scientists do not always follow the steps in the order shown, the authors do not describe any other ways that scientists approach investigations. Hence, the tacit message is that the scientific method is the only method scientists really follow, or at least the only one worth describing in the book.

At the heart of all these versions of "the scientific method" is the notion of creating and testing hypotheses. You may recall that the hypothesis is often loosely defined as "an educated guess." Stated more formally, a hypothesis is a testable, proposed answer to a research question. However you define it, in the view of these (and most other) science textbooks the hypothesis is central to scientific methodology.

Closely connected to the idea of hypothesizing is experimentation. An experiment is a controlled situation in which the scientist puts the hypothesis to the test. As typically presented in science textbooks, experiments involve a single independent variable, a dependent variable, a control group, and repeated trials. Through controlled experimentation, the scientist objectively assesses the validity of the hypothesis. Thus, following the scientific method means that you must create hypotheses and test them through experimentation—anything less and you are not doing science.

If this textbook view of the scientific method is correct, then the judges who dismissed my hydroponics project were correct. I had not completed a science project because I did not formulate and test a hypothesis. On the other hand, the textbook view may be too narrow. In addition to conducting controlled experiments, scientists may work in other, less structured ways that do not involve testing hypotheses. If this is the case, then the judges were out to lunch and my science fair project should have been accepted as science after all.

The following activity is one that addresses the question of whether all science follows the scientific method and teaches important lessons about the nature of science in the process.

The Activity: Fossil Fragments[1]

LESSON AT A GLANCE

1. Students list the steps of the scientific method.
2. Working in pairs, students make drawings of a fossil fragment.
3. Students use inferences to draw the rest of the organism in its habitat.
4. Students explain how they were able to infer a complete organism and environment from a tiny piece of fossil.
5. Students compare the process they used to that of paleontologists.
6. Students compare the process they used to the steps of the scientific method.
7. Conclusions:
   - Scientific knowledge is made of observation and inference.
   - Scientific knowledge is tentative.
   - The scientific method is not the only way scientists do science.

_____

[1] The lesson described here greatly expands upon an idea originally presented in the article, "Real Fossils, Real Science," by Luchessa and Lederman (1992) in *The Science Teacher, 59*(4), pp. 68–69.

Preassessment

Begin the activity by reviewing what your students know about the scientific method. Review the purposes of science and what makes science different from other ways of knowing (this activity is a great follow-up lesson to the ones presented in Chapters 1 and 2). As we saw in Chapter 2, science seeks to understand nature through the investigation of natural phenomena. Science values such things as systematic observation, inference, creative thought, reason, and logic. Although science generally seeks to be objective, it recognizes the fallibility of human nature and that 100% objectivity is an unobtainable goal.

After discussing the goals and values of science, ask students what method(s) scientists use to obtain these goals. Odds are, older students will respond overwhelmingly with "the scientific method." Explain to them that this question and their responses to it are the focus of today's activity and that by the end of the lesson they are likely to gain a new perspective on the scientific method and the work of scientists.

Next, you may either have students state the steps of the scientific method while you write them on the board (see Figure 7.2), or you can have them look up the scientific method in their textbooks and write the steps in their notebooks. Either way, be sure to lead a class discussion with the goal of reaching consensus on the steps of the scientific method before starting the main part of the activity—applying these steps to an investigation.

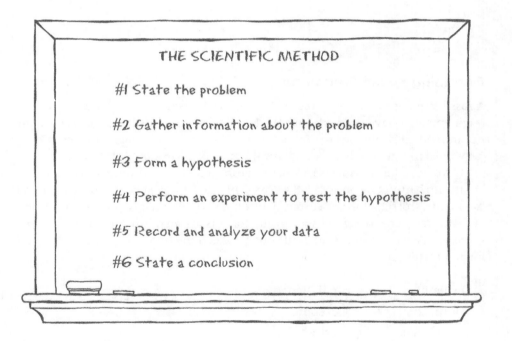

THE SCIENTIFIC METHOD

#1 State the problem

#2 Gather information about the problem

#3 Form a hypothesis

#4 Perform an experiment to test the hypothesis

#5 Record and analyze your data

#6 State a conclusion

Figure 7.2
The typically stated scientific method.

Observing a Fossil Fragment

After recording the steps of the so-called scientific method, have students select a partner. For each pair of students pass out the following:

- A blank overhead transparency
- Two different colored overhead transparency pens (e.g., black and red)

- A fossil fragment (See the Obtaining Fossil Fragments box for information on obtaining fossil fragments.)
- A ruler (optional)
- A magnifying glass (optional)

With a fossil fragment in hand, task each pair of students with making and recording careful observations. I usually ask students what the rock samples are. They shouldn't have any difficulty identifying the samples as fossils, but you'll likely need to point out that they are *fragments* of fossils. None of the samples represents an entire organism.

If your students have been studying the rock cycle, you can even ask what type of rock they have (the majority of fossils are made of sedimentary rock).

Once the students' interest is piqued, inform them that the goal is to accurately record their fossils on the overhead transparency using one of their two pens. Remind them that they are to be as accurate as possible. Depending on the available time, you can have them observe the fossil carefully with the magnifying glass and even use the ruler to take measurements. Providing specific guidelines for their drawings will facilitate the second part of the activity.

- Use only one color when drawing your fossil fragment.
- Place the drawing near the middle of the sheet.
- You may enlarge your drawing of the fossil to show more detail.

STRATEGY 7.1

Obtaining Fossil Fragments

A fossil fragment is simply a piece of a fossil organism. You may use any fossil fragments you have available, but the key is to choose fossil organisms that are not immediately obvious to your students. You can create fragments by carefully breaking intact fossils, or obtain them from a fossil collector or dealer.

We have found Howard Merk of Veronica Matthews Minerals (e-mail: vmattmin@att.net or phone: 1-800-284-2499) to be an excellent source of fossil fragments. In fact, Howard currently offers a very reasonably priced collection of fossil fragments designed specifically for this activity. Just ask for the "Fossil Fragment Activity Collection." Although collection contents will vary, the following fossils are typically included in the collection:

Belemnite	Shark Vertebra
Horn Coral	Coprolite
Orthoceras	Blastoid
Bryozoan	Archimedes Screw
Crinoid	Shark Tooth
Sting Ray barb	

We provided drawings of what scientists think these organisms look like in the handout at the end of this chapter.

- Be sure to include a scale (1x for life-size, 2x for twice life-size, etc.)
- You'll be adding to the drawing, so don't make your drawing so big that you cannot add to it later in the activity.

Finished drawings should look something like the one in Figure 7.3.

Once your students have completed their fossil drawings, it's time for the real challenge of the activity. Tell students to use a pen of another color to draw the rest of the organism represented by their fossil fragment. You may also challenge them to include other features of the organism's habitat that are indicative of the way the organism fits into its environment (what it eats and other factors related to its survival).

Figure 7.3
Belemnite fossil fragment.

STRATEGY 7.2

Fossil Fragment Images

If you are unable to obtain a set of fossil fragments, you may want to try the activity using the following images of fossil fragments.

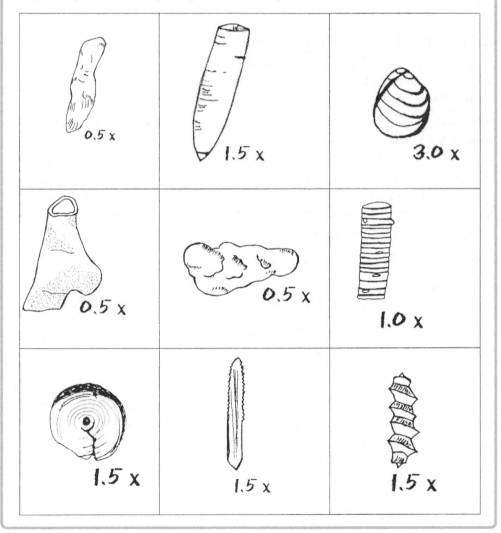

Students will need some time to complete this task, and it helps if you tell them not to worry about coming up with the "right" answer. Rather, encourage them simply to "take their drawings where their fossils lead them." Completed drawings should look something like the example in Figure 7.4.

Sharing Results

When the student pairs have completed the drawings of the fossil organisms in their environments, it's time to share their results with the rest of the class. Have each group present their drawings on the overhead projector for the rest of the class to see. If you have already taught your students to distinguish between observation and inference (see Chapter 3), then you can ask them to identify the observation part of the drawing (drawing of the original fossil fragment in one color) and the inference part of the drawing (drawing of the rest of the organism and its habitat in the alternative color). As pairs of students present their work, ask them what it was about their original fossil fragments that led them to infer this particular organism and environment. Encourage students to be specific in regard to the fossil characteristics that were most influential to their work.

Reflecting on the Experience

Once all of the presentations are completed, have students reflect on how the fossil fragment activity relates to science. You can do this by asking students a series of key questions:

"How were you able to infer a complete organism and environment from a tiny piece of fossil?"

The key idea for students to understand is that they used both observation and inference to construct their drawings. Observation alone was insufficient for them to come up with their final drawings of the fossil organism in its environment. Also, it is important to highlight the role creativity played in the activity. When viewed only from the perspective of the scientific method, science can appear

Figure 7.4
Student observation and inference based on a belemnite fossil fragment.

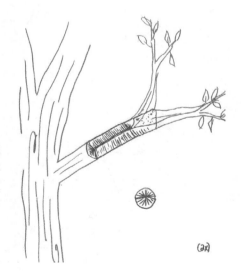

rather sterile and dry. Viewed from the perspective of actually doing science, it is clear that the process of observing and inferring can be very creative and exciting.

"Is the process you used to do this similar to the process paleontologists use to reconstruct prehistoric organisms?"

You're looking for class consensus that the students' work in reconstructing the fossil organism and its environment was similar to the work of paleontologists. Essentially, both the scientists and the students use comparative anatomy to reconstruct unfamiliar organisms—they compare the structures of prehistoric organisms to similar structures in modern organisms. They then infer the prehistoric organism's form and function in light of what they know about the form and function of modern organisms.

"Is this science?"

Students will readily agree that this is clearly a scientific process. Otherwise, we would not call those who study dinosaurs scientists, nor would paleontology be considered a branch of science.

"Why did some of you who received similar-looking fossil fragments draw very different creatures?"

I like to make sure that some of the student pairs receive essentially the same fossil fragment, just so that I can ask this question. For example, Figure 7.5 shows a second student's observations and inferences based on a belemnite fossil fragment. Compare it with the drawing in Figure 7.4. The answer to the question, of course, lies with the different background knowledge of the observers. Different background knowledge results in different inferences and interpretations, even when starting with the same data. This is true in all branches of science, not just paleontology.

The Influence of Background Knowledge

A good example of the influence of different background knowledge on interpretation is the variety of scientific explanations for the extinction of the dinosaurs. About 65 million years ago, toward the end of the Cretaceous period, a mass

Figure 7.5
Another student's observations and inferences based on a belemnite fossil.

extinction obliterated the dinosaurs and many of the other plants and animals living at the time. While no one knows for sure what caused the catastrophic die-off, many causes have been proposed to support the available data. Two ideas have gained wide support among scientists, and it turns out that the explanation a particular scientist prefers tends to be related to his or her background.

For example, in my college astronomy classes, professors have emphasized the asteroid impact theory, in which an asteroid struck the Earth near the Yucatán Peninsula in the Gulf of Mexico. The resulting explosion would have raised a huge dust cloud that could have shrouded the Earth for months or years, obscuring the sun and lowering the Earth's temperature. This ongoing winter, in turn, would kill off the plants and animals (including dinosaurs) that could not adapt to the new, harsher climate. You can read David Raup's (1992) book, *Extinction: Bad Genes or Bad Luck?* for an engaging account of the development of this theory.

My geology professors, on the other hand, tended to attribute the demise of the dinosaurs to a more earthly cause. The late Cretaceous period was a time of high tectonic activity, resulting in greater numbers and intensity of volcanic eruptions. It is postulated that ash from this increased volcanic activity could have obscured the sun in much the same way as a large meteor impact would have, resulting in the observed mass extinctions. Vincent Courtillot's (2002) book, *Evolutionary Catastrophes: The Science of Mass Extinctions,* presents the details of this alternative to asteroid impact theory.

I'm not saying that *all* astronomers explain the dinosaurs' demise by the impact theory or that *all* geologists subscribe to the idea of increased volcanology. However, it is not surprising that astronomers would look toward the heavens for an explanation of the dinosaur extinctions, while geologists would look underfoot. The point is that background knowledge and specific schools of thought within a discipline influence how scientists interpret data, just as your students' differing background knowledge resulted in different inferences and interpretations of the fossil data they were given.

Other Factors Influencing Inferences

Ask your students:

"Would paleontologists reach the same conclusions about the identity of the organisms and their environments as the class did?"

The answer to this question is, of course, "probably not," and the reason is closely related to the answer to the previous question. If inference and interpretation rely on background knowledge, then paleontologists' greater knowledge of fossil organisms and ancient environments will result in more complete reconstructions. At a general level, the process that students go through in this activity is very similar to that of paleontologists; however, the outcome is likely to differ due to the paleontologists' more complete knowledge and deeper understandings. This is the reason it is not true that "anything goes" in science. Interpretations and inferences must be consistent with current understandings before the scientific community accepts them.

If you would like to emphasize this point further, you can show your students drawings of what scientists view as the organisms represented by their fossil fragments. You'll find drawings based on scientists' interpretations in Handout 7.1 at the end of this chapter. The purpose here is not to emphasize obtaining "the right answer." Rather, you can use this extension of the activity to help students understand that scientists' inferences and interpretations differ from their own because:

1. Scientists are working with a lot more background knowledge.
2. Scientists base their inferences on a greater amount of fossil evidence.

Occasionally, a student pair will draw and present some fanciful organism like the one depicted in Figure 7.6. This never fails to get a laugh from the rest of the class, and rightly so. When this happens, I ask the class what is so funny about the drawing. The answer I receive is almost always that "There is no such thing as a _____." or "No animal could look like that!" So even with the limited background knowledge my students possess, it is not true that anything goes. The class automatically applies norms to the each student pair's work. Any proposed organisms that fall outside of these norms are not accepted.

The same thing is true in science—to be accepted by the scientific community, a scientists' work usually must fall within the norms set by the group. Work deemed too fanciful is held to greater scrutiny and skepticism—hence, Carl Sagan's well-known assertion mentioned in an earlier chapter that "extraordinary claims require extraordinary evidence."

Determining Whose Inference is Right

By definition, inferences are based upon our background knowledge (see Chapter 3). Since there is no way to know everything about extinct organisms' structures and environments, there is no way to be 100% sure about the accuracy of our inferences. On the other hand, scientists usually possess lots of background knowledge about the issues and entities they investigate. Although they must always acknowledge that new evidence can come to light (or new ways of interpreting existing

Figure 7.6
Unicorn reconstructed from a fossil fragment.

evidence) that requires them to modify their understandings, scientists can be very confident about their understandings, particularly when the preponderance of evidence points them in a particular direction.

In relation to this concept, I like to ask students:

"Can we know with 100% certainty that our reconstructed organisms and habitats are correct?"

My students usually respond that the only way we could know with 100% certainty would be to travel back in time to observe the organism in its environment and to observe its fossil forming. Of course, this is impossible, so 100% certainty is an unattainable goal. But as we've seen with this activity and our discussion about the work of scientists, this doesn't mean that we can't have fun inferring fossil organisms. With the right background knowledge, scientists' inferences can be useful and accurate.

LESSON WRAP-UP

As a final part of the fossil fragment activity, have students compare the process they went through to reconstruct their fossil organisms and environments to the steps of the scientific method on the chalkboard or in their textbooks. In doing so, they will see that they did not follow all of the steps. For example, they did not state a formal hypothesis, nor did they perform experiments to test hypotheses (see Figure 7.7).

As we saw earlier, in the absence of these two critical steps the students were not following the scientific method. Likewise, scientists simply may not be able to perform controlled tests of a hypothesis when they are dealing with organisms that have been extinct for millions of years. Thus, not all scientists follow one method when doing science.

Figure 7.7
Fossil activity method.

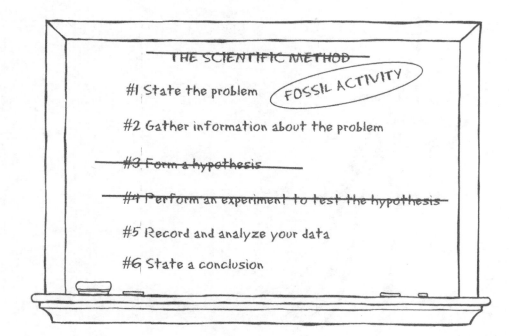

Here's another example: Astronomers do not come to understand the life cycles of stars and internal structures of galaxies by conducting experiments that involve manipulating and controlling variables. After all, how would you control variables when investigating a galaxy that lies 100 million light years away? Or how about Darwin's famous observations while serving as naturalist on the good ship *Beagle*? He collected specimens, made extensive observations, and recorded detailed field notes, all of which eventually led him to develop his theory of natural selection—without conducting a single controlled experiment! In fact, much of science involves descriptive studies that do more to generate hypotheses than to test them. This is still science, but it's a different kind of science than is emphasized in most textbooks.

It may be useful to think of two very broad approaches to generating scientific knowledge: more descriptive methods that rely heavily on observation and inference, and more experimental methods in which variables can be controlled and hypotheses can be tested. Thus, rather than teaching my students that there is a single step-by-step method that all scientists follow, I teach them that the knowledge we have in science is developed through many creative approaches. Some rely heavily on observation and inference. Others focus more on experimentation. Sometimes serendipity plays a role. My goal is to help students understand that science is much more varied and creative in its approaches than is implied by a single scientific method.

Figure 7.8 illustrates the connection between the three aspects of science that the fossil fragment activity addresses. Your goal should be to explicitly teach the concepts listed in each of the three boxes as you share the lesson with your students.

ASSESSMENT

There are many possibilities for assessing students' understandings of the process skills and nature of science understandings targeted in the fossil fragment activity. You could simply require students to show you their drawings of the fossil organism and its environment, with the observation and inference portions of the drawings clearly labeled. This would cover the process-skills portion of the assessment. The nature-of-science portion of the assessment could parallel the discussion that follows the presentation of their drawings. You could ask them a series of short-answer essay questions like the ones in Notebook Assignment 7.1.

A more humorous way to assess students' understandings of the target concepts of this activity is to have them complete Notebook Assignment 7.2 and/or 7.3.

Figure 7.8
Connection among the three
aspects of science for the
Fossil Fragment activity.

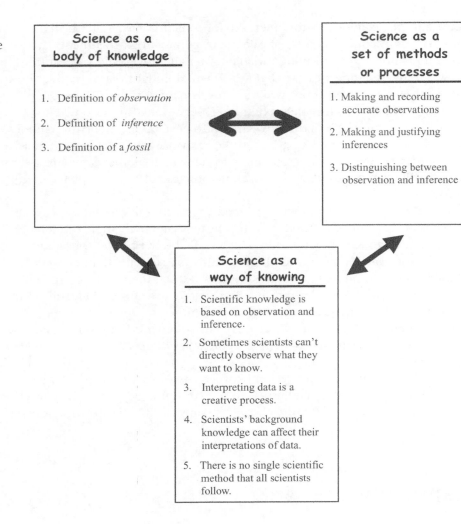

Science as a body of knowledge

1. Definition of *observation*

2. Definition of *inference*

3. Definition of a *fossil*

Science as a set of methods or processes

1. Making and recording accurate observations

2. Making and justifying inferences

3. Distinguishing between observation and inference

Science as a way of knowing

1. Scientific knowledge is based on observation and inference.

2. Sometimes scientists can't directly observe what they want to know.

3. Interpreting data is a creative process.

4. Scientists' background knowledge can affect their interpretations of data.

5. There is no single scientific method that all scientists follow.

Fossil Fragment Activity

Name: _____ Date: _____

Answer each of the following questions with a short paragraph.

1. How were you able to infer a complete organism and environment (habitat) from a tiny piece of fossil?

   _____

   _____

   _____

2. Why did different groups who received fossil fragments similar to yours draw very different organisms?

   _____

   _____

   _____

3. In your opinion, was the process that you followed to re-create your organism in its habitat scientific? Why or why not?

   _____

   _____

   _____

4. Can you (or a scientist for that matter) know with 100% certainty that your re-created organism and habitat are correct?

   _____

   _____

   _____

5. One of the things that we learned in this activity is that scientists do not always exactly follow what is often called "the scientific method." Describe other ways that scientists come to understand the world.

   _____

   _____

   _____

Fossil Fragment Activity

Name: _____ Date: _____

Look carefully at the comic panel and label the portions that represent observations and those that represent inferences. Then answer the questions below.

1. What is funny about this comic? How does it relate to science?

   _____

   _____

   _____

2. Are all of scientists' inferences based on such small amounts of data? Explain.

   _____

   _____

   _____

3. Can scientists ever be confident of their inferences? Explain.

   _____

   _____

   _____

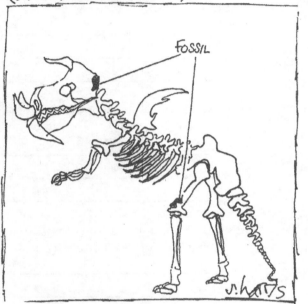

SKELETON OF NEWLY DISCOVERED DINOSAUR SPECIES RECONSTRUCTED FROM TWO FOSSILS (DISPUTED BY SOME EXPERTS)

FOSSIL

ScienceCartoonsPlus.com. Used with permission.

Fossil Fragment Activity

Name: _____ Date: _____

1. Briefly describe what is happening in each section of the comic panel.

   Section 1.
   _____
   _____
   _____

   Section 2.
   _____
   _____
   _____

   Section 3.
   _____
   _____
   _____

   Section 4.
   _____
   _____
   _____

ScienceCartoonsPlus.com. Used with permission.

2. What makes this comic funny?
   _____
   _____
   _____

3. Can a situation similar to the one portrayed in the comic happen in science as well? If so, how can scientists have confidence in their inferences and interpretations of data?
   _____
   _____
   _____

The following are images of fossil fragments (and scientists views of the actual organisms) that are included in Veronica Matthews Minerals' "Fossil Fragment Activity Collection" (e-mail: vmattmin@att. net or phone: 1-800-284-2499).

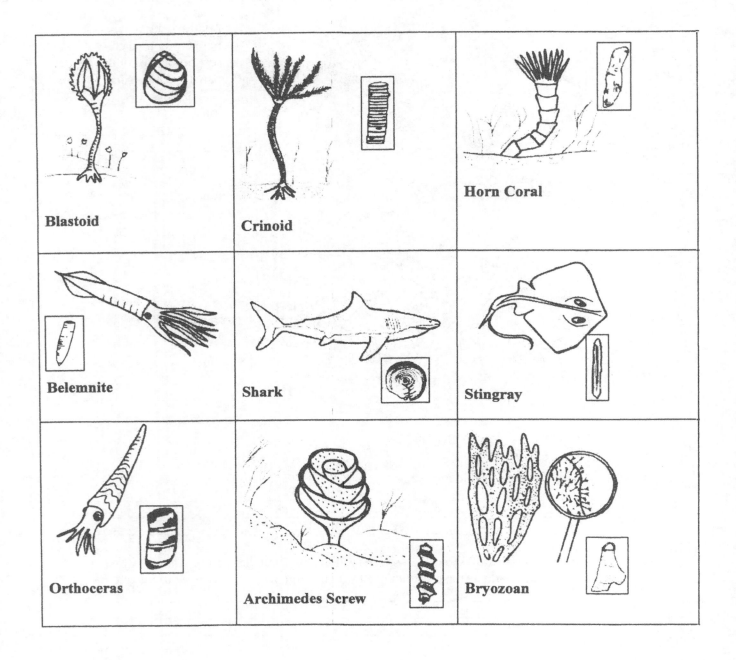

8

Of Cannon Balls and Tissue Paper

This Web-based, black-box activity focuses on the roles of observation and inference in the development of our understanding of the internal structure of the atom. As part of the lesson, students attempt to discern hidden shapes within a box by observing the flight pattern of projectiles that rebound off the hidden object. After completing the activity, students will discuss how observation and inference permitted them to develop a model of the internal structure of the black box, the characteristics of this model, and the way it relates to the work of scientists and the models they develop.

LAYING THE GROUNDWORK

As I write this book, my younger daughter Adrianne is 12 years old. Of course, this is a time of great change, both in her body and her emotions. Adri is peeking around the corner of womanhood, but still is a little girl at heart (and a quite fine one at that, I might add). I suspect that you can remember the awkwardness of that time and all the questions it raised.

Sure enough, the other day Adri (who is studying physical science in school) asked me the inevitable question all parents have come to dread: "Dad, how can we know what's inside of an atom, if it's too small to see inside?" What a question! If only she were taking biology this year and had asked about the birds and the bees, or some similarly easy topic!

The way we can know about objects and phenomena that cannot be directly observed is a critical aspect of the nature of science. Science is full of examples of knowledge that does not come from direct observation. After all, no one has actually seen the dinosaurs, or flown to distant stars, or journeyed to the center of earth. Yet scientists have good reason to believe that they understand the characteristics of dinosaurs, the distance to remote stars and galaxies, and the internal structure of the Earth. When direct evidence is unavailable, scientists base knowledge on inference and indirect evidence. They build logical arguments based upon the direct and indirect evidence available and over time can amass a high degree of confidence that their inferences and conclusions work well enough to be considered "true" for the present. Even so, the journey to this place of confident bliss can be long and arduous and full of false starts and mistaken inferences. Such is the case with the development of our understanding of the atom, which I'll share with you in much the same way I shared with my daughter.

Matter

You may remember from your school days that all materials are made of matter and that *matter* is defined as anything that has mass and takes up space. But what is matter made of?

This question has plagued philosophers and scientists for thousands of years (and eventually led many students to question, "What's it matter, anyway?" But I digress). The basic building blocks of matter are far too small to be observed directly, even with today's most powerful microscopes. Therefore, scientists have had to rely on observing how matter behaves, rather than on direct observation, to understand its tiniest units. Such observations are referred to as *indirect* observations or evidence. Indirect observations are employed in science whenever we cannot directly study the object or phenomenon of interest with our five senses (or with technology that enhances our senses).

Indirect observations can be a powerful tool for understanding what cannot be seen. As scientists collect more and more indirect evidence, they begin to construct a mental picture or model of the object or phenomenon. As we shall see in the case of the atom, these models are subject to change as new evidence becomes available, and as new ways of thinking about existing evidence come into play. Thus models, like all other scientific ideas, should be seen as tentative in the sense that they have the potential to change, even though scientists may be very confident that they are on the right track. In the following sections I will recount the ways that creativity, imagination, and indirect evidence have all been used to construct the contemporary model of the atom.

The Greek Philosophers

The philosopher Democritus is credited as one of the first to formally consider the nature of matter. Democritus lived more than 2,400 years ago, before the discipline we call science had developed. He, along with other philosophers of his day, puzzled (as only philosophers can) over the question of whether matter could be divided into smaller and smaller pieces *ad infinitum*, or whether there was a smallest unit of matter that could not be further divided. Democritus concluded (based on logic and argument, rather than evidence) that matter could not be forever divided into smaller pieces. Cut a block of lead in two, then do it again and again and again, and Democritus argued, you will eventually obtain the smallest piece of lead possible. This smallest piece would be indivisible, so Democritus called it the *atom*, which means "not to be cut" in Greek.

Democritus' ideas about the atom were not accepted by many philosophers of his day. In fact, his ideas about atoms were largely forgotten over time and only resurfaced after a widely accepted model of matter was developed in the early 1800s by an English chemist.

Dalton's Atomic Theory

John Dalton (1766–1844) was a meteorologist whose interest in how gases interact led him to develop a series of ideas about matter that eventually became known as

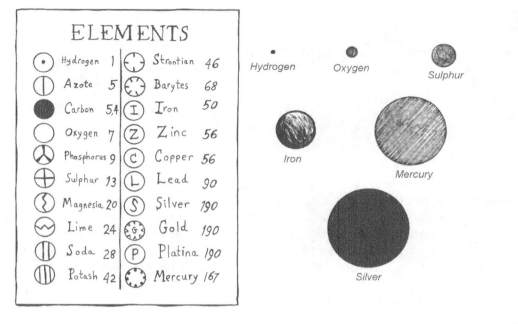

Figure 8.1
Dalton's table of
elements and relative
sizes of atoms.

Dalton's Atomic Theory. To develop the theory, Dalton used experimental data about how certain gases mixed and combined, in conjunction with Democritus' ideas about atoms proposed more than 2,000 years earlier. Dalton's theory differed from the Greek model in that it was based on evidence, as opposed to being solely a philosophical statement that atoms exist because they should exist. In short, his atomic theory consisted of four postulates.

1. Elements consist of tiny particles called atoms. Atoms are tiny, indivisible, and indestructible.
2. All atoms of an element are identical and have the same mass.
3. Atoms of each element differ from one another; particularly, they have different masses.
4. Compounds consist of atoms of different elements combined together. When elements react, they combine in whole-number ratios.

Dalton's Atomic Theory represented a huge leap forward in our understanding of atoms. Even though some of Dalton's postulates were later found to be incorrect, the heart of his theory (that atoms have distinguishing properties and that new compounds are formed by combining and separating atoms) is still considered a foundation of modern chemistry.

Thomson's Model

In 1897 English scientist J. J. Thomson provided evidence that atoms are made up of even smaller particles and in so doing demonstrated that Dalton's model of the atom should be revised.

Thomson conducted a series of investigations in which he passed electric current through an evacuated tube containing tiny amounts of gas. This caused a beam of particles to be produced in the tube. Thomson called these particles "corpuscles," but today they're known as electrons. Even though the particles were

Figure 8.2
Thomson's apparatus
with which he discovered
the electron.

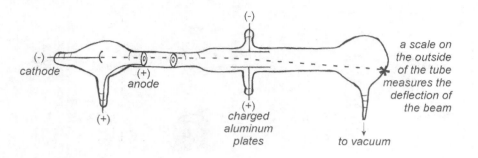

too small to be seen, Thomson was able to determine that they had a negative
charge. He did this by passing the beam of particles through a charged field and
noting that it was attracted toward positively charged plates. The beam of electrons
struck the end of the glass tube, where they caused a glowing spot (Figure 8.2). So,
while the individual particles were too small to see directly, Thomson could observe them indirectly through their interaction with the glass tube, and he could
see that they were attracted to a positively charged plate. This led Thomson to infer that the electrons must be negatively charged, since he knew that opposite
charges attract.

But where did the negatively charged electrons come from, since the gas inside
the tube was neutral? Thomson figured that the electrons must be coming from
within the atoms of the gas. Atoms were divisible after all! Furthermore, since atoms
were known to be neutral, there must be positive charges within the atom to balance
the negatively charged electrons. Thus, Thomson's model of the atom, commonly
called the "plum pudding" model, consisted of the negatively charged electrons em-
bedded in a positively charged substrate (Figure 8.3). Thomson's model of the atom
eventually became known as the "plum pudding" model, due to its similarity to the
old English dessert consisting of candied fruit mixed throughout a bread pudding.

Rutherford's Model

A little more than a decade later, a scientist originally from New Zealand, Ernest
Rutherford, and others at Manchester University in England conducted experiments

Figure 8.3
Thomson's "plum pudding" model of
the atom.

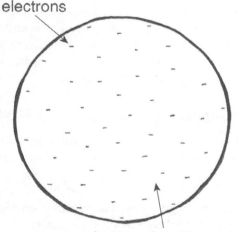

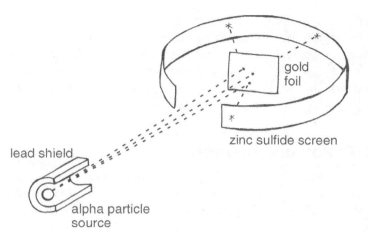

Figure 8.4
Rutherford's gold foil investigation.

that challenged Thomson's plum pudding model of the atom. Rutherford and his colleagues were bombarding a very thin sheet of gold foil with alpha particles and observing the scattering of these particles. Alpha particles are identical to helium nuclei and they are naturally emitted by radioactive materials such as uranium. They could not directly observe the alpha particles, because they were far too small. Instead, the procedure required many hours in a darkened room watching for tiny flashes of light as the scattered particles struck a special screen (Figure 8.4).

Rutherford was surprised to observe (indirectly) that most of the particles passed through the foil without any deflection; under the plum pudding model, charge would be distributed thickly in the foil, and few particles would avoid deflection. This result led Rutherford to infer that most of the apparently solid metal was, in fact, empty space. Even more surprising, a tiny number of the particles underwent larger deflections in their paths—some even bounced back from the foil! (See Figure 8.4.) This could never happen in Thomson's plum pudding model, which included no particles large enough for alpha particles to bounce off. In fact, Rutherford was so amazed at this result that he described it as akin to cannon balls bouncing off of tissue paper!

These findings led Rutherford to the conclusion that the atom is mostly empty space, with most of the atom's mass concentrated in a relatively tiny center, the nucleus. Rutherford included Thomson's electrons in his new model and concluded that they were much smaller than the nucleus, which they orbit like planets orbit the sun (Figure 8.5).

Figure 8.5
Rutherford's planetary model of the atom.

electron orbits

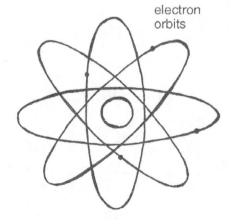

Once again, indirect evidence was used to further revise the atomic model. Rutherford couldn't possibly see the nucleus in the atom, but he could infer its existence based upon the way charged particles behaved when they were fired through the gold foil. At the time, he still didn't know what this newly discovered nucleus was made of, but within the next 20 years, Rutherford and other scientists at Manchester University would solve more pieces of the atomic puzzle.

Discovery of the Proton and Neutron

In 1918, Ernest Rutherford made another "striking" (pun intended!) discovery while firing alpha particles into nitrogen gas in much the same way he fired them at gold foil. Instead of alpha particles striking his scintillant screen as expected, it appeared that hydrogen nuclei were hitting it instead. How could this be? Rutherford was actually changing nitrogen atoms into more massive oxygen atoms, and leftover hydrogen nuclei were flying about. He inferred that the nucleus of a hydrogen atom must be an elementary particle and that it was broken away after the nitrogen nucleus was struck by the alpha particle, creating a more massive oxygen nucleus in its place.

Rutherford named this new discovery *proton* after the Greek word *protos*, meaning "first." He certainly couldn't see these protons, but he inferred they were there, and he inferred that the hydrogen nucleus was made up of one. It's elementary particle mathematics! A nitrogen nucleus + an alpha particle = an oxygen nucleus + a hydrogen nucleus (Figure 8.6).

A few years later, he hypothesized that there must be another particle inside the nucleus, because the nucleus was too massive to be accounted for by protons alone. Rutherford searched diligently for evidence of the neutron, but never found it. Years later one of his colleagues at Manchester University, James Chadwick, discovered the neutron while shooting alpha particles into a piece of beryllium. A strange mysterious ray emanated from the fired-upon beryllium, and this ray could knock atoms loose from different target materials that were put in the ray's path. It turned out that this mysterious neutral ray was composed of neutrons (Figure 8.7).

Figure 8.6
Rutherford transmutes nitrogen into oxygen and discovers the proton.

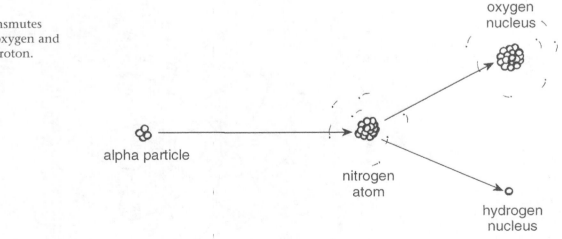

oxygen nucleus

alpha particle

nitrogen atom

hydrogen nucleus

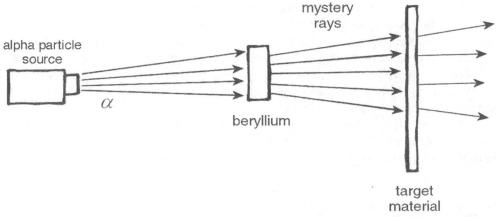

Figure 8.7
Chadwick's investigation.

Finally, scientists had a modern-day conception that an atom is made of electrons orbiting a very small but heavy nucleus composed of tightly bound protons and neutrons (Figure 8.8).

Today's Model of the Atom

By 1932 the last of the subatomic elementary particles had finally been discovered through the interplay of observation and inference when English physicist James Chadwick discovered the neutrally charged particle in the nucleus of atoms, later called the neutron (Figure 8.8). But was this really the final piece to the atomic puzzle? In the decade that followed, the positron, the meson, the muon, and the pion were discovered. Furthermore, the development of quantum mechanics helped scientists understand that electrons are located in "energy levels" about the nucleus and that these energy levels take on various shapes depending on the probability of the electron being there.

Electrons do not orbit the nucleus in prescribed orbits as previously thought, but they rapidly move in "clouds" of probability. In other words, we cannot know exactly where an electron is going to be (as would be the case if the orbit was fixed), but can only predict the region where it's likely to be (probability "cloud"). Also, the current thinking is that protons and neutrons themselves are actually

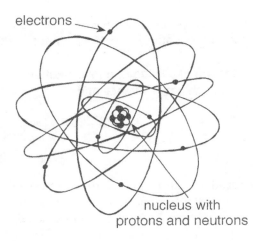

Figure 8.8
Chadwick's model of the atom with protons, neutrons, and electrons.

composed of two types of particles called quarks, the up quarks and the down quarks. While two up quarks and one down quark make a proton, two down quarks and one up quark make a neutron. An explanation of quantum mechanics is outside the scope of this book, *and* my 12-year-old daughter's realm of comprehension, but if you want to know more, the following Intro to Quantum Mechanics Web site by Todd Stedl is an excellent place to start: http://www.hi.is/~hj/QuantumMechanics/quantum.html.

Our view of the atom has certainly changed over the past 2,400 years. To date, more than 200 other particles are thought to comprise the atom. Democritus may very well be rolling over in his grave for calling the atom, "not to be cut"!

THE ACTIVITY: MYSTERY SHAPES GAME

LESSON AT A GLANCE

1. The teacher tells the stories of Democritus, Dalton, Thomson, Rutherford, and Chadwick in order to give students an understanding of how atomic theories have changed over time.

2. The teacher introduces students to the Mystery Shapes guessing game and shows them how it works.

3. Working in pairs, students play the first level of the game, trying to get three correct guesses in a row. They shoot particles at a covered mystery object and guess its shape from the way the particles bounce off it.

4. After mastering the first level, students are given three mystery objects and must infer their shapes and draw them on a handout. They are not given choices.

5. Students explain how they were able to infer the shape of the mystery objects from the way the particles bounced off it.

6. Students compare the process they used to that of atomic physicists.

7. Students compare the process they used to that of other scientists who use indirect evidence.

8. Conclusions.
   - Scientific knowledge is gained through observation and inference.
   - Scientists use indirect evidence to learn a lot about objects they cannot directly observe.
   - Scientists rely on creativity and imagination at all stages of investigation.
   - Scientific theories can change over time with new evidence and technological advances.

Preassessment

Begin the activity by reviewing what your students know about the structure of an atom. They may be familiar with the basic subatomic particles that make up an atom, but even with secondary students, few will be able to tell you how scientists know what an atom looks like. Many will say, erroneously, that because we've seen atoms with electron microscopes, we've seen electrons, and since protons and neutrons are larger than electrons, surely we've seen them too. In fact, the scanning tunneling microscope provides only rough surface details of metal surfaces. It certainly does not allow scientists to see subatomic particles or peer inside of an atom, and the scanning tunneling microscope is the best yet developed.

Review the concepts of observation and inference and indirect evidence and tell students some of the stories in this chapter, stories about how early philosophers used creativity and imagination to model their ideas about atomic structure, stories about how later scientists set up an apparatus that measured the reactions of alpha particles to infer what was being fired upon.

Explain to students that they will be able to infer the shape of a mystery object in today's activity much the same way Thomson, Rutherford, and Chadwick inferred the existence of subatomic particles. By the end of the lesson they should have a greater appreciation of the roles indirect evidence, creativity, and imagination play in scientific endeavors.

Playing the Mystery Shapes Game

Demonstrate the Mystery Shapes gizmo found at the Curry School of Education Web site: http://www.teacherlink.org/mysteryshapes. Show students how to move the particle firing device and how to shoot particles out of it. Have them make observations and try to infer the shape of one mystery object.

After students have a good understanding of how the game works, use Notebook Assignment 8.1 as a guide for students as they work in pairs and practice guessing the shapes.

After students have guessed correctly three times in a row, the game will proceed to another level that more closely approximates the true nature of science. In science, we don't usually have answers revealed to us so easily! In the second level of the game, your students will be asked to infer the shape of three hidden objects, and they will have to draw what they think the objects look like instead of choosing from a list. As with science, the game will never reveal the true nature of the hidden mystery object. It's up to your scientist-students to make their best guesses based on the data available to them.

Sharing Results

After students have completed the activity and drawn the three mystery objects based on their observations and inferences, have them share these shapes with the class. Have each group present their drawings on the overhead projector, or draw the shapes on the board for the rest of the class to see. It will be interesting to see if all your student groups come up with the same findings. Probably not! That's how it is in science; it's often quite open to interpretation, even though all groups were presented with the same data. As each pair of students presents their work, ask them what it was about their observations that led them to infer the particular shapes.

Reflecting on the Experience

Once all of the presentations are completed, have students reflect on how the Mystery Shapes activity relates to science. You can do this by asking students the following series of questions and then having them answer them in their science notebooks (see Notebook Assignment 8.1).

"How were you able to infer the shape of an unseen object from the way little particles bounced off it?"

Help your students to understand that they used both careful observation and inference to construct their drawings. Observation is often insufficient for determining the unknown—in such cases inference is used to fill the gaps in our knowledge. In addition, creativity played a strong role in the activity as students used their imaginations to see the unseen in the mind's eye.

"How is the process you used to infer the mystery shapes similar to the process physicists use to construct models of the atom?"

In a classroom full of students who may have thought that powerful microscopes allowed physicists to see subatomic particles with their own eyes, you're looking for class consensus that students' work in determining the shape of a hidden object was similar to the ways Rutherford, Thomson, and Chadwick inferred the existence of subatomic particles.

Even Albert Einstein used this type of process in 1905 when he observed the swarming Brownian motion of grains of pollen suspended in water under a microscope. As the pollen grain moved about, he inferred the action of very tiny kinetic molecules of fluid impacting on the pollen grain. Thus, he inferred the motion of invisible molecules based on how a visible object reacted. In the Mystery Shapes game, students infer the shape of a nonvisible object based on how tiny particles react. Your students used their observations and inferences to construct unfamiliar objects, essentially just as Einstein did.

"Why did some of you draw very different mystery shapes even though you were given identical computer games to play?"

You may find your students debating whether they did in fact receive the same computer game! They may find it hard to believe that different interpretations can result from the same data. Each of your students may have different background knowledge about the science of light reflection, about playing the game of billiards, or about basic geometry. Different background knowledge results in different inferences and interpretations, even when starting with the same data. This is true in science, as well. It is not uncommon for different groups of scientists to reach different conclusions from the same data, especially in areas where the data are very complex and/or incomplete.

"Would a particle physicist reach the same conclusions about the identity of the mystery shape as the class did?"

Your students may respond that one person's interpretation is a good as another's. But, in actuality, someone with more complete background knowledge, whether a champion miniature golf player or a particle physicist, will most definitely have a more sophisticated interpretation of the mystery shapes data. If inference and interpretation rely on background knowledge, then those with more thorough knowledge of impacts and collisions have more accurate constructions of the shapes.

To emphasize this point further, show your students drawings of what a particle physicist might infer the three mystery shapes to be (Figure 8.9). Although

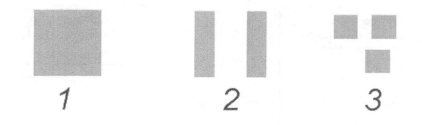

Figure 8.9
Scientists' inferences of mystery shapes.

these are the "right" answers, try not to do this in a way that makes your students "right" or "wrong." The point in showing these interpretations to students is to help them understand that scientists' inferences and interpretations differ from students' because scientists begin their work with a lot more background knowledge.

"Can we know with 100% certainty that our mystery shape depictions are correct?"

Your students may assert that in this case, you, the teacher, probably have the answer key. Maybe you do, maybe you don't, but it's important to remind students that scientists *never* have the answer key. In scientific endeavors, it's impossible to ever be 100% certain about phenomena that cannot be observed. With a lot of effort, careful observation, and creative and intelligent inferences, however, scientists are able to develop models and understandings that work well enough to be convincing. Even the most convincing scientific models and explanations may change in the future as new data or perspectives on existing data become available.

LESSON WRAP-UP

One goal of this activity is for your students to have a better historical understanding of the development of ideas about the structure of the atom. Another goal is for your students to understand that scientists developed those ideas over time through indirect evidence and that the evidence could become more precisely interpreted as technological apparatuses improved. Scientific theories can change over time as new minds come into play and as technological advances allow for more precise measurements and observations.

The closure of this activity might be a good time to introduce the concept of scanning electron microscopy. These microscopes fire particles at a substance. The way the particles bounce off the substance determines the image the microscope displays on the screen. In a way, through mathematical calculations, the microscope is doing the inferring for us!

The Molecular Expressions™ Web site has a virtual scanning electron microscope that is sure to fascinate your students. By bouncing electrons off of golddust-plated insects and other critters, the complex shapes of miniature objects can be inferred! Visit the Web site at: http://micro.magnet.fsu.edu/primer/java/electronmicroscopy/magnify1/index.html.

Figure 8.10 provides a quick overview of how the three aspects of science are addressed by the Mystery Shapes game.

Figure 8.10
Connection among the three aspects of science for the Mystery Shapes game.

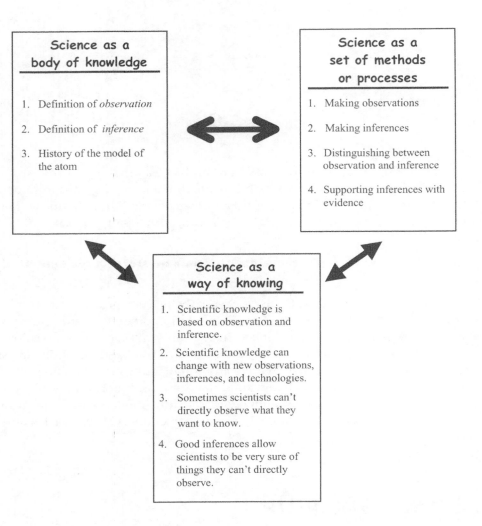

Science as a body of knowledge

1. Definition of *observation*
2. Definition of *inference*
3. History of the model of the atom

Science as a set of methods or processes

1. Making observations
2. Making inferences
3. Distinguishing between observation and inference
4. Supporting inferences with evidence

Science as a way of knowing

1. Scientific knowledge is based on observation and inference.
2. Scientific knowledge can change with new observations, inferences, and technologies.
3. Sometimes scientists can't directly observe what they want to know.
4. Good inferences allow scientists to be very sure of things they can't directly observe.

ASSESSMENT

Notebook Assignment 8.1 should be used for your students to make inferences with the Mystery Shapes game. In addition, the questions will help you assess their understandings of how atomic models have changed over time. More importantly, question 3 addresses the way scientific conclusions are often subjective. The students can see this play out as they debate the true nature of the hidden shapes, and you can help them understand that it's common for scientists to debate their ideas and conclusions, as well.

Notebook Assignment 8.2 allows your students to take a trip back in time, as they are asked to construct a timeline of some historical events that led to the modern-day model of the atom. Be sure they include both the observations and inferences made by scientists.

Mystery Shapes Activity

Name: _____ Date: _____

Use your observations in the Mystery Shapes game to infer the shapes of the three mystery objects. Draw what you think they look like.

Shape 1	Shape 2	Shape 3

Answer each of the following questions in your own words.

1. How were you able to infer the shape of an unseen object?

   _____

   _____

   _____

2. Describe how the process you used is similar to the process physicists use to construct models of the atom.

   _____

   _____

   _____

3. Did all of your classmates agree on the shapes of the mystery objects? How does this compare to the way scientists agree or disagree with one another?

   _____

   _____

   _____

Timeline Activity

Name: _____ Date: _____

Using resources your teacher provides and/or the Internet, construct a timeline of some historical events that led to the modern-day model of the atom. Be sure to include both the observations made by scientists and their inferences.

9

Laying Down the Law

n this activity, students learn about scientific laws, in general, and the Law of Superposition, in particular. They examine books placed on a desk and are challenged to devise an inferred chronological list of when the books were read by the teacher, who placed them there one at a time after reading them. After students list the books in terms of when they were probably read, the teacher announces that earlier someone disrupted the pile, thus changing the order. This activity reinforces the idea that scientific laws are not absolute.

LAYING THE GROUNDWORK

Among the things I learned in science class as a junior high school student were the definitions of scientific facts, hypotheses, laws, and theories. You probably learned these, too. A fact was any information presented as true and accurate. I learned that a hypothesis was an "educated guess" (although this was never elaborated upon). A theory was a hypothesis that had been tested and found worthy of tentative support, but was not yet proven. And finally, a scientific law was a theory that had been proven beyond the shadow of a doubt. These definitions implied a certain progression of scientific ideas—starting with the fact and ending with the scientific law (Figure 9.1). According to this view, scientific laws are the most powerful ideas in science, because they are the most certain.

The only problem with these definitions and this view of science is that it is completely wrong! It turns out that no idea in science is ever "proven beyond a shadow of a doubt," nor has any scientific theory in the history of science ever become a scientific law. It simply can't happen.

But if this is true, why was I taught otherwise? Although the answer to this question is complicated, I suspect that the biggest part of it lies in the everyday meaning of words that scientists have adopted.

What Is a Scientific Law?

Scientific laws are generalizations derived from facts. A scientific law is a description of a natural relationship or principle, often expressed in mathematical terms.

Figure 9.1
The commonly taught (but inaccurate) relationship among key scientific ideas.

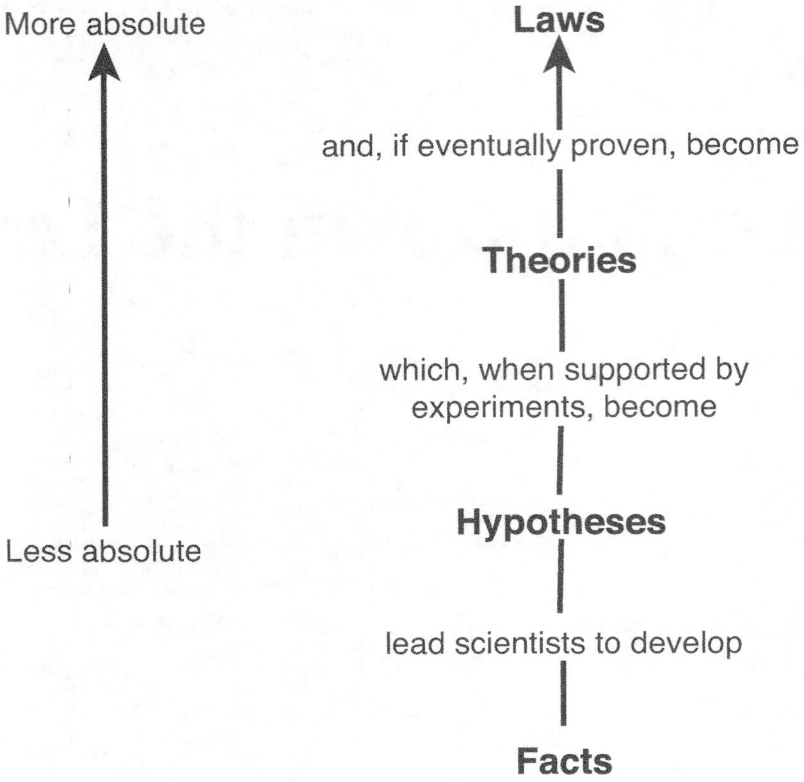

More absolute

Less absolute

Laws

and, if eventually proven, become

Theories

which, when supported by experiments, become

Hypotheses

lead scientists to develop

Facts

Or as Krimsley (1995) so succinctly put it, a scientific law is

A set of observed regularities expressed in a concise verbal or mathematical statement.

In short, scientific laws are descriptive in that they are statements of generalizations or patterns in nature. They offer concise descriptions of *what* happens, but no explanation for *how* it happens. I sometimes see definitions of scientific laws that include wording that they "invariably hold true" or are "universal." Such absolute knowledge has no place in science. Succinctly stated, a scientific law is an observed, well-tested, and confirmed generalization. It describes a pattern in nature under given circumstances. Often, scientific laws are expressed mathematically (e.g., Einstein's famous law, $E = mc^2$). It is important to remember that scientific laws generally hold true, but aren't meant to absolutely hold true for every possible circumstance. Some examples of scientific laws are included in Table 9.1.

Note that each scientific law example in Table 9.1 is descriptive in that it states a generalization of what happens, but offers no explanation for why. Thus, the Ideal Gas Law provides a mathematical relationship describing the behavior of a gas in relation to temperature, volume, and pressure, but offers no explanation for why this relationship exists. As you will learn in the next chapter on scientific theories, an explanation for the Ideal Gas Law is provided by the Kinetic Molecular Theory.

It's important to realize that we do not have explanations for every scientific law. For example, Newton's First Law of Motion states that all objects possess inertia, but it does not explain why they have inertia. In fact, we currently have no theory or good explanation for why objects should have inertia—they just do.

Table 9.1

Examples of Scientific Laws.

Scientific Law	Facts on Which the Law is Based
Newton's Laws of Motion—three laws proposed by Isaac Newton in the mid-seventeenth century that describe the motion of material objects. The first law describes inertia, the second describes the relationship $F = ma$, and the third is often described in terms of actions and reactions.	A hockey puck travels farther on ice than on carpet when the same force is applied to it. While riding up an accelerating elevator, a force is felt pushing against the feet. To move forward on a skateboard, you have to push backward with your foot.
The Law of Conservation of Matter—first clearly described by eighteenth-century chemist Antoine Lavoisier, this law states that in a closed system, matter is not created or destroyed.	The mass of the reactants in a chemical reaction equals the mass of the products. A melted ice cube has the same mass as it did when it was frozen.
The Ideal Gas Law—three simple gas laws developed over two centuries, including Boyle's Law and Charles's Law, can be combined to describe the behavior of an ideal gas with the equation $PV = nRT$.	The volume and temperature of an enclosed gas are directly proportional. The pressure and volume of an enclosed gas are inversely proportional. The pressure and temperature of an enclosed gas are directly proportional.
Mendel's Laws—developed by Gregor Mendel in the mid-nineteenth-century. The law of independent assortment states that traits are passed on to offspring independent of each other; the law of segregation states that offspring receive one factor for a trait from the mother and one from the father.	When purple-flowered pea plants are bred with white-flowered pea plants, all offspring in the first generation have purple flowers. When these first generation purple-flowered plants cross, white-flowered plants appear in the second generation in one fourth of the plants.
Ohm's Law—German physicist (and school teacher) Georg Simon Ohm developed the law in the early 1800s. Ohm's law deals with the relationship between voltage and current in an ideal conductor. It is often expressed as a mathematical formula: Voltage = Current × Resistance	Accurate measurements of an electrical circuit reveal that current and voltage are directly proportional to each other. The more voltage applied, the higher the current.
The Law of Superposition—proposed in the seventeenth century by Nicolas Steno, this law states that in undeformed layers of rock, the oldest rock will be at the bottom.	Dinosaur fossils and trilobite fossils are not found in the same stratum of rock. The trilobites will be beneath the dinosaurs. Trilobite fossils become rare in rock strata where shark fossils first appear.

Scientific Laws Are Not Absolute

Consider the Law of Conservation of Matter, for example. Originally, the law stated that matter cannot be created or destroyed. However, after Einstein developed his famous equation relating matter and energy ($E = mc^2$), the law was revised to include the concept that matter can be viewed as a form of energy and that the two can be converted into each other. In other words, this fundamental law of nature required a fundamental change!

In fact, if you think about it, all scientific laws share this characteristic. They are not absolute laws of nature, but useful approximations and descriptions of scientists' best ideas (backed by evidence) of the way nature works. When a law is useful and fits the data, it is generally accepted by the scientific community. Consider the examples of scientific laws in Table 9.2. In each case, the scientific law is not "true" in any universal or absolute sense of the word.

Finding a Fossil and Forming a Law

A few years ago, a student of mine brought a strangely shaped rock to class. She'd found it in the woods outside her mountaintop home, and we agreed that it looked like a seashell fossil. She was quite puzzled as to how a seashell fossil ended up on her mountain, and we got out a few field guides to see if we could name the thing. It was too worn down to identify properly, but it seemed to be of the phylum Brachiopoda. As we flipped through the field guide, we could see that many of the fossils in that section of the book could be found in the Appalachian Mountains as well as many other mountain ranges. My student wondered if this shell was evidence of the great biblical flood of Noah's time.

It turns out, my young student's experience wasn't unique. Since ancient times, people have found shell-shaped rocks on mountains and in fields, and wondered what they really were and how they could have gotten there. Back in the 1600s the prevailing idea was that these rocks just simply grew on their own—like crystals, but the biblical flood idea was a popular one too.

Nicolas Steno's Law of Superposition

In 1666, a Danish anatomist named Nicolas Steno dissected a shark, took out its teeth, and stated that fossils were remains of living creatures because he had noticed that the shark's teeth looked remarkably like "tongue stones" (or *glossopetrae*), tooth-shaped objects that were thought to fall from the sky. However, it was one thing to accept that fossils were once living things and another thing altogether to accept that sea creatures lived on top of mountains.

Fortunately, Nicolas Steno struggled with that idea as well, and turned his study of anatomy to the study of fossils and rocks and rock layers. He published his ideas in a document called *De Solido Intra Solidum Naturaliter Contento Dissertationis Prodromus,* asserting that mountains and valleys formed as waters flooded the land, eroding and collapsing the areas that would be the valleys. He didn't know about plate tectonics and the monumental forces that form mountains when plates collide, but his idea made sense at the time. He also wrote about layers of rock called strata, and said that as sediments settled they could form a layer called a stratum, trapping the would-be fossils with the rest of the silt, sand, and debris. By thinking

Figure 9.2
Sandstone cliffs in southern Utah.

about how these strata would be laid down, Steno developed what came to be known as the Law of Superposition. It stated that the deepest layers of stratified rock were deposited first, and in this way the relative ages of rock strata and the fossils they contain could be estimated. See Figure 9.2, a photo of sandstone cliffs in Utah, for an example of this stratification.

So my student with the mystery seashell learned that her mountaintop home was once at the bottom of an ancient sea. I told her that fossils form when minerals replace the original organic material and that fossils found in lower strata of rock are older—according to Steno's Law of Superposition. What we didn't talk about that day was the old axiom, "Laws are meant to be broken." Steno knew that his Law of Superposition didn't always hold true, that there were exceptions to many rules in nature. Although lower layers of sedimentary rock are indeed formed first, he realized that caves might form, collapse, and remove lower strata. He also realized that underground forces might push layers of rock upward, disrupting the order of the strata. Just because one stratum was beneath another didn't always mean it formed first.

Today we recognize that the superpositional order of strata can be difficult to determine when geological events flip the strata like a deck of cards. We also know about unconformities and igneous inclusions that can disrupt the natural order of strata.

Common Laws

Your students may be familiar with many common "laws," or proverbs about life that don't hold true in every situation. Benjamin Franklin said that a stitch in time saves nine, but perhaps it could save eight or fourteen! There's an old Latin saying,

Table 9.2
Exceptions to the Rule.

Scientific Law	Exceptions to the Law
Newton's Laws of Motion—three laws proposed by Isaac Newton in the mid-seventeenth century that describe the motion of material objects. The first law describes inertia, the second describes the relationship $F = ma$, and the third is often described in terms of actions and reactions.	While Newton's laws of motion work very well in most cases, scientists eventually began to recognize some subtle inconsistencies between what the laws predicted and what was observed in nature. Einstein began to develop his theories of relativity to deal with these issues. His ideas required a revision of Newton's Laws for objects moving at high speeds or in very strong gravitational fields.
The Law of Conservation of Matter—first clearly described by eighteenth-century chemist Antoine Lavoisier, this law states that in a closed system, matter is not created or destroyed.	Today, we know that in nuclear processes, matter is converted to energy and therefore not strictly conserved. The law has been modified, and is now called the Law of Conservation of Mass and Energy.
The Ideal Gas Law—three simple gas laws developed over two centuries, including Boyle's Law and Charles's Law, can be combined to describe the behavior of an ideal gas with the equation $PV = nRT$.	There is no such thing as an ideal gas. No gas has ever been found to exhibit ideal characteristics. However, normal gases behave closely enough to the hypothetical ideal gas to make the law useful.
Mendel's Laws—developed by Gregor Mendel in the mid-nineteenth-century. The law of independent assortment states that traits are passed on to offspring independent of each other; the law of segregation states that offspring receive one factor for a trait from the mother and one from the father.	More recent genetic research has revealed that independent assortment is not always the case when genes are closely located on the same chromosome.
Ohm's Law—German physicist (and school teacher) Georg Simon Ohm developed the law in the early 1800s. Ohm's law deals with the relationship between voltage and current in an ideal conductor. It is often expressed as a mathematical formula: Voltage = Current × Resistance	In order for Ohm's Law to be accurate, the conductor (e.g., wire) must be "ohmic," or ideal. But no real conductor is an ideal one. The imperfections of real conductors must be taken into account when applying the law.
The Law of Superposition—proposed in the seventeenth century by Nicolas Steno, this law states that in undeformed layers of rock, the oldest rock will be at the bottom.	Rocks can be overturned by subterranean forces. Caves can erode layers of rock, then collapse and bring higher strata downward.

"*Audaces fortuna iuvat,*" which means "Fortune favors the brave," but I'm sure we could find at least one filthy rich coward. Ask your students to brainstorm some common "laws" about life and exceptions to them. Remember, there's an exception to every rule! Here are some possibilities to get you going.

- A bird in the hand is worth two in the bush.
- Absence makes the heart grow fonder.
- An apple a day keeps the doctor away.
- A watched pot never boils.
- Doctors make the worst patients.
- No pain, no gain.
- Two heads are better than one.

As your students remind themselves that common "laws" about life don't always hold true, they may have an easier time accepting the fact that scientific laws aren't absolute either.

THE ACTIVITY: BOOK STACKING

LESSON AT A GLANCE

1. Teacher displays the arrangement of books on a desk.
2. As a class, students make observations about the placement of books.
3. Teacher asks for predictions about which books were read before others.
4. Students devise a chronological list of when the books were probably read.
5. Teacher discloses a secret that the books were rearranged, and places them back in the original locations.
6. Teacher and students discuss how this activity relates to the Law of Superposition and scientific laws in general.
7. Conclusions.
   - A scientific law is a description of a natural relationship or principle, often expressed in mathematical terms.
   - Scientific laws are not meant to be absolutely true for every circumstance.
   - Scientific laws may change with new evidence.

The Law of Superposition doesn't apply only to rock strata. Lunar geologists use it to determine the relative order of when craters, lava flows, and other lunar events occurred. You can use it in your classroom to determine the order books or other items were placed on a desk.

Setting the Stage

Begin by stacking books or colored sheets of paper in a semihaphazard fashion on a display table. While your own desk may already boast such a display, I find it's

Figure 9.3
Books initially placed on table.

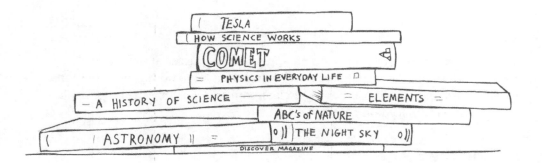

easier for students to participate in this activity when different pieces are easily identifiable. Colored construction paper will work well, but books are easy to come by and the titles are easy to see. Your stack may look something like the one in Figure 9.3. If you have a digital camera handy, you may even want to photograph the original order of books to use later in the activity.

From this stack, you can imagine that I read *Comet*, then *How Science Works*, then *Tesla*, then *Discover Magazine*, then probably *The Night Sky*, *Astronomy*, *ABC's of Nature*, *Elements*, *A History of Science*, then finally *Physics in Everyday Life*. But it's debatable. Several books look as if they were placed at the same time, and perhaps they were. It's hard to tell unless you were there.

Now, it's time to do some shuffling. Pull some of the books or papers out from the bottom of the pile and place them on top. Perhaps a colleague asked to borrow three books on the bottom, so you slid them out. When the books were returned the next day, you just stuck them on top. This new arrangement is the one you show to your students as you assign the questions in Notebook Assignment 9.1.

Making Observations

Have your students take a look at the new arrangement (Figure 9.4), and tell them that after you had read each book, you placed it on the table. That's a fact. After YOU read each book, that's what you did. Ask your students to make observations and then inferences in order to discern the order in which you read the books. Have them record these observations and inferences in their science notebooks (see Notebook Assignment 9.1). In this example, the top four books are the easiest to determine. *A History of Science* may have been placed down before *Elements*, but it's

Figure 9.4
The books after a disruption.

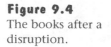

hard to tell. The same goes for *Astronomy* and *The Night Sky*, and the first read book was probably *Discover Magazine*. Right?

Revealing the Unconformity

After students have had sufficient time to complete their inferences, you can reveal the fact that the stack was disrupted. Tell students about the colleague who borrowed books from the bottom of the stack, and perhaps display your photo of the original arrangement or simply replace what was removed. As you do so, remind students of Nicolas Steno's Law of Superposition and the exceptions to the rule he stated as he devised the law. Not everything is as it appears to be, or to quote an old proverb, "You can't judge a book by its cover!"

LESSON WRAP-UP

Scientific laws are similar to ordinary laws we experience in everyday life in that they can be broken, but the similarity ends there. Scientific laws are quite different from everyday laws because they are based upon observations of natural phenomena. Can you imagine a traffic cop clocking the speed of cars on a highway, then making a speed-limit law based upon the top speed attained by a car? Can you imagine an undercover cop observing the frequency of shoplifting in a department store, then making a shoplifting law based on the number of items stolen per day? "NO SHOPLIFTING MORE THAN TWO ITEMS PER PERSON PER WEEK." What a joke!

Now imagine Nicolas Steno observing layers of different colored fossil-containing stone, making notes, drawing pictures, and noticing that different types of fossils exist in different strata. This is how scientific laws are created—by people formulating generalizations from observations about nature, and then confirming these generalizations against still more observations. Because scientists, like all people, have limited abilities to observe and infer, and because nature is infinitely more complex than we can ever imagine, scientific laws are not absolute. They can change, they may not fit every situation, and they can be disregarded altogether over time. As *Star Trek*'s Scotty said, "*I canna' change the laws of physics, Captain, but I can find ye a loophole.*"

Figure 9.5 provides an overview of the main ideas about science that you will want to explicitly address during the Book Stacking activity.

ASSESSMENT

As you do this activity with your students, have them complete Notebook Assignment 9.1. This will help them document, and you assess, their ideas about the tentative nature of scientific laws.

Figure 9.5
Connection among the three
aspects of science for the Book
Stacking activity.

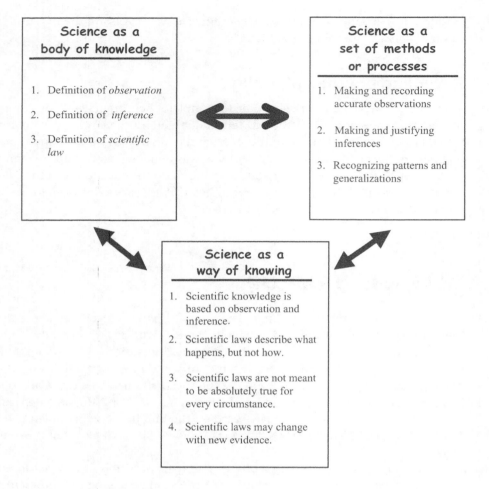

Book Activity

Name: _____ Date: _____

1. Draw a picture or diagram of the stack of books displayed by your teacher. Take care to accurately record the relative position of each book in the stack.

2. Assuming that your teacher placed books on the stack immediately after they were read, in what order do you think the books were read? Remember, this is your *inference*, and your inference may differ from others in your group.

_____

_____

_____

_____

3. What might have affected your teacher's pile of books and made your inference incorrect?

_____

_____

4. What is a scientific law?

_____

_____

5. As used in geology, what is the Law of Superposition?

_____

_____

6. What might cause the Law of Superposition to not hold true in a given situation?

_____

_____

7. If scientific laws are not always true, what good are they?

_____

_____

10

Scientific Theories and the Mystery Tube

I n this activity, students observe the behavior of strings that are pulled through holes in a tube and infer the internal arrangement of the strings that best explains their behavior. In addition to providing another engaging way to practice observing and inferring, students learn the differences between facts, hypotheses, theories, and laws by creating their own "tube string theory" and "law of tube strings."

LAYING THE GROUNDWORK

In 2002, the Cobb County School District in Georgia required stickers with the following text to be applied to science textbooks that addressed the concept of evolution:

> This textbook contains material on evolution. Evolution is a theory, not a fact, regarding the origin of living things. This material should be approached with an open mind, studied carefully and critically considered.

In all, school officials affixed 34,452 stickers in the school system's textbooks. Two years later, U.S. District Judge Clarence Cooper ruled that labeling evolution a "theory, rather than fact" could confuse students by playing on the popular use of the word as a "hunch." The ruling required that all of the stickers had to be scraped off of the textbooks. Apparently, Cobb County school officials could have saved themselves a lot of work had they understood some key terms in science, such as *fact*, *theory*, and *law*.

To help your students think about their understanding of these terms, here's an exercise that you can do with your class. Ask students, "What ideas come to mind when you hear the word *theory*?" If your students are like most, their responses will be similar to the following list.

- an idea
- a hunch
- a guess

Figure 10.1
Is it "just a theory"?

If your students are older, they may add more advanced terms like:

- an assumption
- speculation
- abstract reasoning

The point is that in the everyday sense of the word, "theory" connotes a high degree of speculation and uncertainty (see Figure 10.2 for an example).

Figure 10.2
Everyday use of the term *theory*.

Now, ask your students "What ideas come to mind when you hear the word *law*?" If you've conducted the activity from Chapter 9 with your students, they will hopefully say that a scientific law is an observed and tested generalization that describes a pattern in nature for a certain circumstance. It *generally* holds true, but like any other product of science, we cannot say that it *absolutely* holds true for all circumstances and conditions. Otherwise, your students may associate the word *law* with such ideas as:

- rules you have to follow
- fact
- something that is proven true

And perhaps, if they are really creative they might come up with:

- a piece of enacted legislation
- the first five books of the Hebrew Scriptures
- a police officer or other authority figure (as in the title of the Sonny Curtis song, "I Fought the Law")
- a general principle or rule in mathematics that has been proven to hold between expressions

What all of these ideas have in common is the notion of absoluteness and authority. Typically, laws are viewed as ideas and principles that are unlikely or impossible to change.

In everyday terms, a theory is a hunch or speculation that may or may not be factual and thus does not warrant a great deal of confidence. Laws, on the other hand, denote rules that are factual, proven, and unchanging. Apply these everyday definitions to science and it's no wonder that you wind up with the relationship depicted in Figure 10.1. But do the colloquial uses of these terms apply to science?

Let's look at what scientists mean when they use the terms *fact, theory,* and *law*. In science, facts are the data scientists use in confirming or disputing their ideas. Thus, valid observations, whether quantitative or qualitative, can be viewed as facts. Facts usually engender a high degree of confidence and correspondence among scientists.

This is not to say that scientific facts can never change (not even facts in science are absolute). Rather, as Stephen J. Gould (1981) put it, facts are "confirmed to such a degree that it would be perverse to withhold provisional consent"—emphasis on *provisional*. It is always possible that new data will emerge in the future that disputes currently accepted facts. For example, at one time, the scientific community considered it fact that only hominids were capable of creating and using tools, a characteristic setting us apart from other animals. Now it has been observed that not only do primates create and use tools, but so do woodpecker finches, Egyptian vultures, otters, and even green herons who "fish" with bait!

Theories in science are structures of ideas used to explain and interpret facts (Gould, 1981). Theories are not simply conjectures or hunches—they are based upon, and account for, copious amounts of data. Theories provide interpretive frameworks that help scientists know which questions are important, what types of data to collect, and how to explain the facts (see Chapter 16). Contrary to the popular notion, theories are too complex to stem from a single confirmed hypothesis—rather, they are collections of ideas that evolve over time.

Generally speaking, theories involve inference and indirect observations. We cannot directly observe the motion of molecules and atoms (as in the kinetic molecular theory), or the evolution of one species into another (as in Darwin's theory of natural selection), due to the tiny scale and huge time frame of these respective phenomena. However, what theories lack in terms of being directly observable, they make up for in terms of the explanations they provide for existing data and predictions they make that can often be tested with future technologies. Thus, as Lincoln, Boxshall, and Clark (1990) so succinctly described it, a scientific theory can be defined as:

> A general principle supported by a substantial body of evidence offered to provide an explanation of observed facts and as a basis for future discussion or investigation.

To illustrate this definition further, I've listed a few theories and the facts that they explain in Table 10.1.

The most powerful theories are the ones that best account for existing data and that consistently predict new phenomena that are subsequently observed. But even the most powerful theories undergo revisions as new data become available that show discrepancies between how nature works and what the theory predicts. Thus, theories, like facts, should never be viewed as absolutely true. When an accepted theory fails to account for new data, this creates a "problem" that is of great interest to scientists. Consequently, much energy and effort is put into solving the discrepancy, and what emerges over time is a revised theory that not only explains the new data, but also accounts for all of the old data. Thus, over time, theories become more powerful in that they are revised to better account for greater quantities and variety of scientific facts.

THE ACTIVITY: THE MYSTERY TUBE[1]

LESSON AT A GLANCE

1. Teacher displays the Mystery Tube.
2. As a class, students make observations about the tube.
3. Teacher asks class for suggestions of what could be done to provide more information for observations.
4. Teacher asks for predictions, then demonstrates what happens as different strings are pulled.
5. Students devise general statements that accurately describe the behavior of the strings.
6. Students devise a theory for what makes the strings behave as they do and present their ideas to the class.
7. Students construct working models of the tube.
8. Conclusions.
   - Scientific laws are descriptive while scientific theories offer explanations.
   - Neither scientific laws nor scientific theories are proven in any absolute way.
   - Scientific theories never become scientific laws. They are different kinds of ideas.

---

[1] An early version of this activity dealing with observation, inference, and tentativeness appears in the National Academy of Sciences publication, *Teaching About Evolution and the Nature of Science* (1998), pp. 22–25. The activity in this chapter elaborates on the prior activity by addressing the nature of theories and laws.

Table 10.1
Examples of Scientific Theories.

Scientific Theory	Some Facts the Theory Explains
Atomic Theory—developed by John Dalton in the mid-eighteenth century, the theory states that all matter is composed of elements made from indestructible particles called atoms. It describes the structure, properties, and behavior of atoms.	When liquids evaporate, they do not disappear, but become gases. A small piece of steel has the same density as a large piece.
Kinetic Molecular Theory—developed in the mid-eighteenth century by James Clerk Maxwell, the theory states that gases consist of tiny particles in constant motion colliding elastically, the velocity of which is in direct proportion to the temperature.	As the temperature of a gas in a fixed volume is lowered, its pressure decreases. As the volume of a gas at a fixed temperature is increased, its pressure decreases.
Germ Theory—developed by Louis Pasteur in 1861, the theory states that contagious diseases are caused by microorganisms.	Malaria is spread by *Anopheles* mosquitoes that carry protozoan parasites. Influenza is spread by contact with an infected person rather than exposure to cold temperatures.
Theory of Natural Selection—described by Charles Darwin in the mid-nineteenth century, this theory explains that organisms best adapted to their environments survive and pass on heritable traits. In this manner, favorable heritable traits become more common in the next generation. The process can eventually lead to new adaptations and species.	99.9% of all species that ever lived on earth are now extinct. Different fossil organisms are present in rock from different geological epochs.
Theory of Continental Drift—proposed by Alfred Wegener in the early twentieth century, the theory states that there originally was one giant continent, which broke into smaller continents that drifted into their current locations. Wegner's theory did not enjoy wide support in his day, but was eventually accepted and adopted into the Theory of Plate Tectonics.	Continents roughly fit together like a puzzle; fossils and rocks on different continents are similar where they were once joined.

I hope that by now you are convinced that it is inappropriate to teach that theories become laws when proven to be true and that explicitly teaching the definitions and functions of scientific theories and laws is important. Great! Now, all you need is an engaging activity to address these issues and to connect them to students' previous knowledge about observations and inference. That's where the "Mystery Tube" comes in!

Displaying the Tube

Imagine that you begin a lesson by showing the class a tube like the one in Figure 10.3. The tube is about 25 cm long and about 8 cm in diameter, and can be made from an empty potato chip can with holes drilled in it. Protruding from holes in the tube are two pairs of strings, with each string opposite its partner. Each of the four strings has a knot about 5 cm from the end. The strings cross or interconnect as indicated in either Figure 10.6, 10.7, or 10.8 on page 133. From experience, using a metal or plastic key ring and constructing the tube as indicated in Figure 10.8 provides the best results. After putting the lid on the potato chip can, cover the can in paper or contact paper so the strings inside cannot be seen.

Making Observations

Begin the lesson by reviewing the terms *observation* and *inference* with the class. Then ask students to make a list of observations about the tube. Being practiced at the skill of observing by now, your students should quickly develop a list similar to the one in Figure 10.4.

Demonstrating the Tube

Now, point out to students that up to this point they have made passive observations about the tube, meaning that they haven't done anything to it. Often in

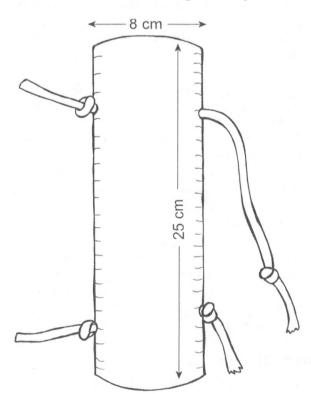

Figure 10.3
The Mystery Tube.

Figure 10.4
Typical student observations of the Mystery Tube.

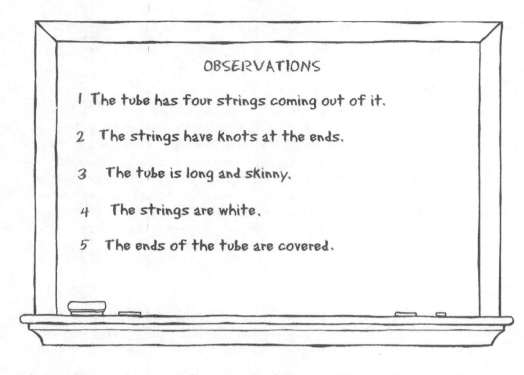

OBSERVATIONS

1 The tube has four strings coming out of it.

2 The strings have knots at the ends.

3 The tube is long and skinny.

4 The strings are white.

5 The ends of the tube are covered.

science, we can gain more information by *doing* something to what we're observing. When we begin to manipulate the thing that we observe, we are entering into the world of experimentation. Now, ask your students if anyone would like to suggest something you could do to the tube to provide more information for the observation list. Naturally, someone will suggest that you pull one of the strings protruding from the tube. Now, grab hold of the short string directly across from the long string as if you're about to pull it. Before taking action, ask the class to write down a prediction of what they think will happen. Most students will simply predict that the short string you pull will slide out of the tube and lengthen, while the long string protruding goes in and becomes shorter.

Once the class has settled on a prediction, go ahead and conduct the experiment. The class will quickly observe that their prediction was correct: The short string was lengthened by your pull and the long string on the opposite side of the tube was shortened. Now, before students have an opportunity to suggest that the two strings are connected (remember, the class is only making observations at this point), ask students to predict what will happen when you pull one of the short strings at the bottom of the tube. Since both strings in this pair are short, and there appears to be no slack between them, students will naturally assume that nothing will happen. However, when you pull one of the bottom strings, it gets longer, while the long string from the first pull gets shorter! (Figure 10.5).

Next, to really pique your students' curiosity, begin pulling short strings at random around the tube. Each time you do, the string you pull lengthens, while the long string shortens. It's amazing, and your students will immediately begin asking how the tube can behave this way. Of course, you're not about to tell them—rather, you will expect them to figure it out.

The First and Second Laws of Tube Strings

Challenge the class with the task of coming up with a general statement that accurately describes the behavior of the strings when pulled. It's a good idea to have students

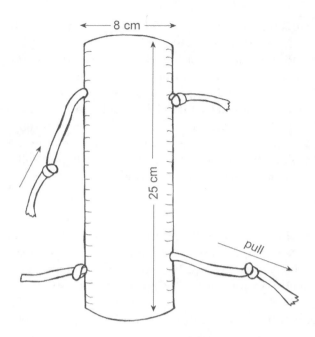

Figure 10.5
The strings behaving unexpectedly.

work in pairs or small groups to come up with the statement, which should read something like this:

> Any short string that is pulled gets longer, while the long string gets shorter.

A second more quantitative generalization that older students may come up with (with a little prompting) is:

> The amount the pulled string lengthens is directly proportional to the amount the long string shortens. (You can use a ruler to verify this).

Where's the Science?

Now it's time to relate all of this string pulling to science. It turns out that accepted generalizations in science that are supported by lots of evidence are often referred to as laws. Like scientific laws, the statements your students developed for the behavior of the strings are descriptive in that they summarize how the strings behave when pulled. Consider Newton's First Law of Motion. It describes the property of inertia that tends to keep moving objects moving and resting objects resting. However, the law offers no explanation for why inertia exists. This is true of all scientific laws. The same is true with your students' "First Law of Tube Strings." It describes the general behavior of the strings without offering any explanation for why the strings behave the way they do.

Your students' "Second Law of Tube Strings" exhibits another feature common to scientific laws—it shows a relationship among variables via a mathematical formula. Like Newton's Second Law of Motion (Force = mass × acceleration), the Second Law of Tube Strings is expressed as a mathematical formula (in this case, Pulled string lengthening = Long string shortening).

A third similarity that your students' laws of tube strings have in common with real scientific laws is that they are not proven in any absolute way. Even if you try all of the combinations of pulls and find the results consistent with the first and second laws, there's always the chance that some future action will result in something new. You cannot rule out the possibility. Albert Einstein showed this to be the case with Newton's Second Law of Motion, when he stated that it did not hold true at velocities near light speed. He developed the theory of relativity and his famous equation, $E = mc^2$. The point is that while scientific laws are useful generelizations, they are not proven and cannot be viewed as absolutely true. As you learned in Chapter 9, it's not unusual for scientists to revise scientific laws when new evidence warrants it.

Tube Strings Theory

Now that students have settled on the behavior of the strings and have even developed a law or two to describe this behavior, it's time for them to work on an explanation for what makes the strings behave as they do. To be convincing, the explanation must account for all of the observations up to this point, as well as be reasonable to the rest of the class.

It's a good idea to let students work in groups of three or four for this part of the activity. To help them get started, hand out Worksheet 10.1. You will find that it facilitates sharing explanations at the end of the activity if you copy the diagram of the tube onto an overhead transparency for each group. The task for each group is to come up with a diagram that accounts for all of the observations the class has made about the mystery tube.

Sharing Results

After students have had ample time to develop their ideas (usually about 20 minutes or so), have them share their ideas with the rest of the class. This process is facilitated by having a single spokesperson from each group bring their transparency to the overhead projector. Group spokespersons can then present their group's explanation, using the Mystery Tube as a prop, if desired. Typically, you'll find that the students come up with a variety of creative explanations, more than one of which could possibly work. Figures 10.6–10.9 depict some of the student explanations I have seen over the years.

Note that all of these explanations could possibly work, but not all are equally plausible. Figure 10.9 is a bit too fanciful to be accepted as a reasonable explanation, something your students will readily acknowledge with their laughter should anyone propose something similar. This provides a good opportunity to make the point that not just anything goes in science—explanations must not only account for the data, but they must be reasonable to science peers (i.e., they fit within accepted theories and norms).

Reflecting on the Experience

Once all explanations have been shared and any "unreasonable" explanations have been weeded out, the natural question that follows is, "How can we know which of these explanations is 'right'?" Of course, someone in the class will respond that we can open the Mystery Tube to see. However, this is a good time to remind students that we often cannot "open the tube" in science. For instance, no one has observed the inner structure of an atom; we cannot see for ourselves what caused the mass extinction of the dinosaurs, and we cannot directly observe the Big Bang. Yet, scientists know much

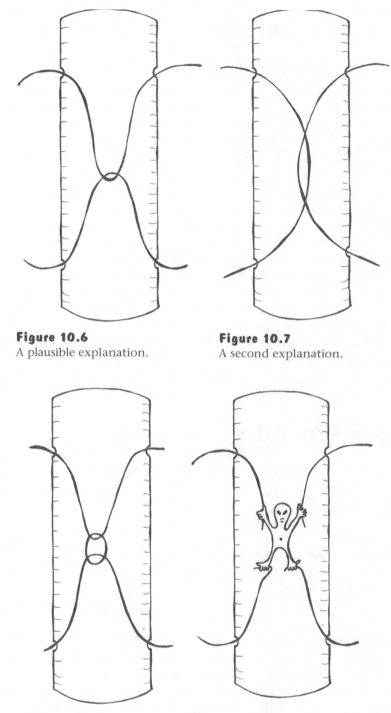

Figure 10.6
A plausible explanation.

Figure 10.7
A second explanation.

Figure 10.8
A third explanation.

Figure 10.9
This explanation is NOT plausible.

about all of these things. So, just as is often the case in science, you will have to attempt to answer the question of which explanation is "right" without opening the tube.

Constructing a Working Model

If you can't open the tube, the next best thing is to construct the models that the students have proposed and see which of them (if any) works just like the Mystery Tube. This is a great project to assign at this point—challenge each group to construct their models of the Mystery Tube to see if their explanations work. You can have a set of potato chip cans, along with string, tape, etc., to provide students with the materials they need to construct their tubes, or you can challenge them to find their own materials (toilet tissue tubes and thread, or shoe boxes and yarn will work) and construct their tubes at home.

At any rate, as students bring models in, you can test them against the Mystery Tube to see which ones actually work like the real thing. The models that do not work can be eliminated from further consideration (but be sure to remind students that even such "negative" results are useful in that they narrow down the field). When you test a model that appears to behave in a similar fashion to the Mystery Tube, ask if this "proves" that the tested model is constructed the same way as the Mystery Tube. Of course, the answer is "no." The only way to know for sure what's inside the Mystery Tube is to open it up, which we've already said we cannot do. So the best that we can come up with is an explanation (or set of explanations) that work, but that may need to be modified in the future as more data become available.

LESSON WRAP-UP

The explanations students develop to explain the behavior of the Mystery Tube are analogous to scientific theories. As we have seen earlier in this chapter, a scientific theory can be defined as:

> A general principle supported by a substantial body of evidence offered to provide an explanation of observed facts and as a basis for future discussion or investigation
>
> (Lincoln et al., 1990).

Note that your students' explanations for how the Mystery Tube works reflect the main points of this explanation quite nicely. Their drawings are models based upon a body of evidence to explain observed facts. Once proposed, they sought to test their explanations, which thus became the basis for future investigations. Unlike scientific laws, which are descriptive by nature, scientific theories are explanatory. Both are based on copious amounts of data, and both can change when new data and new perspectives of looking at existing data become available. Neither theories nor laws are ever "proven." Additionally, it's important to remind students that scientific laws and theories serve different purposes and are, in fact, different kinds of ideas. Therefore, a scientific theory can never be transformed into a scientific law, despite what they may have previously heard.

Figure 10.10 provides an overview of the connections among the knowledge, processes, and nature of science addressed by this lesson.

ASSESSMENT

Your students can use Worksheet 10.1 to draw and explain their ideas about how the Mystery Tube works. Notebook Assignment 10.1 provides opportunities for them to reflect upon the lesson, and to relate it to the nature of scientific theories. Worksheet 10.2 and Notebook Assignment 10.2 are designed to go along with the alternative "Cans Activity."

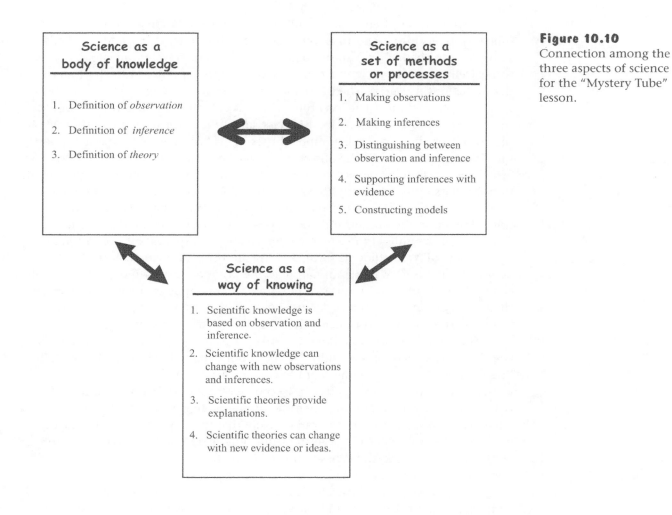

Figure 10.10
Connection among the three aspects of science for the "Mystery Tube" lesson.

MORE FUN WITH THEORIES: THE CANS ACTIVITY[2]

Here is another demonstration you can do with some containers and tubing that's sure to thrill your students and spark animated discussions about theories. It takes some time and effort to set up, but it can be a great resource for years to come. As shown in Figure 10.11, the setup consists of metal cans with two-hole stoppers inserted tightly into the openings. You'll need some glass or plastic tubing, rubber hose, and a glass funnel, too.

As you can see, Can A and Can B both have two tubes inserted through the rubber stoppers into each can, a long one and a short one. Can A and Can B also have water in them. Can A starts about 3/4 full of colored water (blue food coloring works well). Can B starts with a couple of centimeters of water in the bottom (no need to color this water). The water should be just deep enough to cover the bottom of the funnel tube. The long tube in Can A extends almost to the bottom of the can. The funnel is glass, Tube 1 is glass, and Tube 2 has an optional short glass tube piece for viewing between rubber hoses. (This "window" provides an opportunity for students to make the observation that no liquid flows in Tube 2.)

Now, try to imagine what will happen when you pour a different colored fluid into the glass funnel; let's say it's water with red food coloring. It runs down into Can B, and after a few seconds, blue fluid emerges from Tube 1! The blue water flows down into the funnel, and you stop pouring. The blue liquid continues to flow, and for a while, it looks like you've created a perpetual motion machine!

What will your students think is going on inside of the metal cans? This demonstration is very similar in nature to the Mystery Tube activity. Your students can't see inside the cans, but they can observe what happens outside the cans. From their observations, they can make inferences, which can in turn, be combined to form theories about what is inside the cans that make them work.

This setup is based on an old idea called "Hero's Fountain," named after its Greek inventor, Hero of Alexandria. It's been done many ways, including with 2-liter soda bottles, and you may want to create your own variation as well. The cans and other parts can be ordered from Carolina Biological (www.carolina.com) or another scientific supply catalog, if you don't happen to have a few old metal cans in the garage. Note that the cans you want are the ones used for the "Collapsible Cans" air pressure demonstration. Size 8 two-hole stoppers work well with the cans. If cans are not available, you can always use large Erlenmeyer Flasks instead (be sure to cover the glass so students cannot see the insides).

It's amazing what a little air pressure and gravity will do! Worksheet 10.2 and Notebook Assignment 10.2 can be used in conjunction with this demonstration and your discussion of the "Theory of the Cans"!

---

[2] An earlier version of this activity is described by Lederman, Abd-El-Khalick, and Bell in *Professional Development: Planning and Design* (2001) pp. 31–33, published by NSTA Press.

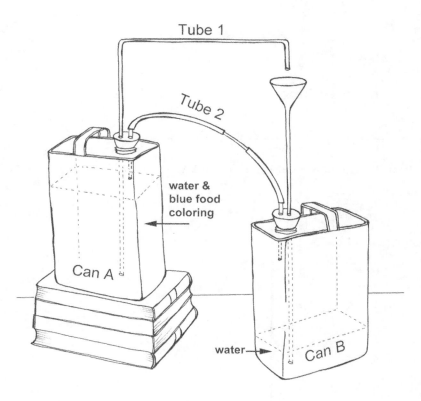

Tube 1

Tube 2

water &
blue food
coloring

Can A

water

Can B

Figure 10.11
The cans demonstration.

Mystery Tube

Name: _____ Date: _____

Use your observations from class to infer and draw what is inside the Mystery Tube that makes it behave the way it does.

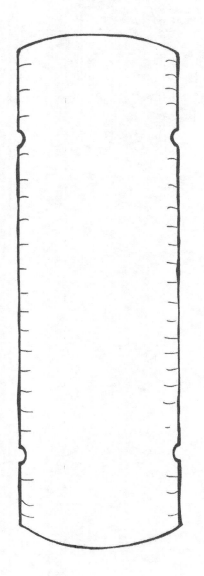

Mystery Cans

Name: _____ Date: _____

Use the drawing below to help you draw and explain your theory for why the cans function as they do when a colored liquid is poured into the funnel.

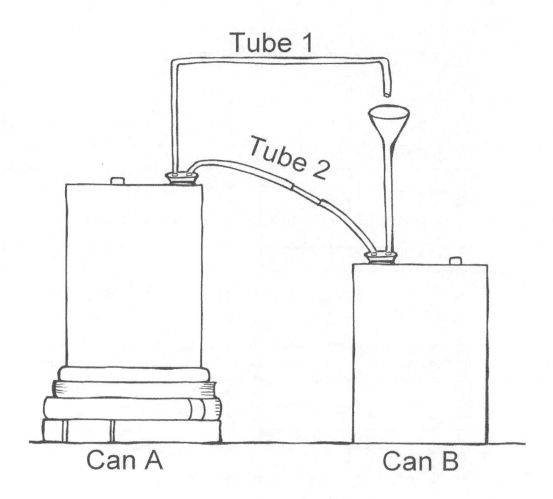

Tube 1

Tube 2

Can A

Can B

Mystery Tubes

Name: _____ Date: _____

1. Based upon your observations, devise two general statements that describe the behavior of the tube strings. Label these statements, "1st Law of Tube Strings" and "2nd Law of Tube Strings."

_____

_____

_____

_____

_____

_____

_____

_____

2. What is a scientific theory, and how is it different from a scientific law?

_____

_____

_____

_____

3. Scientific laws and theories can change as new evidence comes to light. Use the Web sites www.answers.com or http://en.wikipedia.org to research scientific laws and theories. Describe three laws or theories that have changed since they were first devised.

_____

_____

_____

_____

_____

_____

_____

_____

_____

_____

Mystery Cans

Name: _____ Date: _____

1. Define the term, *scientific theory,* and explain whether scientific theories can change.

_____

_____

_____

_____

_____

_____

_____

_____

_____

_____

_____

2. Can scientific laws become theories? Can scientific theories become laws? Explain your answers.

_____

_____

_____

_____

_____

_____

_____

_____

_____

_____

_____

_____

_____

11

Patterns, Patterns, Everywhere

The activities in this chapter use engaging pattern-seeking games to help students improve their skills at recognizing patterns, while they come to see that pattern-seeking is a goal of science. Students will be challenged to consider the issue of whether patterns in nature are invented or discovered by scientists. This chapter will serve as an introduction to the process skill of classification, since recognizing and applying patterns is at the heart of classification in science.

LAYING THE GROUNDWORK

Chris Schnittka, a science educator who provided the artwork for this book, vividly remembers the first time she had an allergic reaction to eating a mango. The reaction wasn't immediate, but within the day her mouth had broken out in what appeared to be a bad case of poison ivy. Since she had been eating mangos for years without trouble, this phenomenon was quite a mystery, and she didn't associate the mango with the itchy mouth at all. Instead, she thought that perhaps she had eaten a piece of fruit that had come in contact with poison ivy. In central Virginia, where she lives, poison ivy vines often climb up apple trees.

One day, approximately a month later, the rash returned, and her mind went racing. What did that day have in common with the other one? It had seemed to be such an anomaly, but now it appeared to be a pattern without an explanation. Since she eats a lot of fruit, the poison-ivy-on-fruit explanation seemed to be the most plausible, and she tried to recall all the different types of fruit she'd eaten in the last month. She looked for a pattern, but came up with none until . . . her third episode of an itchy mouth. It turned out to be mangos! She had finally recognized the pattern, and upon further research she learned that many people have allergic reactions to mango skin.

Looking for patterns seems to come naturally for humans; indeed, it is basic to our survival. If our ancient ancestors hadn't looked for patterns in how they reacted to foods or plants or insects or snakes, they wouldn't have learned to anticipate dangers in the environment. Recall the old folk saying, "A ring around the moon or sun means snow or rain is sure to come." Surely it was written as a result of many years of pattern recognition.

Scientists look for patterns too, sometimes where none exist, but it is a basic scientific habit of mind to seek pattern and invent pattern whenever possible. Recognizing patterns in the natural world can be a challenge. Whereas some patterns are obvious (such as the pattern that most sea stars have five arms), other patterns are more obscure. Scientists record weather patterns in order to understand and predict climate. They examine patterns in our DNA sequences to look for mutations and differences among individuals. The patterns in the growth rings of trees help scientists understand atmospheric conditions of the past, while the pattern of volcanic eruptions around the globe are still a mystery. Why does Pavlof, an Alaskan volcano, usually erupt in the fall of each year, as do the two Japanese volcanoes, Oshima and Mikakejima? Questions about patterns in science will continue to challenge us as we explore them.

The following pattern recognition games will challenge your students as they search for solutions and set the context for you to lead discussions about the many ways pattern seeking contributes to science.

THE ACTIVITIES

LESSON AT A GLANCE

1. Students are challenged to discuss whether patterns in nature are discovered or invented.
2. Students play up to three different types of pattern recognition games.
3. Students discuss that in science, patterns are often difficult to discern and that they can never be proven true for all cases.
4. Relate pattern-seeking to science.
   - Scientists use patterns to create models, make predictions, and develop scientific laws.
   - Scientists can be very sure that the patterns they develop fit the available evidence.
   - Scientists can never absolutely know that the patterns they develop hold for every possible circumstance.

Petals Around the Rose

Ask students, "Are patterns in nature discovered or invented?" The riddle dice game, Petals Around the Rose, might help you and your students answer that tricky question.

Figure 11.1
The first roll of the dice.

Supposedly, it has been played since the thirteenth century, and it could keep you stumped for days, weeks, or months, so be prepared!

The best way to learn the game is to have someone play it with you. That someone could be a person who knows the solution to the riddle, or it could be a computer simulation that "rolls" the five dice, gives you a chance to type in your guess, and then gives you the correct answer.

The game goes like this: Five traditional, six-sided dice are rolled. They might look like the dice in Figure 11.1. The roller, also called the "Potentate (or Ruler) of the Rose," tells you the rules. There are three rules.

1. The name of the game is, "Petals Around the Rose."
2. The name of the game is significant.
3. The number of petals around the rose is always an even number, including zero.

For the first few rolls of the dice, the Potentate will tell you the solution, the number of "petals around the rose." For Figure 11.1, the solution is 14. Your job is to discern a pattern as future rolls are cast and come up with the method for calculating the number of petals around the rose. Once you have figured out the method, you are a Potentate of the Rose and can teach the game to your students. Want to try again? Try and figure out the solution to the roll in Figure 11.2.

Figure 11.2
Another roll of the dice.

Internet Sites for a Simulation of the Game

Petals Around the Rose (Weaver vs. World)
http://weavervsworld.com/docs/think/rose/
This simulation shows you the previous roll, which is helpful.

Play Petals Around the Rose (Lloyd Robert Borrett)
http://www.borrett.id.au/computing/petals-j.htm
This simulation is well designed and the Web site has some interesting anecdotes about the game.

Petals Around the Rose (Chris Davis)
http://crux.baker.edu/cdavis09/roses.html
This simulation is simply designed and easy to use.

Do you think you have a solution? Did you guess four? The number of petals around the rose is indeed four. It's not too difficult to figure this out—try not to think too hard! This game can be played by kindergarteners, it's so simple. All you need to be able to do is count and recognize the pattern!

Okay, I'll give you one more hint before showing you the last roll of the dice. Sometimes this game is called "Polar Bears Around the Ice Hole,"—you are to count the bears. Take a look at the dice in Figure 11.3 and see if you can determine the number of petals around the rose, or the number of bears around the ice hole. In this case, the solution is two. I hope you got it right! There are several simulations of this game on the Internet. You can use these simulations to keep playing yourself, and then you can use them with your students. Either project the simulation from your computer and conduct a whole-class demonstration, or provide students with computers to work on by themselves. See the Strategy box above for a list of some of the better simulations available.

As a Potentate of the Rose, I am sworn to secrecy and must never divulge the method of determining the number of petals on the rose. If one of your students thinks he or she has determined the method, this must be shown by successfully determining the correct solution six times in a row. As tradition goes, this student is then dubbed a Potentate and must also keep the solution to the riddle secret.

Figure 11.3
The last roll of the dice.

Figure 11.4
Four petals around the rose.

If you haven't become a Potentate of the Rose yourself, and you've tried all the Internet simulations and are truly stumped, perhaps the drawing in Figure 11.4 will help. This is my last and final hint!

Inquiry Cubes[1]

Perhaps after your students learn the Petals Around the Rose game, they may be interested in devising their own rules and inventing similar games. For example, they could invent a game called, Fish in the Well, and the solution might be the sum of all the dots (called "pips") on the dice NOT showing. To calculate that sum, you would have to know which set of pips is opposite the set on top. There are four pips opposite the "three" and two pips opposite the "five." With this rule, the sum of the face-down dice sides in Figure 11.1 would be 16. The student could ask, "How many fish are at the bottom of the well?" and the answer would be 16.

An Inquiry Cube works like the well game. However, an inquiry cube is not covered with dots; it may have words or letters or pictures. Just like the made-up game Fish in the Well, students try and discern what is on the facedown side of the cube. They base their guesses on the patterns they see on the sides that are visible. Scientists make inferences like this all the time as they survey the natural world for patterns then infer some unknown or unknowable entity. What do you think would be on the blank facedown side of the Inquiry Cube in Figure 11.5 if the sides were folded and taped together? It's easy to see the pattern here. Opposite sides of the cube contain words representing a particular animal and its offspring. Your students would easily see the pattern and guess that the word on the bottom of the assembled cube would be "Kid."

Of course, you can make Inquiry Cubes for older students with patterns that are more challenging to discern, and you can make them for younger students out of pictures or symbols. Go ahead and guess what is on the facedown side of the

---

[1] An earlier version of this activity can be found in the National Academy of Sciences book, *Teaching About Evolution and the Nature of Science* (1998), pp. 66–73.

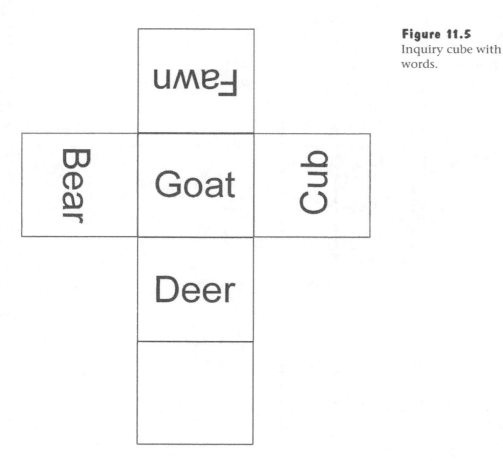

Figure 11.5
Inquiry cube with words.

picture-based Inquiry Cube in Figure 11.6. The theme here is "personal care," and opposite sides of the cube relate a tool to a body part. The image on the facedown side of the cube might be a fingernail or a toenail. But what if the theme isn't personal care? Could the facedown side of the cube be the image of a misspelled word? That bottle of "fingernail polish" might actually be a container of correction fluid! We can never be absolutely sure, unless we turn the cube over, which is not allowed in this activity! Likewise, in science, we can develop patterns from our observations, but cannot always "turn the cube over" to see what lies underneath.

You can read more about Inquiry Cubes in the book, *Teaching About Evolution and the Nature of Science* (1998), which is published in print and on the Internet by the National Academy of Sciences. Find the activity online at http://www.nap.edu/readingroom/books/evolution98/ as Activity 1 in Chapter 6.

Tricky Cards

An Inquiry Cube has six sides and several clues for students to discern a pattern. The Petals Around the Rose game uses five dice and multiple rolls of the dice for students to pick up on the pattern. A Tricky Card has only two sides, but you can make as many as you want, hiding a pattern within the two sides. For instance, one side might contain a number from 1 to 26, with the other side containing the corresponding letter of the alphabet. Thus, the card with the number 3 would have the letter C on the opposite side. How many cards would you need to show a student before he or she recognizes the pattern? How many cards would be necessary to

Figure 11.6
Inquiry cube
with pictures.

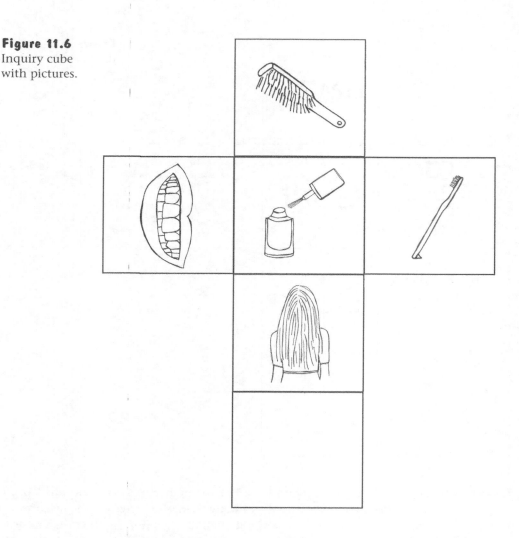

disprove the pattern? It might take five or six cards for a student to suppose that the pattern is 1 = A, 2 = B, 3 = C, etc., but only one card that has a 15 on one side and an M on the other to disprove the pattern. It's that way in science too—as science philosopher Karl Popper (1963) said, it only takes one black swan to disprove the notion that all swans are white.

The first thing you need to do is make a deck of cards. You can do this quickly with a magic marker and some index cards. A more challenging pattern than the 1 = A, 2 = B pattern is the one in Table 11.1. Take a look at the card arrangement and see if you can determine a pattern. It's tricky!

Shuffle the cards. It doesn't matter whether the front side is on top, but deal out some cards where your students can see them. Perhaps if each card is large enough, you can tape the cards to the chalkboard. Ask students to determine whether the cards follow a generalized rule. Then turn some of the cards over. Challenge the students to guess the pattern based on what they've observed from the turned-over cards. Remember that the instructional goal is not to find the "right answer" but to encourage students to test and defend their answers.

One guess your students may give is the following: *If a card has a number on one side, it will have a letter on the other.* They can then test this idea by simply having you turn over some more cards. Sooner or later you will deal a card that falsifies this guess because several cards have numbers on both sides.

Front	Back
A	2
B	4
3	5
E	6
F	1
5	6
I	4
K	2
U	8
M	3
9	8
O	10

Table 11.1
One possibility for the card arrangement.

Students may eventually propose the pattern that works: *Every vowel is paired with an even number.* If no one proposes this pattern, you may suggest it to them and have students test it. Note that the pattern does not work in reverse. Not all even numbers are paired with a vowel. Sometimes even numbers are paired with consonants.

When do you decide that a pattern has been tested enough that you can be confident it is true? That's best left for the class to decide, but it probably shouldn't happen until both sides of all cards have been revealed. Remember though, that in science we don't ever know whether we have the whole deck of cards at our disposal. Nature is never that straightforward and simple. Even after many convincing trials, we can never prove a pattern to be true for all possible cases, but we can be reasonably certain that our ideas are valid and that our scientific discoveries work.

You can simulate this concept by waiting until the class is very certain it has discovered the pattern, then pull out an additional card (or two) that was ostensibly separated from the original deck. Make sure that the card does not fit the arrangement in Table 11.1. For example, if the new card has a "Y" on one side and a "7" on the other, they may decide they need to modify the original pattern. Of course, first they'll need to decide whether "Y" is a vowel or consonant—remember, these cards are tricky!

And as your students debate this last card, you can remind them that it often happens that just when we think nature has shown us all her cards, she throws us for a loop.

LESSON WRAP-UP

In order for students to attain general scientific literacy, they need to be exposed to patterns and relationships in nature and sometimes use those patterns in solving practical problems. The American Association for the Advancement of Science (1993) has devoted a section of its book, *Benchmarks for Science Literacy*, to describing pattern recognition standards of comprehension and application at all grade levels. As early as kindergarten, students should know about shapes in nature and learn how to put together and take apart patterned shapes. Later on, pattern identification takes on a prominent role as students learn about astronomy and weather, the water and rock cycles, population dynamics, and anatomy and physiology. Discuss with your students that patterns are often difficult to discern and that sometimes patterns cannot be found at all. Oftentimes, a pattern emerges only to be refuted by an anomaly. Patterns are human constructions, and nature has a way of not always following the rules!

Be sure that your students understand and value the importance of pattern recognition in science. Scientists use patterns to create models, make predictions, describe laws, and develop theories. Patterns are often used as evidence in the construction of theories—take for example, the discovery of alternating bands of magnetized rock on the ocean floor. That pattern was used to help support the theory of plate tectonics.

Patterns are also used in the construction of scientific laws. When the voltage in a closed electrical circuit is increased, the current increases as well, in proportion to the circuit's resistance. This pattern was noted and studied by Georg Ohm, and published in 1827 as Ohm's Law. Although it doesn't hold true for all cases, it is nevertheless a worthwhile product of the human quest to find pattern in the universe.

Figure 11.7 provides an overview of the connections among the knowledge, processes, and nature of science addressed in this lesson. Feel free to include specific

Figure 11.7
Connection among the three aspects of science for the three pattern-seeking games.

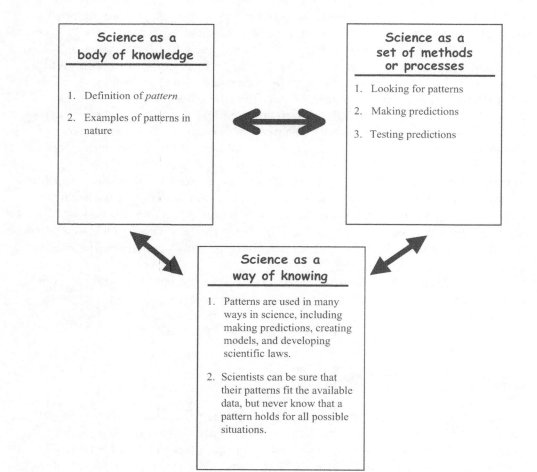

Science as a body of knowledge

1. Definition of *pattern*
2. Examples of patterns in nature

Science as a set of methods or processes

1. Looking for patterns
2. Making predictions
3. Testing predictions

Science as a way of knowing

1. Patterns are used in many ways in science, including making predictions, creating models, and developing scientific laws.
2. Scientists can be sure that their patterns fit the available data, but never know that a pattern holds for all possible situations.

patterns found in nature in the Science as a Body of Knowledge box, such as the Fibonacci sequence, fractals, and exponential growth.

ASSESSMENT

The objective of this chapter is to help you teach your students about recognizing and describing patterns and understanding that patterns are human inventions aimed at describing and explaining the natural world. Scientists use patterns to help them create theories and describe laws of nature, but ultimately nature doesn't always follow a pattern, and sometimes one can't be found at all. The questions in Notebook Assignment 11.1 can be used for class discussion or written reflection in a science notebook, or you can incorporate them into a unit quiz. You may be able to photocopy them as is, or rewrite them for the grade level you teach.

Patterns, Patterns, Everywhere

Name: _____ Date: _____

1. What is a pattern? How do you know if you've found one?

   _____

   _____

   _____

   _____

2. What are some ways that scientists use patterns?

   _____

   _____

   _____

   _____

3. Describe some examples of patterns you see in nature.

   _____

   _____

   _____

   _____

4. Is it more accurate to say that patterns exist in nature and are waiting to be discovered, or are they invented by the people who "discover" them?

   _____

   _____

   _____

   _____

Creativity and Constellations

Students will create their own constellations from star maps and compare their creations with the patterns created by diverse peoples throughout history. They will see how cultural perspective influences the star patterns people have seen in the sky. This activity will lead to the understanding that creativity and culture, as well as our perspective in time and space, all affect the patterns we see in the sky.

LAYING THE GROUNDWORK

A few years back, when I was teaching high school science, we lived in a small and remote desert community in eastern Oregon. It wouldn't be accurate to say that we lived at the end of the Earth, but my wife always claimed that you could see it from there! One of the benefits of living in the high desert was the sky—the low humidity resulted in great weather (over 300 sunny days each year) and deep, azure skies. At night, the dry air combined with low light pollution to create absolutely magnificent views of the heavens. Even from town you could routinely see the Milky Way, along with thousands of bright stars set against the pitch black sky.

My older daughter, Jessi, who was two at the time, used to sit with me in our front yard and watch the stars on summer evenings. I remember pointing out some of the more familiar star patterns, starting with the Big Dipper. For several nights in a row, I would point toward the seven bright stars of the dipper and ask Jessi to name the group. She would always shout out "Big Dipper!" and squeal with joy when I told her she was right and gave her a big hug. Being an astronomy-loving dad, I was more than a little pleased that she not only enjoyed looking at the stars with me but could even recognize at least one star group at such an early age.

One evening I decided to begin the evening's star-gazing session with a little test of her understanding. So, I pointed toward a different group of stars (this time the Northern Cross) and asked her to name the group. Imagine my chagrin when she once again shouted, "Big Dipper!" just like before. In fact, I could have pointed at anything in the sky and Jessi would have identified it as the Big Dipper. All of this time she had no idea of what I was trying to teach her, only that she got some very positive reinforcements from dad when she shouted "Big Dipper!" while looking up at the night sky. Of course, I still gave her a big hug, and she still laughed in delight at her great knowledge of the night sky. But I learned a lesson that night about how easy it is to mistake learning the name of a thing for learning *about* the thing. I also started thinking about how we have come to recognize and name star patterns at night, which in turn, led me to the lesson I now share with you.

THE ACTIVITY: CREATIVE CONSTELLATIONS

LESSON AT A GLANCE

1. Students and teacher discuss what a constellation is.
2. Students use a map of the sky to create their own constellation and myth.
3. The teacher tells different stories from different cultures about one constellation, and students research different cultures' versions of a constellation myth.
4. Conclusions:
   - Creativity and imagination play a role in science.
   - There is not always one right answer in science.
   - Constellations have more to say about the culture that created them than the stars themselves.
   - Subjectivity can play a role in science.

Begin the lesson by asking your students if they know any constellations in the night sky. Students will usually respond with some of the more familiar star patterns, including the Big Dipper and the Little Dipper. It turns out that these familiar star patterns are not really complete constellations, but are groups of bright stars within the larger constellations of Ursa Major and Ursa Minor, respectively. For example, Figures 12.1 and 12.2 show the *asterism* (star pattern) commonly known as the Big Dipper and the "stick figure" of the constellation Ursa Major that it lies within.

To help students understand this difference, ask them to define the term *constellation*. Typical student answers will include such ideas as "pictures in the sky," "groups of stars that show shapes in the sky," and "images of famous people

Figure 12.1
The Big Dipper.

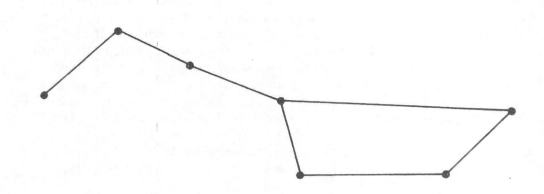

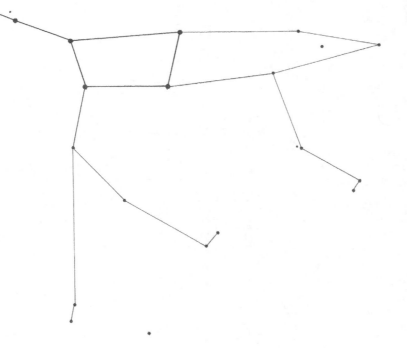

Figure 12.2
The Big Bear stick figure.

and animals formed by stars." Explain to students that these ideas are certainly part of the definition of the term *constellation*, but that a complete definition involves more than just pictures in the sky.

To astronomers, a constellation is actually a region of the sky, much like a state is a region of a country (Figure 12.3). That explains why many constellations do not really look like the figures that they are supposed to represent. You wouldn't expect the constellation Andromeda to look like a damsel in distress any more than you would expect the state of Washington to look like the father of the United States!

The following activity will give you a chance to create your own constellation. In doing so, you will learn more about the roles of culture and creativity in science, both important nature of science concepts.

Begin the activity by passing out star maps of a region of the summer sky (see Worksheet 12.1 at the end of this chapter) to students working in pairs. You can facilitate the subsequent sharing of student work if you transfer the star map to overhead transparencies. Challenge each pair of students to create their own constellation by drawing lines to connect principal stars and constructing pictures of the figures that the constellation represents. Additionally, challenge your students to write a brief story or myth that goes with the constellation they have created.

Once students have completed their constellation drawings and pictures, select a few pairs to share their creations with the rest of the class. Your students will have fun sharing their work and seeing the creativity of others during this part of the lesson. It will quickly become apparent that no two groups' constellations and myths are the same, even though all started with exactly the same star map. Ask your students why this might be the case. Of course, they will respond that creativity and imagination play a large role in the activity, and that there is no single right answer to the challenge.

Figure 12.3
Ursa Major—the official constellation.

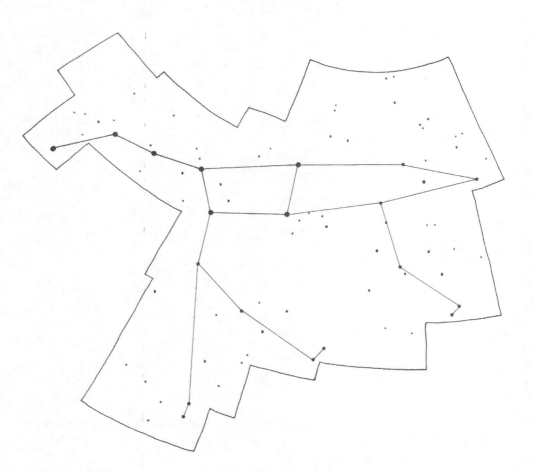

Constellations and Culture

This is the perfect opportunity to point out that science doesn't always produce a single "right" answer. In fact, some concepts in science are downright arbitrary. The naming of the constellations is a case in point. As the activity illustrates, many valid patterns and stories can be created to describe and account for the patterns of stars we see in the sky. Consider The Big Dipper asterism discussed earlier. The Egyptians saw these seven stars as The Bull's Hind Leg (Figure 12.4). The Ostyak of Siberia envisioned a moose. Northern Europeans imagined the group of stars as a plow. And the Native American Sioux tribes pictured the stars as a skunk. These figures are all based upon the same stars, but in every case the image the observers saw closely reflected their own culture and experiences.

Additionally, each culture had a different story or myth to go along with the image they saw in the seven stars of our Big Dipper. Probably the most famous of these accounts comes from the ancient Greeks, who depicted the stars in this region of the sky as the Great Bear and Lesser Bear (Figure 12.5). As the story goes, the Bear was originally Callisto, a beautiful maiden who to her misfortune caught the eye of Zeus, the king of the Greek gods. Recognizing a golden opportunity for one of his many secret love affairs, Zeus set about the task of seducing Callisto, who being mortal, could not resist Zeus's advances. Subsequently, she gave birth to a son, whom she named Arcas.

When Zeus' wife Hera learned of the affair, she turned Callisto into a Great Bear to roam the woods in disgrace. One day, Callisto happened upon Arcas, who

The Bull's Hind Leg (Egypt)

The Moose (Siberia)

The Plow (Northern Europe)

The Skunk (The Sioux of North America)

Figure 12.5
The Great and Lesser Bears.

was now a grown man. Upon seeing her son, she rushed toward him to embrace him. When he saw the bear charge, Arcas drew his bow and would have surely slain his own mother had Zeus not intervened. Zeus changed Arcas into a bear, too, and swept mother and son into the heavens where they settled among the stars. The strength of Zeus' mighty grasp stretched the bears' stubby tails into the elongated ones depicted in Greek constellations.

Native American peoples had different stories to go along with the images they constructed from the seven stars of the Big Dipper. For example, the Iroquois viewed the four stars of the Big Dipper's bowl as a bear and the handle of the dipper as hunters pursuing the bear. The hunt begins each spring, with the bear emerging from its den of hibernation. All through the summer, the hunters pursue the bear. They eventually slay the bear in the autumn, whose spilled blood turns the leaves of trees on Earth red.

The figures people identified in the night sky correlated to objects and people of importance in their culture, and the people developed myths to explain these figures. In the end, constellations have much more to say about the cultures that developed them than about the stars themselves.

Space-Time Discontinuity

The majority of stars that make up the constellations have no association with one another other than that they appear aligned when viewed from Earth. Viewed from other places in the galaxy the stars would appear differently. Consider once again the stars in the region of the sky we call Ursa Major. As we have seen, it's easy to recognize the asterism of the Big Dipper within this constellation, and with a little imagination you can see the constellation's namesake of the Big Bear (Figure 12.6).

Figure 12.6
The stars in the region of Ursa Major as viewed from Earth.

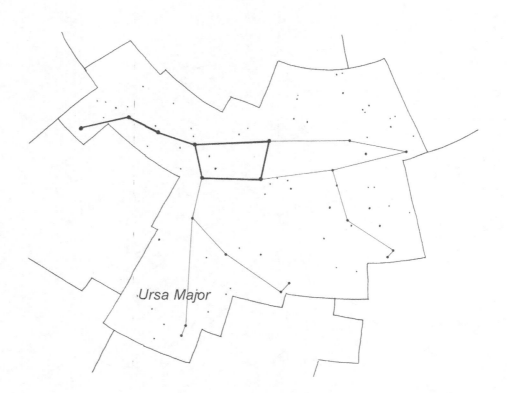

Ursa Major

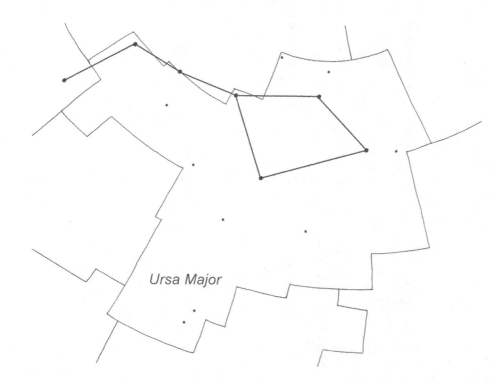

Figure 12.7
The stars in the region of Ursa Major, as viewed from the star Chara, about 27 light years away from Earth.

However, viewed from 27 light years away from Earth (about 158,000,000,000,000 miles), the stars take on an entirely different perspective. The Big Dipper is beginning to look a little warped and the Big Bear is nowhere to be seen! (Figure 12.7). Viewed from even farther out, say at 110 light years, and there are hardly any bright stars in the region at all (Figure 12.8). So the constellations as we know them are artifacts of our position in space.

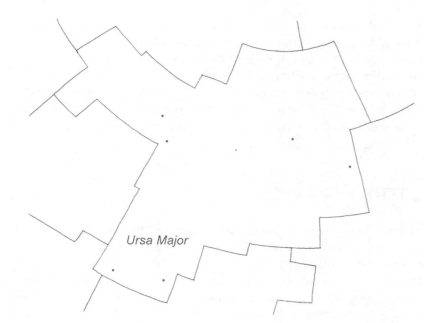

Figure 12.8
The stars in the region of Ursa Major as viewed from the star Cor Caroli, about 110 light years from Earth. From this perspective, the dipper asterism is gone!

Figure 12.9
How the Big Dipper asterism
changes over the course of
100,000 years.

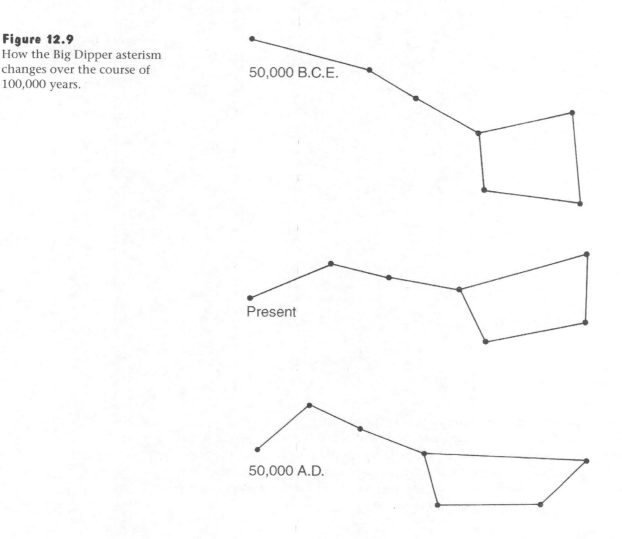

50,000 B.C.E.

Present

50,000 A.D.

It turns out that each star in our Milky Way galaxy is in an orbit around the center of the galaxy, so each star traverses a particular path at a particular speed through space. Astronomers call such stellar movement "proper motion." We don't usually notice the proper motion of stars because they are very far away. However, given enough time the proper motion of stars can be detected from Earth. The star patterns we are familiar with are also artifacts of time. Observe how the "Big Dipper" asterism changes over the course of 100,000 years (Figure 12.9).

LESSON WRAP-UP

It appears that the star patterns we call *constellations* are anything but constant. With an infinite number of possible star patterns across time and space, and the wide variety of patterns identified by the various cultures on Earth, how do astronomers decide to which constellations they will refer in their work and on star maps? After all, it would not do for astronomers in Africa to refer to different constellations when describing the same region of the sky as Australian astronomers.

The International Astronomical Union (IAU), the governing body of astronomy, is responsible for assigning names to celestial objects and the recognizable features on those objects. At its inaugural meeting in Rome in May 1922, the IAU officially adopted the list of 88 constellations still in use today. These 88 constellations include 14 men and women, 42 creatures, a head of hair, a river, and 29 other inanimate objects (including scales, a table, and a telescope). Boundaries between constellations, extending beyond the imagined stick figures, were adopted two years later so that every celestial object, no matter how faint, would lie within the boundary of a single constellation. As we saw earlier, constellations refer more properly to *areas of the sky* than to patterns of stars.

The constellations play an important role for both astronomers and lay people. The constellations facilitate communication about celestial objects by providing a means to concisely describe their locations. Furthermore, the constellations divide the sky into smaller chunks—finding one constellation can help us find other constellations that border it.

The main point to emphasize to your students in regard to the nature of science is that the naming of the constellations and the subsequent defining of their boundaries was arbitrary. An infinite variety of star patterns can be imagined—the official 88 were selected by convention and historical precedence, rather than any intrinsic properties of the stars themselves. In science we call such classifications "artificial," meaning that the classification scheme is not meant to convey any information about the objects being classified. In fact, the constellations actually have much more to tell us about the people and cultures who invented them than about the stars contained within their borders. But that's part of the beauty of science and constellations. Who would have guessed that you can learn about other cultures through studying the stars?

Figure 12.10 provides an overview of the connections among the knowledge, processes, and nature of science addressed in this lesson.

ASSESSMENT

Worksheet 12.1 can be a fun way for your students to express their creativity. Not only do they get to draw their own constellations, but they create stories to go along with them. This activity reinforces the fact that constellations are human constructs based on cultures, religions, early attempts at science, myths, and popular stories of the time. You can follow this activity by telling your students about some of the more familiar constellations accepted by the International Astronomical Union.

Notebook Assignment 12.1 gives your students the opportunity to do some research about how different cultures have interpreted the same sky. It's a nice way to bring in the multicultural aspect of science, but more importantly, it reinforces the idea you've taught them—that science is a creative endeavor and that it's affected by the social and cultural values of the group doing the investigating.

Figure 12.10
Connection among the three aspects of science for the "Creativity and Constellations" lesson.

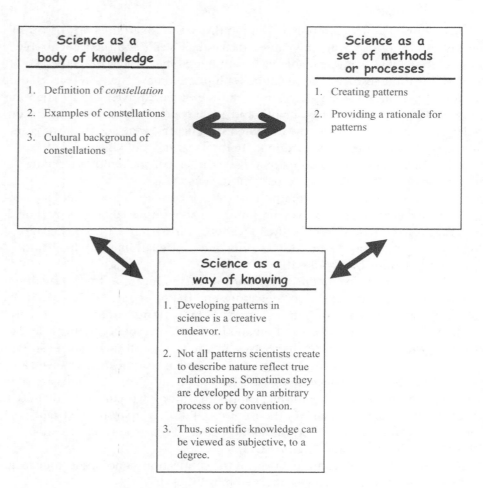

Science as a body of knowledge

1. Definition of *constellation*

2. Examples of constellations

3. Cultural background of constellations

Science as a set of methods or processes

1. Creating patterns

2. Providing a rationale for patterns

Science as a way of knowing

1. Developing patterns in science is a creative endeavor.

2. Not all patterns scientists create to describe nature reflect true relationships. Sometimes they are developed by an arbitrary process or by convention.

3. Thus, scientific knowledge can be viewed as subjective, to a degree.

Constellation Creation Activity

Name: _____ Date: _____

Work with your partner to create at least one constellation from the stars in the star map below. Connect the principle stars of your constellation with lines to form a stick figure. Also, write a short paragraph describing the story or myth behind your constellation.

Constellation Story or Myth

_____
_____
_____
_____
_____
_____
_____
_____

Star Map Showing Actual Constellations as Recognized by Astronomers

(Addendum to Worksheet 12.1)

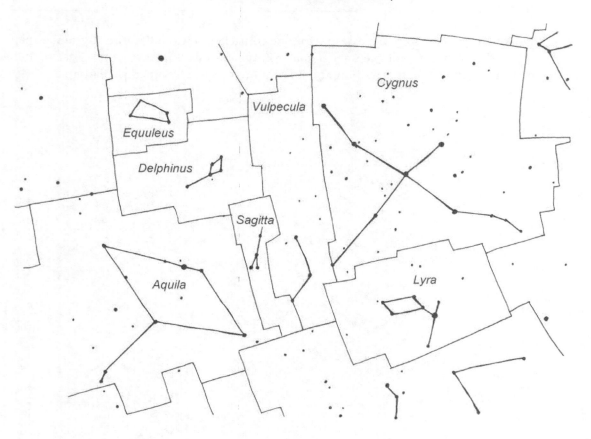

Constellation Research Activity

Name: _____ Date: _____

Choose a familiar constellation or asterism and research at least three myths about it created by different cultures. Draw the constellation image as each culture saw it, and briefly tell the story from that culture.

Drawings from Different Cultures	Stories from Different Cultures

Classified Information

Students will use their observation skills to develop classification schemes for sets of common household objects. Next, they will discuss whether these schemes are primarily based on the physical characteristics of the objects (known in taxonomy circles as "artificial" classification), or whether they reflect functional relationships between objects (known as "natural" classification). This discussion will lead to the concept that inferences (in this case, implied relationships in a classification system) may tell us more about the classifier than the classified.

LAYING THE GROUNDWORK

Consider all of the different kinds of places that exist on Earth. There are mountains and valleys, cliffs and plains, swamps and deserts, and glaciers and rock outcrops, just to name a few. Diversity of habitat and diversity of life are closely linked. Life is adept at taking advantage of every available place to live and way of existing. Considering the multitude of different places and ways to exist on our planet, it is not surprising that there are so many diverse life forms. Although the full extent of this diversity remains unknown, biologist Edward O. Wilson of the Museum of Comparative Zoology at Harvard University has concluded that approximately 1.7 million different life forms (or species) are currently recognized, including over 250,000 plants, 750,000 insects, and 47,000 vertebrates, or animals with backbones (Wilson, 1992). New species are being added to these lists every day. Estimates of the total diversity of life on Earth, including species yet to be described, range anywhere from 5 to 30 million species or more!

Even with the millions of species alive on Earth and the untold millions that are extinct, we still find ways to organize and classify them. We human beings have a strong propensity to find patterns nearly everywhere we look. From the moment of birth, we look for patterns in human faces—a special region of our brains is devoted to this type of pattern recognition. We sort and compare, group, and name the apparent chaos of life.

Look around you. You will find that whatever you see belongs to a more general category. For example, a chair or a table belongs to the higher category of "furniture." The text you are reading belongs to the category of "books." The gold-fish in your aquarium belongs to the general category of "fish." Classification comes so naturally to us that you would probably receive quite a shock should you ever find something that you are unable to classify.

The human tendency for classification has long been applied to the diversity of life on Earth. The Greek philosopher Aristotle (384–322 B.C.E) divided all living things into two categories: plants and creatures. He further divided the creatures into the two subcategories of animals and humans. This straightforward form of classification was used for many centuries. Gradually, however, it was unable to accommodate the diversity of life forms humans encountered. Philosophers and scientists began to propose new classification systems to deal with this difficulty.

The modern form of classification has its roots in the 18th century when Carolus Linnaeus (1707–1778) developed a more complex classification scheme. Similar to Aristotle, Linnaeus divided all known organisms into two primary categories, which he called *kingdoms*. These included the Plantae (plants) and Animalia (animals). However, Linnaeus' classification system differed from Aristotle's in that it included many more subcategories within each of the two kingdoms. Thus, each kingdom was subdivided into sequentially more specific groups, which he called *class, order, genus,* and *species.* You could use a description of a specific location as an analogy to illustrate the increasing specificity in Linnaeus' system. In this case, *kingdom* would be Earth; *class*, country (say, United States); *order*, state (West Virginia); *genus*, city (Charleston); and *species*, street address (200 Civic Center Drive). Over time, scientists added additional subdivisions to Linnaeus' original classification hierarchy. These include the phylum (between the kingdom and class) and the family (between the order and genus).

Table 13.1 demonstrates how the modified version of Linnaeus' hierarchy works for three common organisms. Note that the full classification of the domestic cat would make it a member of the animal kingdom, the vertebrates phylum, class of mammals, order of carnivores, the feline family, genus of *Felis*, and *catus* species (Figure 13.1). Linnaeus realized such naming of organisms would be unwieldy, and so he developed a shorthand method of identifying organisms by their genus and species names only. Thus, the sugar maple becomes *Acer saccharum*, the domestic cat *Felis catus*, and humans *Homo sapiens*.

Linnaeus' two-kingdom classification system worked well enough to classify the organisms that biologists encountered in the early eighteenth century. However, the development of the microscope brought a whole new world of microorganisms into view. Many of the newly discovered microorganisms possessed characteristics

	Sugar Maple	Domestic Cat	Human
Kingdom	Plantae	Animalia	Animalia
Phylum	Tracheophyta	Chordata	Chordata
Class	Angiospermae	Mammalia	Mammalia
Order	Sapindales	Carnivora	Primate
Family	Aceraceae	Felidae	Hominoidea
Genus	Acer	Felis	Homo
Species	saccharum	catus	sapiens

Table 13.1
A comparison of the modern taxonomic classification of a sugar maple, a domestic cat, and a human.

Figure 13.1

The taxonomy of *Felis catus*, "the house cat."

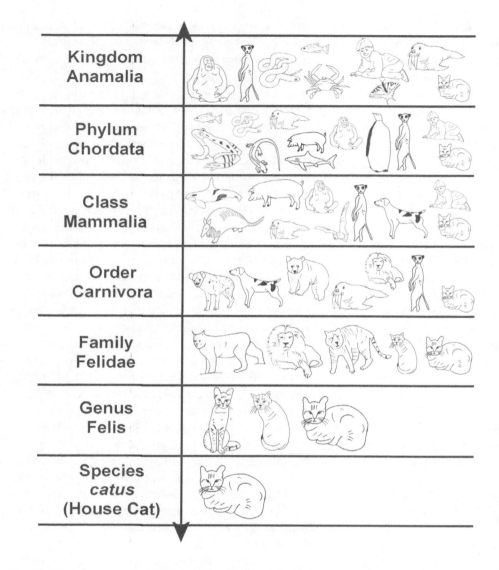

Kingdom
Anamalia

Phylum
Chordata

Class
Mammalia

Order
Carnivora

Family
Felidae

Genus
Felis

Species
catus
(House Cat)

of both plants and animals. For example, the Euglena is a single-celled organism that possesses chlorophyll, which allows it to transform sunlight into sugar, just like green plants. However, unlike plants, it also has a whip-like flagellum with which it swims like an animal. The increasing numbers of microscopic organisms being discovered that possessed both plant and animal characteristics were difficult to place comfortably in either of Linnaeus' two kingdoms.

This difficulty prompted scientists to propose (and debate) the creation of a third kingdom for these microscopic organisms, which was eventually called the *Protista*. As various other difficulties in classification arose over the next century, two more kingdoms were proposed, debated, and eventually added. These include the *Monera* (bacteria and blue-green algae) and the *Fungi* (mushrooms, yeasts, molds, etc.). These five kingdoms are the ones commonly described in older public school science textbooks. However, scientists discovered a difference between the types of prokaryotes (organisms without nuclei) and divided the kingdom Monera into two separate kingdoms: *Eubacteria* (common bacteria) and *Archaebacteria* (once classified as unusual bacteria). Thus, the classification system in common use today consists of six kingdoms: Eubacteria, Archaebacteria, Protista, Fungi, Plantae, and Animalia (Table 13.2).

Table 13.2
The Six Kingdoms.

Kingdom	Structure of Organism	Means of Getting Food	Examples
Eubacteria	Prokaryotes (no nucleus), single-celled	Photosynthesis, Decomposition, Parasitism	Bacteria Blue-green algae
Archaebacteria	Prokaryotes, single-celled	Chemical synthesis using hydrogen gas, carbon dioxide, and sulfur	Crenarchaeota, Euryarchaeota Korarchaeota
Protista	Eukaryotes, (contains a nucleus) mostly one-celled, some multicelled	Absorption, Engulfing, Photosynthesis	Plankton, Algae, Diatoms, amoeba, Paramecium
Fungi	Eukaryotes, mostly multicelled, some one-celled	Decomposition, Parasitism, Absorption, Partnership	Mushrooms, Molds, Mildews, Yeasts
Plantae	Eukaryotes, multicelled	Mostly photosynthesis, Some decomposition Parasitism	Mosses, Ferns, Conifers, Flowering plants
Animalia	Eukaryotes, multicelled	Herbivory, Predation, Parasitism	Sponges, Worms, Insects, Fish, Amphibians, Reptiles, Birds, Mammals

Keep in mind that this six-kingdom system is about fitting the needs of human labeling, and nature doesn't always care much about such human needs. For instance *viruses*, parasites that cause a wide range of diseases in plants and animals, defy classification under the modern system. In fact, due to their simple structure and inability to grow and reproduce outside of a host, scientists have debated whether viruses should even be considered as life. Remember that no classification system is perfect! Classification systems are created by humans to address human needs and, therefore, reflect all of the incomplete knowledge and fallibility that comes with the territory. Still, they prove incredibly useful to scientists and laypeople alike, and it is this usefulness that makes the modern classification system such a powerful part of science.

Classification schemes based on physical characteristics rather than any inferred theoretical underpinnings are known as artificial classification systems. There are myriad possible artificial classification schemes. Go to a bookstore and peruse a few wildflower identification books and you'll see what I mean. Some attempt to classify flowers by color, others by the shape of the flowers, and still others by when and where the flowers typically grow. As described in Chapter 12, naming constellations

Pluto Ponderings

The subjectivity of classification schemes became a public issue when in 2006 the International Astronomical Union (IAU) met to construct and vote on the definition of *planet*. Surprisingly, a technical definition had never been agreed upon by the scientific community.

Clyde Tombaugh discovered Pluto in 1930 after a long and painstaking search of photographic plates. At the time, he was engaged in a systematic search for a trans-Neptune planet (a planet that orbits the sun at a greater distance on average than Neptune), which had been predicted by Percival Lowell and William Pickering. In 1930, and for the next 40+ years, Pluto was thought to be larger than Mercury and maybe even Mars—a clear candidate to be the ninth planet in the solar system.

Since its discovery, astronomers have learned much about Pluto through improved Earth-based telescopes and the Hubble space telescope. For instance, we now know that Pluto's mass is 25 times smaller than Mercury's, and it has a moon, Charon, which is nearly half its size. Astronomers have also found dozens of other bodies in the outer reaches of the solar system with similar characteristics to Pluto.

So it was time for scientists to clarify their scheme of classifying solar system bodies. Either there were many more planets in our solar system than the original nine, or a definition would need to be constructed that might exclude Pluto.

Many scientists on both sides of the ensuing debate had strong feelings about the definition of the category *planet*. An initial proposal by an IAU committee defined the term so broadly that an additional 50 objects in our solar system alone would become planets. Heated debate ensued. "Astronomers, who are normally mild mannered types, are revolting against the IAU proposal," wrote Michael Brown, professor of planetary astronomy at the California Institute of Technology, on his Web site (http://www.gps.caltech.edu/~mbrown/whatsaplanet/revolt.html).

A second, more narrow definition was then proposed that would exclude Pluto as a planet. Brown wrote on his Web site, "If this proposal is accepted, people all over, from school kids to astronomers, will feel like part of their landscape has been ripped away from them, but that is no reason to not accept the scientific reasonableness of this proposal."

In the end, 424 members of the IAU voted and approved the more narrow definition of a "classical" planet and created two new categories: dwarf planets (into which Pluto falls) and solar system bodies.

The story may not be over, however. At the time this book went to press, the definition was being criticized by some as ambigous, and a few hundred IAU members had signed a petition appealing the decision. Depending on the disposition of the members of the IAU, by the time you read this book Pluto may have regained its status as the ninth planet of our solar system.

You can read additional explanations of this debate at the following Web sites:

The Eight Planets, Michael Brown, CalTech
http://www.gps.caltech.edu/~mbrown/eightplanets/

Pluto Demoted: No Longer a Planet in Highly Controversial Definition, August 24, 2006, Space.com
http://www.space.com/scienceastronomy/060824_planet_definition.html

International Astronomical Union
http://www.iau2006.org/

is an artificial classification system of stars. None of these approaches can be seen as "right" or "wrong," as long as they help readers accomplish their goal of identifying wildflowers or star patterns. Still, it can get pretty confusing when people are all using their own classification schemes—not to mention that none of these approaches has any connection to any theory that would support and serve as a rationale for their structure. That's where natural classification systems come in.

In contrast to artificial classification, natural classification systems are based upon a framework that provides some justification for the approach used. As is true with many other aspects of science, theories provide the framework for these natural classification systems. For example, biologists classify plants and animals using a system based upon evolutionary theory. Thus, organisms that biologists classify in the same genus and species are thought to have evolved from common ancestors at the family level. In turn, organisms in the same family are presumed to have common ancestors at the class and order levels. The point is that the classification system used by biologists is designed to reflect paths of evolution that organisms have trod. Thus, the system is based on evolutionary theory and is a natural classification system.

THE ACTIVITY: CLASSIFYING EVERYDAY OBJECTS[1]

LESSON AT A GLANCE

1. Review the development of the Linnaean classification method, highlighting how classification schemes have changed since the time of Aristotle and how living creatures are classified today.

2. Provide students with sets of nuts and bolts to classify as they complete Notebook Assignment 13.1.

3. Ask, "Which scheme is correct?" while pointing out that classification schemes are subjective.

4. Discuss the difference between artificial classification schemes and natural ones, challenging students to create a natural classification scheme.

5. Present students with a new type of fastener and ask them to classify it.

6. Conclusions:
   - There is no single right way to classify natural objects or phenomena.
   - Classification schemes are developed by humans, not discovered directly from nature.
   - Thus, scientific knowledge can be seen as subjective, to a degree.
   - Classification schemes can change with new discoveries.

The Nuts and Bolts of Classification

To prepare for this activity, you will first need to collect objects for students to classify. Although a wide variety of objects can work for this activity, I like to use various fasteners that I find at my local hardware store. These have the advantage of being easy to find and inexpensive, in addition to having many easily observed

---

[1]This activity is based on a classification activity described in *Favorite Labs for Outstanding Teachers, Vol. II,* Linda R. Sanders (Ed.), pp. 8–9.

features that make a wide range of classification schemes possible. Be sure to include a diversity of fasteners in your collection, including nails, screws, bolts, washers, and nuts. Remember that in addition to size you can include a variety of colors, screw heads (flat, round, slotted, Phillips, and Allen), and thread counts. You may also want to include other types of fasteners, such as various paper attachments, rivets, grommets, etc. The point is to come up with a wide variety of items that all serve a common function: fastening objects.

Purchase 15–20 of each fastener. Place one of each in 15–20 small containers, such as food storage bowls or baby food jars. This will create a set of easily stored equivalent sets of objects for the classification activity.

Begin the lesson by reviewing the human tendency toward classification and how it applies to common objects found in the classroom (writing implements, books, paper, etc.). Next, discuss the development of the modern classification system that biologists use today. Key points include the hierarchical classification scheme devised by Linnaeus, the six kingdoms of organisms, and how both have changed over time. To help make these concepts less abstract for your students, you will want to share concrete examples, such as those provided in Tables 13.1 and 13.2 on pages 167–169.

After you have provided this background information, your students should be ready for a hands-on experience developing their own versions of a classification system. Inform your students that they will be working in small groups to observe and classify a set of objects you provide. Pass out the fastener sets to students working in pairs or groups of three. Ask each student group to open its container and to pour out and observe the contents. Students should carefully note as many characteristics as they can about the objects, paying particular attention to similarities and differences among the objects. Next have them give a name to each object, making sure that the name is descriptive and brief. Challenge each group to sort the fasteners into categories based on common characteristics. When they have completed the sorting task, they should have all the fasteners sorted into at least three broad groups. The fasteners within each group should share at least one characteristic that separates them from the other groups, and no fasteners should remain unsorted. Thus, depending on the original mix of fasteners, a student group might form three categories (Figure 13.2):

1. fasteners without shafts
2. spring loaded
3. fasteners with shafts

Figure 13.2
Sorted fasteners.

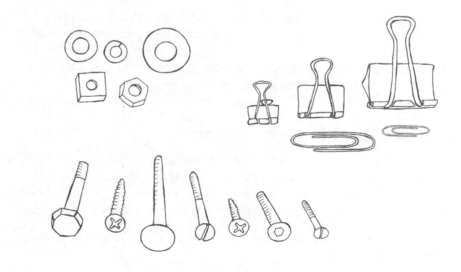

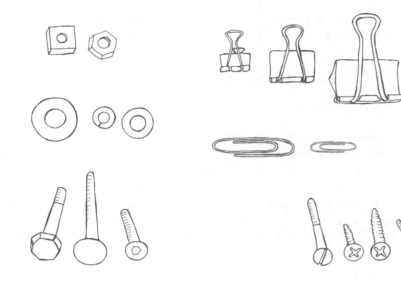

Figure 13.3
Fasteners sorted into subgroups.

Once this sorting is completed, challenge students to sort each of their groups into subgroups. In the previous example they might split the first group into two subgroups: nuts and washers. The second group could be divided into paper clips and paper clamps, and the third group could be split into screws and bolts (Figure 13.3).

Students can continue splitting the groups into subgroups until they are satisfied with their overall classification scheme. At this point, they should record their schemes in their notebooks. Ideally, their classification diagrams should be hierarchical, like the example shown in Figure 13.4.

The wonderful thing about this activity is that there are so many different ways a collection of 20 fasteners can be sorted, so no two student groups are likely to come up with the same classification system. Therefore, you'll want to give the student groups an opportunity to share their classification systems with the rest of the class. At the conclusion of the sharing time, be sure to discuss the fact that everyone started with the same observations for the same set of objects, yet all developed different classification schemes. I like to ask the class which one is "right." Students are

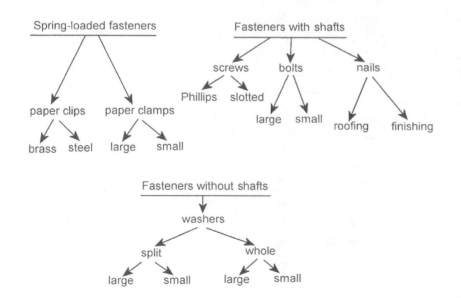

Figure 13.4
One possible classification system diagram.

pretty quick to pick up the concept that no particular scheme is "right," but rather that there is an inherent degree of subjectivity to all classification schemes.

Classifying Classification Systems

A nice extension to the activity is to address the issue of artificial versus natural classification systems. In most cases, you'll find that your students base their classification schemes on physical characteristics. As we saw earlier in the chapter, scientists call these types of systems artificial classification. They are developed arbitrarily for convenience, rather than based on functional relationships between the objects being classified. With no theoretical underpinning, they have more to say about the classifier than the classified. Natural classification systems, on the other hand, are based on theoretical relationships between the objects being classified. Such classification systems are not arbitrary, but are justified by some theoretical underpinning.

To begin the extension activity, ask students whether their classification systems are based on physical characteristics, or whether they are based on the less arbitrary criterion of function. They should readily agree that their classification systems were based on physical characteristics and so were artificial. The arbitrary nature of their artificial classification systems is reflected by the fact that no two were alike. Now challenge students to create a natural classification system for their fasteners. (If time is short, you may show them one that you've created instead). The system is to be natural in that it is to reflect the *natural function* of the fasteners and how they relate to each other. Tell students that, while in this activity they are focusing on function for their fastener classification schemes, scientists don't always use *function* as the basis for classification systems. Biologists, for example, use evolutionary theory to provide the framework for natural classification.

With a little prompting on your part, students should be able to come up with a system based on function similar to the one in Figure 13.5.

One point to note with the class is that having a theoretical underpinning (function in this case) narrows the possibilities a bit resulting in greater similarity between the systems developed by different groups. Also, you should note that natural classification systems, while not necessarily easier to develop and use, are more useful to scientists because they support the theories upon which they are developed, rather than the whims of the scientist who creates them. Even so, natural classification systems are still created by fallible humans and are by no means perfect. One way to illustrate this is to show the class a new fastener not in their collections (Figure 13.6).

Figure 13.5
A natural classification system based upon inferred function.

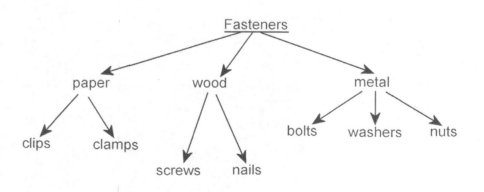

This item is a hollow socket set screw. Typically, it's screwed into something unstable like plywood, and then a bolt is driven through it. Use this item, or one like it, to point out to your students that natural classification schemes have limitations; we may discover new items that do not really fit into our classification systems. Viruses are a good illustration of this point, in that scientists have debated whether they are actually even alive, let alone where they would fit in the six kingdoms.

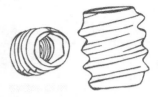

Figure 13.6
Two views of the new fastener.

LESSON WRAP-UP

Your students may have held the misconception that all knowledge in science is absolute and that scientists are about the business of discovering the "truth" in nature. Through this lesson, students can begin to understand that in many instances, there is no single right answer in science and, therefore, the methods and concepts scientists develop reflect a degree of subjectivity.

Figure 13.7 provides an overview of the connections among the knowledge, processes, and nature of science addressed for this lesson.

Figure 13.7
Connection among the three aspects of science for the "Nuts and Bolts" lesson.

Science as a body of knowledge

1. Explanation of the purpose and use of classification systems

2. Characteristics of the six kingdoms used to classify organisms

3. Understanding the difference between artificial and natural classification systems

Science as a set of methods or processes

1. Recognizing patterns as the basis of classification

2. Applying classification schemes

3. Inventing classification schemes

Science as a way of knowing

1. Science does not always produce a single "right" answer.

2. Classification schemes are developed by scientists, not discovered directly from nature.

3. Thus, scientific knowledge can be seen as subjective, to a degree.

4. Classification schemes can change with new discoveries.

ASSESSMENT

The questions in Notebook Assignment 13.1 allow your students to document their work as they attempt to classify the nuts and bolts given them. It also gives them a chance to reflect on how creative they had to be in order to classify these different pieces of hardware, and compare that to the creativity scientists must use in order to classify natural phenomena (insects, stars, subatomic particles, etc.).

The next assignment, Notebook Assignment 13.2, guides your students through an Internet research activity in which they compare and contrast two competing ways of classifying life. Through this activity they will see that, in science, classification is subjective—again, it really depends more on the classifier than the classified!

The Nuts and Bolts of Classification

Name: _____ Date: _____

1. Work in a group to observe and record in the table below several similarities and differences among the set of objects provided by your teacher.

Similarities   **Differences**

_____   _____
_____   _____
_____   _____
_____   _____
_____   _____
_____   _____
_____   _____
_____   _____

2. Record a name for each object in your set in the space below. You can use the proper names if you know them, or invent your own. Just be sure to keep the names descriptive, yet simple.

_____
_____
_____
_____

3. Based on the information in the list above, sort your set of objects into three or more groups. Feel free to create subgroups. Objects in each group must be similar to each other in some way, but different from objects in the other categories. Finally, record your classification scheme as a diagram.

4. Now compare your classification system to those of your classmates. Are they similar or different? Why do you think this is the case?

_____

_____

_____

5. Creativity and subjectivity (being influenced by something other than the data) have roles to play in the development of all kinds of scientific knowledge. Based on your experience with classifying the fasteners, how would you say that creativity and subjectivity affect the work of taxonomists (scientists who develop classification systems)?

_____

_____

_____

_____

_____

Comparing Classification Systems

Name: _____ Date: _____

Linnaeus (1758) originally classified all macroscopic living organisms as either animals or plants, based on whether they moved or not. Later, the invention of the microscope led to the discovery of microorganisms, which were initially classified as plants or animals, or sometimes placed in a separate kingdom. In 1969, R. H. Whittaker developed a widely accepted five-kingdom system that included the Monera, Protista, Fungi, Plant, and Animal kingdoms. Based on rRNA studies, C. R. Woese and his associates discovered a difference between the types of prokaryotes in the Monera kingdom and proposed a six-kingdom system in 1977. This new system included Eubacteria, Archaebacteria, Protista, Fungi, Plant, and Animal kingdoms and was adopted by most biologists.

More recently, some biologists have advocated a new category above the kingdom level called a domain or superkingdom. Using Internet resources, describe the three-domain system of classification and contrast it with the five- or six-kingdom system. Then, state and justify a position on which system you believe is most appropriate, including arguments that scientists use.

Internet Resources to Get You Started

1. *Rediscovering Biology* online textbook

   http://www.learner.org/channel/courses/biology/textbook/compev/compev_2.html

2. Biology classification

   http://www.sirinet.net/~jgjohnso/classification.html

3. The five kingdoms of life

   http://waynesword.palomar.edu/trfeb98.htm

4. The six kingdoms

   http://www.ric.edu/ptiskus/Six_Kingdoms/

5. Alternative classifications of life

   http://www.mun.ca/biology/scarr/Five_Kingdoms_Three_Domains.html

14

Experiencing Experiments

n this activity, students develop deeper understandings of experiments and scientific inquiry. Not all science activities are inquiry-based, and not all inquiry is experimental, but each type has value in science. In completing the activities in this chapter, students will participate in scientific inquiry by designing and conducting a real experiment on an event that is as easy to do as it is spectacular. In so doing, they will gain a greater appreciation of the role of experimentation in science.

LAYING THE GROUNDWORK

My young nieces, ages 8 and 11, were visiting recently from out of town, and in the usual fashion, I offered them some fun science activities. I promised that after they finished drinking their newly purchased glass bottle of strawberry milk, I'd put a hard-boiled egg in the bottle through its narrow opening. Of course, they rapidly drank the milk, and they were thrilled as the egg loudly popped into the bottle after I placed a piece of lit newsprint inside it. They were even more thrilled when the soot-covered egg emerged unscathed after I turned the bottle upside down and ran hot water over it!

Later in the day, they played outside with light-sensitive paper, making shadowy images on the blue paper with natural objects. Finally, I had them take clear straws and try to get four different densities of colored salt water layered inside. They had a glorious time, and said to their mother afterwards, "We were doing science experiments!" Even though my nieces were engaged in some valuable learning experiences, the only true experiment I had planned for the day was yet to come, and that experiment involved much more messy fun. I challenged them to figure out how to get the biggest splash from a bottle of soda and some mint candy.

My nieces' confusion about what constitutes science experiments is common among school-aged children and their teachers as well. It highlights the fact that we need to be careful with our language. Often, we call every science activity an experiment, but experiments are only one way scientists conduct research, and as we shall see later in this chapter, they refer to a very specific research design. Experiments are part of school science, as well, but they are only one type of many activities teachers can use to teach science effectively (see Figure 14.1). Demonstrations,

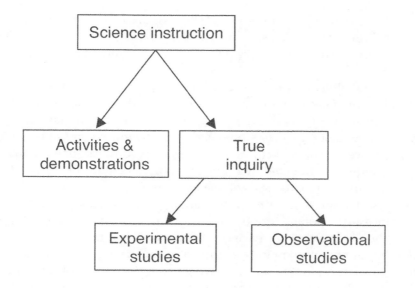

Figure 14.1
A breakdown of activities
in science instruction.

hands-on activities, and building models are all examples of engaging activities that are not necessarily experiments, but are valuable nonetheless in teaching science content and processes.

What Is Inquiry?

The *National Science Education Standards* stress that students should engage in scientific inquiry as one approach to learning about science. At all grade levels, the standards emphasize that students should be able to ask questions, gather data, and construct reasonable explanations. This leads to a very simple and useful definition of inquiry: the process of analyzing data to answer a scientific question (Bell, Smetana, & Binns, 2005). To count as inquiry, a science lesson must involve students in two critical activities.

1. Asking a research question or questions
2. Seeking the answer to the question(s) through the analysis of data

By applying these criteria, we can see that many worthwhile activities are not inquiry based. Collecting and identifying leaves, demonstrating the chemical reaction that occurs when baking soda and vinegar are mixed, and building edible models of cells are examples of good science activities that can be used to teach science content and processes. However, as typically taught, these activities do not include an explicit research question and so cannot really be counted as inquiry. Although using light-sensitive paper to make images of leaves and flowers can be used to teach students about chemical reactions, shadows, and visible light, it is not an inquiry activity unless students are asking a research question and gathering data.

Light-sensitive paper can certainly be used in the process of scientific inquiry—but students must first create a question (often with lots of help from the teacher) and then gather data in order to answer it. Would sunscreen products block the sun and create a shadow on the light-sensitive paper? Would sunscreen products with greater SPF (Sun Protection Factor) values applied to small squares of translucent paper block more sunlight than products with less or no SPF values? With these questions guiding the activity, students can decide what data to collect and how it should be analyzed, turning a fun exploration activity into one that supports scientific inquiry.

Now, if not all hands-on science activities support inquiry, it is equally true that not all examples of scientific inquiry can be labeled as experiments. In the real world of science, astronomers and geologists collect all sorts of data in order to answer questions about the evolution of stars and the movements of tectonic plates. They can't, however, conduct controlled experiments on these natural phenomena. The type of inquiry conducted in a nonexperimental environment is called an observational study. In many fields of science, observational studies are the only way to answer research questions; the manipulation of variables simply cannot occur. Biologists measuring populations of wildlife conduct observational studies in the process of their inquiries. They have guiding research questions and they collect data, but they are not purposefully manipulating anything. If astronomers notice a supernova (distant exploding star) in the night sky, they might observe the object carefully and collect as much data as possible to characterize the star and the changes it undergoes during the explosion. These data help scientists answer the research question, "What is a nova like?" and help them better understand novas. But they are not conducting an experiment. Why not? To answer this question, we must carefully consider what constitutes an experiment in science.

What Is an Experiment?

A science experiment is a controlled activity designed to test a hypothesis in which independent variables are manipulated and dependent variables are measured. The process of manipulating variables to test hypotheses is at the heart of every experiment. A scientist might hypothesize (formally predict) that when a fertilizer containing more nitrogen is applied to plants, the plants will produce more seeds in their fruit. Scientists differentiate between variables they manipulate (independent variables) and those that change as a result of their manipulations (dependent variables). In this case, the independent variable would be the amount of nitrogen in the fertilizer, and the dependent variable would be the number of seeds in the fruit. Hypotheses are not just guesses or hunches; they are formal predictions or explanations based on prior knowledge, research, and other investigations. So by definition any activity said to be a scientific experiment must contain these components:

1. Hypothesis(es)
2. Independent variable(s)
3. Dependent variable(s)

An experiment then, can be seen as a special kind of scientific inquiry involving the formal test of a hypothesis. But how do we go about testing hypotheses?

Hypothesis Testing 101

The British philosopher Karl Popper maintained back in the early 1930s that a hypothesis must be falsifiable; in other words, it should be a statement that can be tested and possibly proven untrue. For example, he proposed that if you saw one white swan you might conclude that all swans are white, but in order to test this hypothesis you would have to locate and observe every swan, an impossible task. A more reasonable way to test the hypothesis is to attempt to falsify it. Once you've found one non-white swan, your search is over, because you've proven the hypothesis untrue.

What works for British philosophers also works for scientists. Scientists typically conduct their experiments in such a manner as to attempt to falsify their hypotheses rather than try and prove them. In the case of the high-nitrogen fertilizer and fruit seeds, the hypothesis, "the higher the nitrogen the greater the seed count" could be easily disproved if plants grown in soil with a higher nitrogen concentration consistently produce less seeds in their fruit.

Scientists' confidence in a hypothesis increases over time, assuming it withstands repeated attempts to disprove it. Thus, hypotheses may be confirmed or validated but never actually proven. To do so would require an infinite amount of resources and time as every possible condition related to the hypothesis is tested, which is totally unrealistic.

The following activity is designed to be an experimental inquiry into how to get the best splash out of some soda and candy. Of course, any time you bring soda and candy into a classroom, it's a big splash! This experiment, however, does not involve eating or drinking, but testing, measuring, observing, predicting, and hypothesizing. Believe me; it's just as fun but a whole lot messier, so be prepared to get wet!

THE ACTIVITY: CANDY AND SODA

LESSON AT A GLANCE

1. Students observe a demonstration of a Mentos® candy in a bottle of soda.
2. Then students research this phenomena and propose an independent variable to test in the quest for the "best splash."
3. The class decides on the definition of the term, "best splash," and also how to measure it.
4. Groups of students conduct inquiry experiments with candy and soda and compile the results.
5. Conclusions:
   - Scientific hypotheses are not simply guesses, they are formal statements created after some investigation and research.
   - Hypotheses can be disproved but never absolutely proven.
   - Inquiry activities involve both observational studies and experimental ones.

There's been a great deal of hype lately about the phenomena of adding Mentos® candy to a two-liter bottle of soda. Video clips abound on the Internet; if you go to www.video.google.com and search the keywords, "mentos soda," you'll see the latest postings. Perhaps your students will have seen this phenomenon, but regardless, it's rife with possibility for exploration. If you design the activity so that you and your students are answering an explicit research question through data collection and analysis, it can be a great inquiry activity.

Go outside and demonstrate the phenomena by dropping one Mentos® mint candy into a two-liter bottle of soda (any brand will work, but diet is less sticky), and observe what happens.

Then ask your students, "What can we do to get the best splash from these two ingredients—candy and soda?" That's your research question. Collecting the data is the fun part. Students can do some research on the Internet to learn more about this reaction and get some ideas to help them propose a hypothesis. A day or two prior to the inquiry activity, have your students answer the questions on Notebook Assignment 14.1. Your students' plans will guide you in purchasing supplies for the inquiry.

How can you get the best splash? Well, first you need to define the term, *best*. Does it mean the highest spout of soda, or does it mean the greatest volume of soda? Or perhaps it means the greatest amount of time that the soda is spurting. Whatever you measure in your quest for the best is your dependent variable.

The next problem to solve is how will you measure this variable? This too should be decided upon ahead of time so that there is a standard way to measure the result. Be warned that with the ideal configuration the spout of soda can reach 10 meters!

What independent variables can your students manipulate? For one thing, they have their choice of all sorts of candy. Mentos are not the only candies that could possibly cause this reaction. Life Savers®, Tic Tacs®, and Altoids® are just a few of the other possibilities you and your students can try. The candies can be put in the soda whole or crushed. One can be added, or more . . . many more. I've seen an entire roll of Mentos dropped into a soda bottle! And think of all the brands and types of soda available, from soda water to caffeinated sugary soda. The temperature of the soda can be manipulated. The soda can be pre-shaken or not. Any of these independent variables can be manipulated in your research.

If you can afford it, divide your students into groups of four and allow them two or three soda bottles and one type of candy per group. If your budget is tight, your students may be enthusiastic enough about this activity to bring in their own supplies. Have them select one independent variable to test—the soda type, candy type, candy amount, or whatever. Have each group record their results, write a conclusion, and then compile all the results into a data table of their own design for further analysis.

LESSON WRAP-UP

So far, you've learned from this book that there's more than one way to conduct scientific investigations and that there is no one method to science. This chapter reinforces the idea that scientists do not follow "cookbook" steps in their search for answers. They practice what we call *inquiry*. By asking questions and collecting data that they analyze to answer their questions, your students can inquire in much the same way as scientists.

One way to connect this activity to the nature of science is to emphasize that in science, the term *experiment* refers to a very specific type of activity. An experiment is a test of a hypothesis that involves changing variables and measuring what

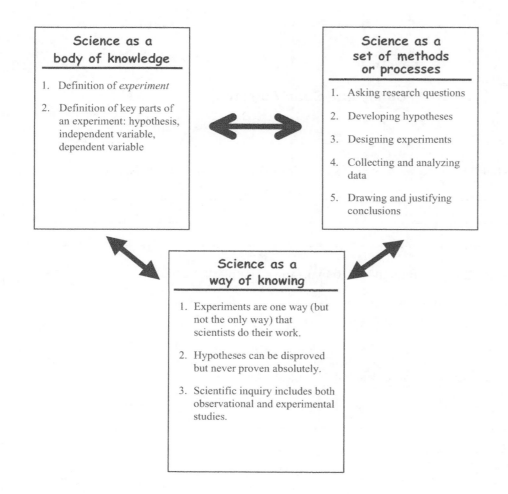

Figure 14.2
Connection among the three aspects of science for the "Experiencing Experiments" lesson.

Science as a body of knowledge

1. Definition of *experiment*

2. Definition of key parts of an experiment: hypothesis, independent variable, dependent variable

Science as a set of methods or processes

1. Asking research questions

2. Developing hypotheses

3. Designing experiments

4. Collecting and analyzing data

5. Drawing and justifying conclusions

Science as a way of knowing

1. Experiments are one way (but not the only way) that scientists do their work.

2. Hypotheses can be disproved but never proven absolutely.

3. Scientific inquiry includes both observational and experimental studies.

happens because of the change. Although experiments are a powerful way to find out what causes things to happen, they are by no means the only way scientists do their work. Some scientists, like astronomers and paleontologists, can go through their whole careers without ever conducting a single experiment! They are still doing inquiry, though, as long as they are answering research questions through data analysis. And it is their inquiries that lead us to so many answers about the world around us, just as your inquiry has led you to many answers about what happens when you add candy to soda.

Figure 14.2 provides an overview of the connections among the knowledge, processes, and nature of science addressed for this lesson.

ASSESSMENT

The following assignment can be used with this lesson as students plan and conduct their experiments, or if your students record all their activities in science notebooks, you can provide the assignment as a guide.

Candy and Soda Activity

Name: _____ Date: _____

1. Describe what happened when your teacher dropped the candy into the soda.

   _____

   _____

   _____

2. What are some things you might try to make the soda splash "better?"

   _____

   _____

   _____

3. What is your class definition of the "BEST" splash?

   _____

   _____

   _____

4. My research question is _____

5. What is your independent variable? _____

6. What is your dependent variable? _____

7. What is your hypothesis? Write it as an "If . . . . . Then . . . . ." statement, including both your independent and dependent variables in the statement:

   _____

   _____

   _____

8. What supplies will your group need to conduct your activity?

   _____

   _____

   _____

9. Briefly describe your procedure.

_____

_____

_____

_____

_____

_____

10. Is this activity an experiment? Use what you've learned about experiments to defend your answer.

_____

_____

_____

_____

_____

_____

11. Create a data table for your results. At a minimum your table should include a title and columns for your independent variable and dependent variable.

_____

_____

_____

_____

_____

12. Write a short paragraph describing your conclusions. Be sure that your statement includes an answer to your research question.

_____

_____

_____

_____

_____

Subjectivity and the Boiling Point of Water

Working in small groups, students are challenged to determine the boiling point of water as accurately as possible. Students will wind up producing a variety of results, typically ranging from about 95° C to 105° C. The teacher then leads a discussion challenging students to explain the wide range of boiling points, given that these results were all based on careful observational data. Finally, students are asked to consider how scientists arrive at a single accepted value for the boiling point of water, despite having to deal with similarly disparate results.

LAYING THE GROUNDWORK

Daniel Gabriel Fahrenheit devised his temperature scale in the early 1700s; there are a variety of stories about how he did it. He had invented a mercury thermometer and needed two fixed points to develop the scale for it. You see, every new temperature scale needs two fixed reference points, and the inventor of the scale then fills in the divisions that go between the points.

One story goes that he used his own internal body temperature as one fixed point and called it 100° F, and the coldest solution he could concoct with water, ice, and salt represented 0° F. He then filled the scale in with a hundred points.

A more humorous variation of this story is that he didn't use his own internal body temperature to represent 100° because, being a scientist, he knew he needed repeated trials to establish a valid number. Instead, he took a herd of pigs . . . yes, pigs . . . and took their temperatures with his thermometer invention. The average pig temperature was the fixed point we now call 100° F.

Who knows what actually happened. We don't have a good historical record of this moment in time 300 years ago. Some say he recorded the winter temperatures in his hometown of Gdańsk, Poland, during the winter of 1708–1709 and called the coldest day 0° F!

Whichever story it true, it goes without saying that 0° F and 100° F are arbitrary values in an invented scheme of measuring temperature. Fahrenheit was *trying* not to use arbitrary values. He really thought that the human body temperature and the coldest winter day in Gdańsk were numbers that could be consistently relied on.

Anders Celsius, the Swedish astronomer, devised a new temperature scale in the mid-1700s. Celsius reported that the temperature of thawing snow or ice was a constant value, independent of geographical latitude, so he chose it to represent one of his

More About the Celsius Temperature Scale

Anders Celsius actually assigned 0° C to be the boiling point of water and 100° C to be the freezing point of water! After his death the scale was flipped around to the version of the scale we use today.

fixed points. Although he realized that barometric pressure affects the boiling point of water, he chose the boiling point of water to be his other fixed point anyway.

We know today that many factors can affect both the boiling and freezing points of water. Minerals or impurities, altitude, and barometric pressure are just some of the variables that can affect these points. In school science labs, user error and faulty equipment also lend themselves to different values of these measurements. Celsius himself noted that when he removed his thermometer from boiling water the temperature seemed to rise for a moment—due to the contraction of the glass! These factors explain why, when you ask a classroom of science students to each determine the boiling point of water, you'll most likely get a range of values.

And what if you asked students from classrooms all over the world? That's just what the Center for Improved Engineering and Science Education (CIESE) did when they started the International Boiling Point Project back in the year 2000. (See http://www.ciese.org/curriculum/boilproj/index.html for more information.) Students participating in this project from all over the world report their elevation, room temperature, location, volume of water, and boiling point class average. The project has continued for six years now, and the results are fascinating. As students post their results each year, they communicate with each other in an online discussion area as well.

Even outside the classroom science can be a messy endeavor with different people coming up with different answers to scientific questions. For example, scientists have been describing "constants of nature" for thousands of years. Back in 2000 B.C.E. the Babylonians found an approximate value for the ratio of a circle's circumference to its diameter (or π): 3 1/8, or 3.125. About the same time, the ancient Egyptians said the value was equal to $4 \times (8/9)^2 = 3.16049. \ldots$

In the sixteenth century, the French mathematician Francois Viète attempted to solve for π with algebra, and he came up with a decimal number that was infinite in sequence, which he rounded to nine decimal places, or $\pi = 3.1415926536$. By 1967, the value of π was known to 500,000 decimal places; however, in today's math and science classrooms students use either the truncated value 3.14 or perhaps 3.14159.

Perhaps you've tried to find the value of π with your students by measuring the circumference and diameter of round or spherical objects. If so, you know how difficult obtaining an accurate and precise value can be.

This constant of nature isn't the only constant scientists have grappled with. For example, scientists have debated about "G," the gravitational constant, ever since Isaac Newton first proposed its existence in 1686 with his Law of Universal Gravitation. Henry Cavendish tried to find the value of "G" in 1798 using a torsion balance, and he determined it to be equal to (6.75×10^{-11}) m^3 kg^{-1} s^{-2}.

Cavendish's torsion balance experiment has been repeated many times over the past 200 years with more sophisticated equipment, and each time scientists have modified the accepted value slightly. The official value of G was published in 1982 by CODATA, the Committee on Data for Science and Technology, and they determined G is equal to $(6.6742 \times 10^{-11} \pm 0.0001)$ m^3 kg^{-1} s^{-2} with an uncertainty of 0.0128%.

To date, groups of scientists all over the world are debating the true value of the gravitational constant. Most physics textbooks simply state the value as equal to 6.67×10^{-11} m^3 kg^{-1} s^{-2}.

Another question regarding constants is whether they really are constant or do they change over time? What if scientists learned that the speed of light had actually changed since the beginning of the universe? Physicists are currently debating that question. A team of physicists in Australia began studying quasars a few years ago to measure the fine-structure constant, and their initial finding suggested that this constant of nature may have changed ever so slightly since the beginning of time, implying that the speed of light may have changed ever so slightly as well.

Scientists will continue to debate each of these points until, over time, they reach some sort of consensus. Your students can more fully understand this aspect of the nature of science if you ask them to conduct the following exercise and discuss their inevitably different findings. The Boiling Point activity (or its alternative Freezing Point Depression activity on page 191) is, in a sense, a microcosm of the scientific endeavor.

THE ACTIVITY: BOILING POINT OF WATER LAB

LESSON AT A GLANCE

1. Introduce students to the idea that standardized measurements are arbitrary with a warm-up activity.

2. Students work in groups to determine a procedure and measure the boiling point of water (or use the alternative activity).

3. Discuss the different results your students may have produced.

4. Describe how the two most familiar temperature scales were invented.

5. Conclusions:

   - Scientific concepts are sometimes based on subjective factors, rather than defining principles of nature (e.g., Fahrenheit's scale).
   - Even scientific "constants" are subject to change with new data or more precise techniques.
   - Scientists sometimes disagree about what should be accepted, and go through a process of debate that may take decades.
   - While scientific knowledge is subject to change, it is durable after it has gone through rigorous testing and debate.

Warm-Up

Get your students warmed up to the idea that measurements are subjective by asking them to tell you what time it is. If students are wearing watches, you will surely get different answers from different students. Even if there is one clock on the wall in your classroom, ask your students if they think the room next door has a clock showing the same time.

You may even get into a debate if you ask a scientist, because the Earth's rotation is slowing down, and the current definition of a "second" is that 86,400 of them equals one Earth day. If the Earth day is getting longer, then what is that doing to time? Just as your classroom students may be debating the current time and temperature, physicists and astronomers are debating whether to use an astronomical definition of time or a physical one. The final decision may significantly affect computer systems, satellites, and every modern electronic device that uses time to keep track of events.

Next, have students measure something simple like a new crayon, a new unsharpened pencil, or an index card. Older students can even be challenged to calculate the area of the index card or the volume of the crayon or pencil. Certainly, regardless of the standardization of crayons, pencils, index cards, measuring tapes, and rulers, your students will all come up with different values. What are the rules? Are they arbitrary, or do you establish them beforehand? True to the nature of science, before the rules for measurement are established, the determined values will all differ.

Finding the Boiling Point

To transition into this activity ask students to define the boiling and freezing points of water. Most likely, you'll have consensus, although some students will be more familiar with the Fahrenheit scale than the Celsius one.

Next, challenge students to determine a procedure for finding the boiling point of water and implement it. They will need to determine how they will heat the water, how they will measure the temperature, and how they will know when the water is boiling. It will take a while for all the lab groups to set up their equipment and wait for the water to come to a rolling boil. If you have enough space and equipment for pairs of students to work together, that's probably best. The more results you get from the class, the easier it will be to make the point that perfect results may be the goal, but are seldom the reality. Also, more data will make for a richer discussion about reaching consensus at the end of the investigation.

Be sure to check students' procedures to make sure they are following safety rules. (Note that an alternate activity that is safer for younger students is presented on the prior page.) Whenever working with a heat source and boiling liquids, have students wear safety goggles and close-toed shoes, with long hair pulled back. Have fire extinguishers readily available. Electric heat sources may be a safer option than open-flamed Bunsen burners. Be sure the container they use for the water is heat-safe and that it is steadily balanced and not likely to tip and spill. Students should have a way to hold the thermometer without burning themselves; avoid using mercury thermometers. See Figure 15.1 for a safe, appropriate lab setup.

Students may record their results in their notebooks using Notebook Assignment 15.1 as a guide. Remind students that they should not "fudge" their data or revise their results to get what they think is the expected "right" answer. After the exercise is complete, have a member from each pair or group present the boiling point they determined. You may want to draw a data table on the board showing the group number in the left column and the boiling point temperature found by that group in the right column.

Have students copy the completed table into their science notebooks (see Notebook Assignment 15.1) and create a frequency histogram, like the example in Figure 15.2. Then ask them, "What is the correct answer?" Your students'

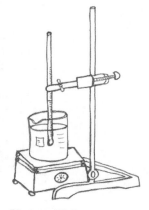

Figure 15.1
Lab setup with hotplate.

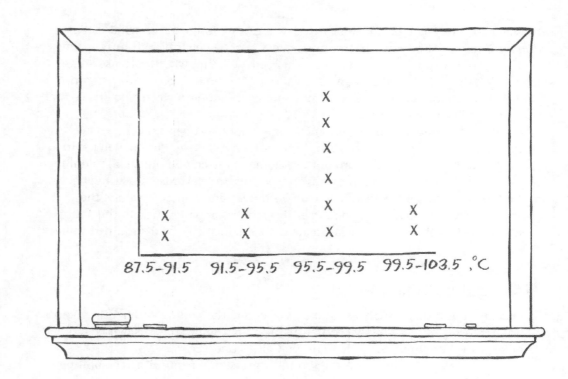

Figure 15.2
Hypothetical class frequency histogram.

87.5–91.5   91.5–95.5   95.5–99.5   99.5–103.5 , °C

range of values for a seemingly simple and straightforward "constant" value will provide the context for an important discussion about the nature and process of science.

Reflecting on the Results

In trying to determine an answer to the boiling point question, some students will suggest taking the average, or the mean, of all the findings. In the case of our hypothetical class data, the mean is 96° C, but only one group actually measured that value. Other students may point out that some of the values don't make sense and should be eliminated rather than averaged in (e.g., 88° C and 101° C). Ask students why there are different answers. They may offer some of the following explanations.

- Some beakers may have been slightly dirty, contaminating the water.
- Some people placed their thermometers too close to the bottom or top of the beaker.
- If digital thermometers were used, some may have had weak batteries.
- Some people may not have read the thermometer properly.

It is not an easy task to come to consensus with an activity such as this! Your students, like all scientists, need to negotiate about this scientific finding and come up with a workable, agreeable solution. That's the way it's always been in science. Some workable ways to accomplish this task are to calculate the statistics, such as median, mean, and mode. Students can throw out the "outliers," those anomalies due to mal-functioned equipment or sloppy science—the numbers no one has confidence in. This might happen when an eager student sees little bubbles form on the bottom of the beaker at 88° C and declares it boiling. It also might occur when the thermometer is not calibrated correctly and reports values that are consistently too high.

ALTERNATIVE ACTIVITY: FINDING THE FREEZING POINT DEPRESSION

If you really like the idea of the boiling point activity but don't think it's prudent to let your students get too close to potentially dangerous heat sources and boiling water, then you can follow the same format but substitute the following freezing point depression activity that uses water, sodium chloride (NaCl, or table salt), and ice.

When Daniel Fahrenheit was establishing the fixed point on his temperature scale, 0° F, he may have used a mixture of water, salt, and ice. If he did, it is because when salt dissolves in water, breaking up into sodium and chlorine ions, the freezing point is lowered. The more ions dissolved in the water, the lower the freezing point will be. But there's a limit—only so much salt will dissolve in cold, icy water before the solution is saturated. Under ideal laboratory conditions, the coldest temperature you can achieve with water, ice, and salt, is −6° F or −21° C. Fahrenheit must not have had ideal laboratory conditions back in 1724, because he called the coldest temperature he reached, 0° F.

Distribute small plastic or glass containers (a 6 oz. plastic drink cup works well), ice cubes, salt, stirring sticks, and thermometers to lab groups of two or three students. Have them proceed as in the boiling point activity except this time the goal is to reach the coldest temperature possible. Have students add five or six ice cubes to the cup and just enough water to make the ice cubes float. Instruct them to slowly add a few teaspoons of salt as they stir and measure the temperature. They can add even more salt if the temperature continues to drop and the salt continues to dissolve.

Another difference between this activity and the boiling point activity is that students are not measuring a constant of a pure substance; they are reenacting a historical moment and trying to come to some consensus about what the "correct" value should be. They will debate their results in much the same way and come to consensus about the coldest temperature they could reach.

Freezing point depression is the name of the process in which the freezing point of water is lowered through the addition of salt or antifreeze. Scientists study freezing point depression in much the same way as your students did, except that scientists use purified water, purified salt, and very accurate instruments. You might also want to lead a discussion about how the freezing point depression of water affects the oceans and how people use it to their advantage in both winter road safety and ice cream making! Notebook Assignments 15.3 and 15.4 may be used with the freezing point depression activity.

LESSON WRAP-UP

What is the difference between this classroom activity and what scientists have had to do to determine an accepted value for the boiling point of water? For one thing, the International Temperature Scale adopted in 1990 (known as ITS-90) by the International Committee of Weights and Measures followed a number of other official temperature scales that had been in place over the years. The new ITS-90 defines the boiling point of pure water to be approximately 99.974° C at 1 atmosphere of pressure—the approximate atmospheric pressure on Earth at sea level.

Additionally, tap water in the United States usually contains fluoride and all sorts of other minerals. These dissolved minerals can slightly raise the boiling point of water. When scientists calibrate the boiling point of water, they use distilled water—pure H_2O. You might want to try distilled water with your students and see if it makes much of a difference.

Be sure to steer your students away from the thinking that there is no accepted boiling point of water, or that anything goes when it comes to constants. Just as we don't want our students viewing scientific knowledge as indisputable facts, we don't want them overcorrecting and deciding that scientists don't know any answers at all. Remember, ideas in science may not be absolute, but they are durable after going through the process of consensus and peer review.

Figure 15.3 provides an overview of the connections between the knowledge, processes, and nature of science addressed for this lesson.

Figure 15.3
Connection among the three aspects of science for the Boiling Point Lesson.

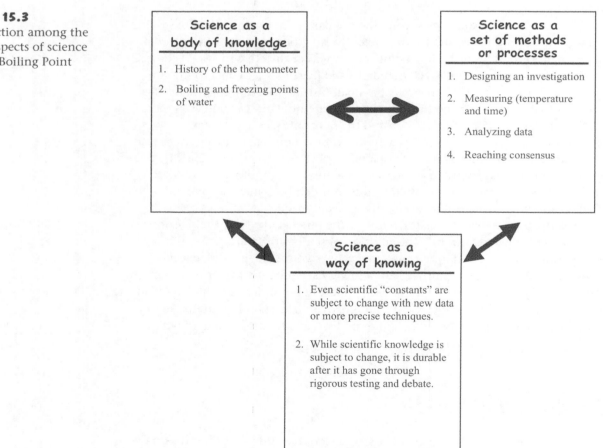

Science as a
body of knowledge

1. History of the thermometer
2. Boiling and freezing points of water

Science as a
set of methods
or processes

1. Designing an investigation
2. Measuring (temperature and time)
3. Analyzing data
4. Reaching consensus

Science as a
way of knowing

1. Even scientific "constants" are subject to change with new data or more precise techniques.

2. While scientific knowledge is subject to change, it is durable after it has gone through rigorous testing and debate.

ASSESSMENT

In this activity, there is no single right answer to assess. Although your students may use the questions in Notebook Assignment 15.1 as a guide to recording their data, they are practicing some basic process skills of measuring temperatures. The bigger point to bring home is that scientists don't just follow a prescribed method to determine the "right" answer when they conduct their investigations. Scientific inquiry involves more thought, creativity, and work than that. The questions in Notebook Assignment 15.2 aim to bring out these points about science. Use it to see if your students got the big picture while watching their pots boil.

Notebook Assignments 15.3 and 15.4 are similar in focus but are designed to accompany the alternative activity on finding the freezing point depression.

Boiling Point of Water Lab

Name: _____ Date: _____

Using the procedure approved by your teacher, work with your partner to determine the point at which water boils. After all lab groups have determined a value, record and graph them all.

Draw the apparatus you used, list the equipment you used, and describe the procedure you used to determine the boiling point of water.

My apparatus looked like this	List of materials

My procedure

What boiling point did you determine? _____

Data Table

Group	Boiling point, °C

Frequency Histogram

°C

Discussion about the Boiling Point of Water

Name: _____ Date: _____

Based on the activity you completed and your discussion about science and scientists, answer the following questions.

1. Why didn't everyone get the same result when measuring the boiling point of water?

   _____

   _____

   _____

2. What was the class consensus (agreement)?

   _____

   _____

   _____

3. How did the class reach a consensus?

   _____

   _____

   _____

4. Do scientists ever have to reach consensus when there are results that vary from person to person or results that vary over time? Explain and give an example.

   _____

   _____

   _____

   _____

5. What did this activity teach you about science?

   _____

   _____

   _____

Coldest Temperature Lab

Name: _____ Date: _____

Using the procedure approved by your teacher, work with your partner to determine the coldest temperature you can reach by adding salt to water. After all lab groups have determined a value, record and graph them all.

Draw the apparatus you used, list the equipment you used, and describe the procedure you used to determine the coldest temperature of the salt and water solution.

My apparatus looked like this	**List of materials**

My procedure

My coldest temperature for the salt water solution was _____

Data Table

Group	Coldest temperature reached (°C)

Frequency Histogram

°C

Discussion about the Coldest Temperature Activity

Name: _____ Date: _____

Based on the activity you completed and your discussion about science and scientists, answer the following questions.

1. Why didn't everyone get the same result when determining the coldest temperature that can be reached in the salt water solution?

   _____

   _____

   _____

2. What was the class consensus (agreement) for the coldest temperature?

   _____

   _____

   _____

3. How did the class reach a consensus?

   _____

   _____

   _____

4. Do scientists ever have to reach consensus when there are results that vary from person to person or results that vary over time? Explain and give an example.

   _____

   _____

   _____

   _____

   _____

5. What did this activity teach you about science?

   _____

   _____

   _____

Perception and Conception: Two Sides of the Same Coin

Students observe confusing pictures of familiar objects and read ambiguous descriptions of familiar experiences. Students can make little sense of these objects and descriptions until the teacher provides some key hints. These hints provide interpretive frameworks (paradigms) that make the identification of the images and meaning of the passages clear. Students then learn that theories play a similar role in interpreting scientific data—there is seldom a direct line from observation to scientific concept—and that theories provide the context in which much of science is done.

LAYING THE GROUNDWORK

I grew up in the days before iPods, Game Boys, and car DVD players. In those days, there was nothing to do on long road trips but look out the window, read books, or pick on my younger brother.

One summer—I think I was about 8—we were driving down a long stretch of Midwestern highway on a sweltering hot day, when I noticed something remarkable while peering out the front windshield. The road some distance ahead appeared to be covered in water, despite the fact that we were in a dry area with no other water in sight. As we got closer to the puddle it disappeared, but then a new puddle materialized further ahead.

This phenomenon repeated itself several times before I asked my dad if he could see the same thing. Smiling, he said he could and told me that what I was seeing was a mirage caused by the hot pavement. I was intrigued by the idea of seeing a real mirage for the first time—until then I had only seen them on the *Bugs Bunny/Road Runner Hour*.

Not until years later did I learn the science behind the mirages commonly seen on the highway. The dark-colored asphalt absorbs energy from the sun and heats to a higher temperature than the surrounding area. The hot pavement warms the air above it to higher temperatures as well, resulting in warmer layers of air just above the pavement.

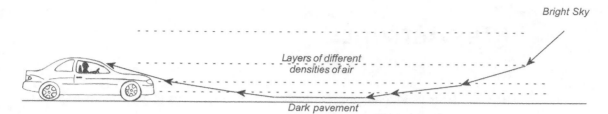

Figure 16.1
Path of light
for a mirage
(angles are
greatly
exaggerated).

Bright Sky

Layers of different
densities of air

Dark pavement

You may remember that light bends as it passes through layers of different densities. Since the warm air above the pavement is less dense than the cool air surrounding it, light from the sky travels a bending path as it passes through layers of different densities (Figure 16.1). The result is that a "false" image of the sky appears on the road, and we interpret the shininess as a puddle of water.

The point of this story is not so much to teach a physics lesson, but to emphasize two different ways of "seeing" a mirage. When I first encountered the phenomenon as a child, I was convinced I was seeing a disappearing puddle of water in the road. My conviction was based upon previous experiences of how water looks when viewed at a distance. Now that I understand the physics behind mirages, I no longer see water, but rather an interesting example of refraction, or the bending of light. The image of the mirage that reaches my eyes hasn't changed, but the way I interpret the image has changed. I have a new interpretive framework, and as we shall see, this makes all the difference in the world.

Throughout the earlier chapters of this book, I have emphasized that scientific knowledge is similar to most other kinds of knowledge, in that it is built upon both observation and inference. As we have seen, because inference plays a role in the development of scientific knowledge, scientific knowledge is necessarily tentative. Inferences, by their very nature, are not directly observable and cannot be considered true in any absolute sense of the word. Therefore, the scientific concepts and theories that depend upon inferences must be considered open to revision, as well.

But remember that scientific ideas are built upon two types of processes—inference and observation. Surely, we can depend on our observations as totally reliable and objective, especially when they're made within the rigors of scientific methodology! In fact, we all know that "seeing is believing." But does this common saying always hold true when it comes to science? The purpose of the activities described in this chapter is to help you and your students explore the possibility that even scientific observations can be influenced by preconceived notions and that this influence is not always a bad thing. In fact, without some kind of preconceived interpretive framework, many of our observations make no sense.

The activities in this chapter serve as analogies to help students better understand the importance of interpretive frameworks in interpreting scientific phenomena. The fourth activity describes an actual instance in science in which different interpretive frameworks made a dramatic difference in scientists' understanding of the planet Saturn. Choose one or more of these activities that will work best for your class.

The Activities

1. Students view ambiguous images or read ambiguous text passages and try to make sense of them.

2. Teacher provides a framework for interpreting the images or text.

3. Teacher discusses the role of interpretive frameworks in art and in science.

4. Conclusions:

   - Sometimes data do not make sense without an interpretive framework.
   - Scientists often need to use or create an interpretive framework to understand what they are observing.
   - Theories contribute heavily to scientists' interpretive frameworks.

Activity 1: Ambiguous Images

I like to demonstrate the necessity of interpretive frameworks by challenging students to make sense of a set of ambiguous images I show them via an overhead projector. For example, carefully look at and describe what you observe in Figure 16.2. Be careful to focus on making detailed observations and to avoid inferences for

Figure 16.2
An ambiguous image.
Source: Photo from *Vision* by David Marr, ©1982 by W.H. Freeman and Company. Reprinted by permission of Henry Holt and Company, LLC.

now. When I ask students to list observations of this confusing figure, I usually get responses like:

- There are black spots and blotches on a white background.
- The black areas appear in various shapes and sizes.
- There is more black in the upper left corner than the lower right.

Once students have had the opportunity to share all their observations, I tell them that these splotches actually are meant to depict an image and ask them if they can see this image in the figure. Students are pretty adept at identifying the Dalmatian dog in the center of the figure, so I can usually have a student come up and point out the dog to the rest of the class. Do you see the Dalmatian? The dog has his nose to the ground and he appears to be walking away from the observer. For those students who still cannot see the dog, I show Figure 16.3. After seeing the dog outlined, students are able to see it in the original figure without any trouble.

Most people find that once they have seen the outline of the Dalmatian, it is difficult to view the figure and not see the dog. The picture (data) has not changed, but now you have a framework that allows you to interpret the data. Without the framework, you could not make sense of the data.

Let's try this again. Look at Figure 16.4 and list as many observations as you can. Remember to observe carefully, but save your inferences for later. When I ask students to make detailed observations of this figure, they usually respond as they did for Figure 16.2.

Figure 16.3
The Dalmatian revealed!
Source: Photo from *Vision* by David Marr, ©1982 by W.H. Freeman and Company. Reprinted by permission of Henry Holt and Company, LLC.

Figure 16.4
Another
ambiguous
image.

Source: Figure
from K. M.
Dallenbach's
article, "A
picture-puzzle
with a new
principle of
concealment,"
©1951 in the
*American Jour-
nal of Psychol-
ogy*, Vol. 64: 3,
pp. 431–433.
Used with per-
mission of the
University of
Illinois Press.

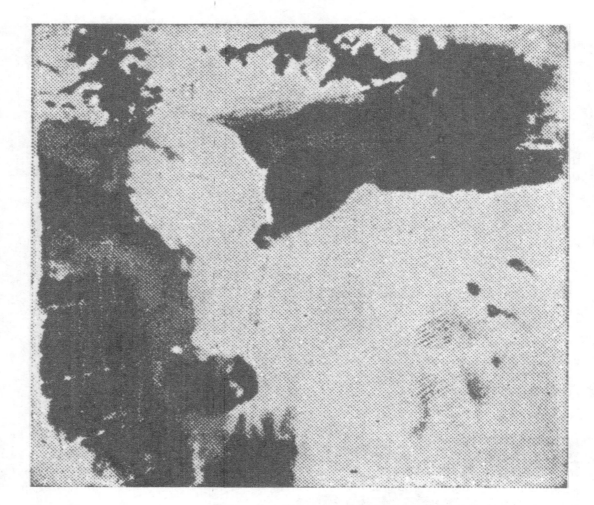

- There are black spots and blotches on a gray background.
- The black areas appear in various shapes and sizes.
- There is more black in the upper right and lower left corners.
- There is a checkered "texture" to most of the gray areas.

Next, I challenge students to identify the image hidden among the confusing splotches in the figure. Most people find this one more difficult than the Dalmatian picture, and students will likely offer a variety of responses, none of which really work. After a bit of consternation on their part, I show them a "key," as in Figure 16.5.

Again, having seen the outline of the cow's head, most people find it difficult to look at the figure and not see the cow. In fact, the cow becomes so obvious that, if you are like me, you wonder how you ever missed it! Nothing about the picture has changed; you simply now have a framework with which to interpret the data.

Figure 16.6 is another image with which to challenge your students. It is a sideways view of North America, with East and West replacing the typical North and South views.

A primary role of perceptual frameworks is to inform us about what to look for. Notebook Assignment 16.1 can be used to record your students' observations and thinking during this activity.

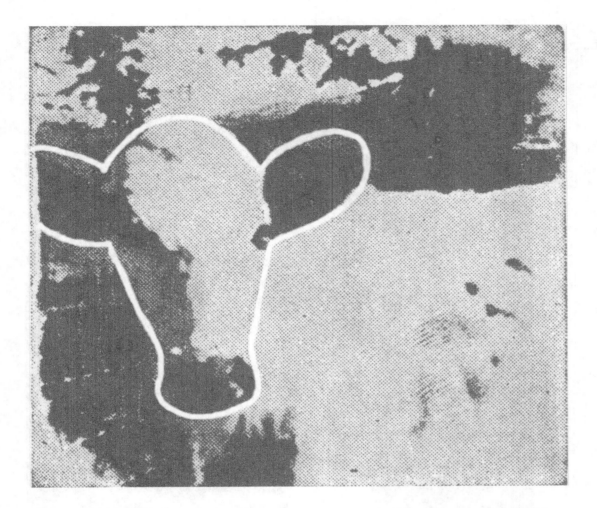

Figure 16.5
The cow revealed!
Source: Figure from K. M. Dallenbach's article, "A picture-puzzle with a new principle of concealment," ©1951 in the *American Journal of Psychology*, Vol. 64: pp. 431–433. Used with permission of the University of Illinois Press.

Activity 2: Reading Is Fundamental (or Is It)?

Interpretive frameworks are just as necessary for verbal data as for visual data. The following activity illustrates this well. Students may use the questions in Notebook Assignment 16.2 to record their responses.

The text passage in Figure 16.7 was originally used in a psychological study by investigators John Bransford and Marcia Johnson (1972). In the study, the investigators read a short text passage to groups of students, and then asked them to complete assessments of their comprehension and recall of the content of the passage. The investigators read the passage to the first group without any context, as you should do for your students when you do this activity.

How would you rate your comprehension and recall of this passage? Does it make sense to you? What procedure is being described? Chances are good that both you and your students will find this text passage difficult to understand, due to its ambiguous nature.

Next, Bransford and Johnson (1972) read the passage to a second group of students, this time prefaced by a short statement designed to provide the context of the passage. When you use this activity in class, read the text passage a second time to your students, but first read the statement the investigators used to set the

Figure 16.6
What will your students
make of this image?

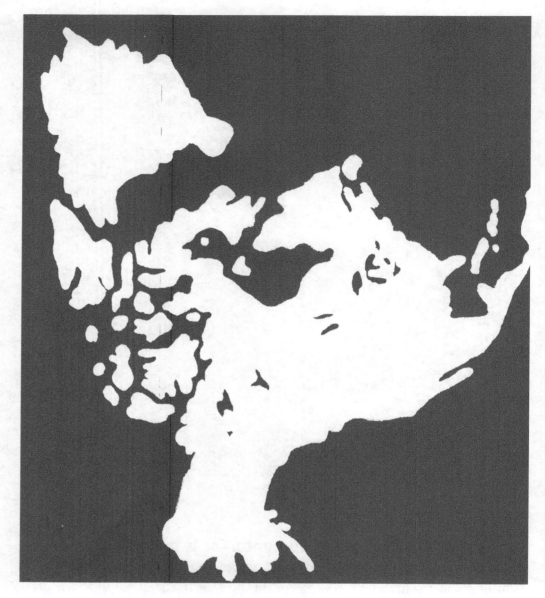

context of the text passage, which I've included as a footnote. After reading the text passage a second time, ask your students whether the passage makes more sense now. They will very likely agree that it does.

Explore with students the reasons why it makes more sense with the context than without. The key point is that context is critical for making sense of what we read or observe. The individual words and sentences by themselves are comprehensible, but make little sense as a whole. Knowing what the text passage is about in a general way helps fill in the gaps of meaning between the sentences, resulting in greater comprehension.

Let's try this again with a second text passage that Bransford and Johnson (1972) used in their study. Read the text in Figure 16.8 out loud to your students.

TEXT 1

The procedure is actually quite simple. First you arrange things into different groups depending on their makeup. Of course, one pile may be sufficient depending on how much there is to do. If you have to go somewhere else due to lack of facilities that is the next step; otherwise you are pretty well set. It is important not to overdo any particular endeavor. That is, it is better to do too few things at once than too many. In the short run this may not seem important, but complications from doing too many can easily arise. A mistake can be expensive as well. The manipulation of the appropriate mechanisms should be self-explanatory, and we need not dwell on it here. At first the whole procedure will seem complicated. Soon, however, it will become just another facet of life. It is difficult to foresee any end to the necessity for this task in the immediate future, but then one can never tell.

'The paragraph you will hear will be about washing clothes.'

Figure 16.7
Paragraph with ambiguous meaning.
Source: Reprinted from *Journal of Verbal Learning and Verbal Behavior*, Vol. 11, John D. Bransford and Marcia K. Johnson, "Contextual prerequisites for understanding: Some investigations of comprehension and recall," pp. 717–726, ©1972, with permission from Elsevier.

TEXT 2

A newspaper is better than a magazine. A seashore is a better place than the street. At first it is better to run than to walk. You may have to try several times. It takes some skill but is easy to learn. Even young children can enjoy it. Once successful, complications are minimal. Birds seldom get too close. Rain, however, soaks in very fast. Too many people doing the same thing can also cause problems. One needs lots of room. If there are no complications it can be very peaceful. A rock will serve as an anchor. If things break loose from it, however, you will not get a second chance.

The context is "making and flying a kite."

Figure 16.8
Another paragraph with ambiguous meaning.
Source: Reprinted from *Journal of Verbal Learning and Verbal Behavior*, Vol. 11, John D. Bransford and Marcia K. Johnson, "Contextual prerequisites for understanding: Some investigations of comprehension and recall," pp. 717–726, ©1972, with permission from Elsevier.

Can you and your students make sense of this passage? Very likely you and your students will find this one just as difficult to comprehend as the first text passage. But as we now know, a little context can go a long way toward making sense of what we see and read, so try reading it to your students a second time, preceded by a short statement to set the context of the paragraph.[2] Once again, your students will find that the paragraph you read makes more sense, as the context allows their minds to fill in the meaning between the words. Nothing about the paragraph has changed; you and your students simply now have a framework with which to interpret what you read. The questions in Notebook Assignment 16.2 are designed to facilitate your students' reflection on this activity and the nature of science.

Activity 3: The Morphing Man

Show the images of the morphing man (Figure 16.9) one at a time to your students. Tell students that you will show them a series of images of a man, but that

Figure 16.9

The Morphing Man.

Source: From H. Haken (1990). "Synergetics as a Tool for the Conceptualization and Mathematization of Cognition and Behavior—How Far Can We Go?" In H. Haken & M. Stadler (Eds.), *Synergetics of Cognition* (p. 23, Figure 19), with permission from Springer Science and Business Media.

the man's appearance will change slightly with each image. Their goal is to see how long they can see the image of the man before he morphs into something else. They should record in their notebooks (see Notebook Assignment 16.3) the number of the image where they last see the man.

If your students are like most, they should easily see the man through the first four images and likely will continue to see him into the fifth and perhaps even the sixth image. By the seventh image, however, it's pretty clear that a new image has emerged—a profile of a woman.

Once your students have seen all eight images, repeat the process, but this time have them record the number of the first image in which they see the woman. You'll likely find that they are able to see the woman much earlier than before, perhaps as early as the third image. Ask your students to compare their results for the two trials—how soon were they able to see the woman the first time vs. the second time through the images? It should be plain to them that the woman appears earlier the second time. But why? Nothing about the images has changed.

With a little probing on your part, the students should come to realize that they could recognize the woman sooner the second time through because they know what to look for. By challenging them to see the woman as soon as possible, you provided an interpretive framework that helped them see details they missed the first time. This explains how scientists are able to see details and reach conclusions that nonscientists miss. Scientists' education and experiences, as well as their commitments to particular theories, all work together to provide an interpretive framework that enables them to "see" and understand what the rest of us can miss.

Notebook Assignment 16.3 includes questions designed to help students reflect on the value of interpretive frameworks to scientists.

Activity 4: Seeing Saturn

LESSON AT A GLANCE

1. Students view a series of drawn telescopic images of Saturn and make observations and inferences.

2. Teacher tells students the story about how these images were created and when.

3. Teacher shows students Huygens' model, showing images of how Saturn looks throughout its year and discusses how knowing what to look for provided an interpretive framework that helped scientists comprehend the diverse images of Saturn.

4. Conclusions:
   - Sometimes data do not make sense without an interpretive framework.
   - Scientists often need to use or create an interpretive framework to understand what they are observing.
   - Theories contribute heavily to scientists' interpretive frameworks. That's one of the reasons theories are so important in science.

Interpretive Frameworks in Science: Believing and Seeing in Science

All of this talk about interpretive frameworks may make sense in regard to interpreting ambiguous figures and texts, but what does it have to do with science? It turns out that scientists rely on interpretive frameworks to make sense of the natural world, too. Let's consider an example of this from the history of science. Galileo Galilei was the first person to observe Saturn with a telescope, and in 1610 he noted that Saturn had bulges like ears to either side, as you can see in his drawing in Figure 16.10. Having recently discovered the four major satellites of Jupiter, Galileo was predisposed to seeing satellites again when he turned his telescope on the planet Saturn.

Thus, he concluded that the "ears" he observed protruding from the planet were also satellites. However, these were very unusual satellites in that they never appeared to shift position until they unexpectedly disappeared in 1612.

Figure 16.10
An early drawing of Saturn by Galileo from
Il Saggiatore (1623).

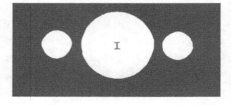

Two years later, the "satellites" reappeared and engendered a great deal of interest among the astronomers of the day as they tried to make sense of what they
observed in their telescopes. Their work produced a variety of drawings (as in
Figure 16.11) and explanations over the next few decades. Among their fanciful
explanations was Gilles de Roberval's proposition that the "satellites" were ex-
pelled vapors from Saturn's equatorial zone, and Honoré Fabri's suggestion that
Saturn's changing appearance could be explained by the eclipsing of two bright
satellites by two darker ones.

Figure 16.11
Early telescopic
views of Saturn,
published by
Christiaan Huygens
in *Systema
Saturnium* (1659).

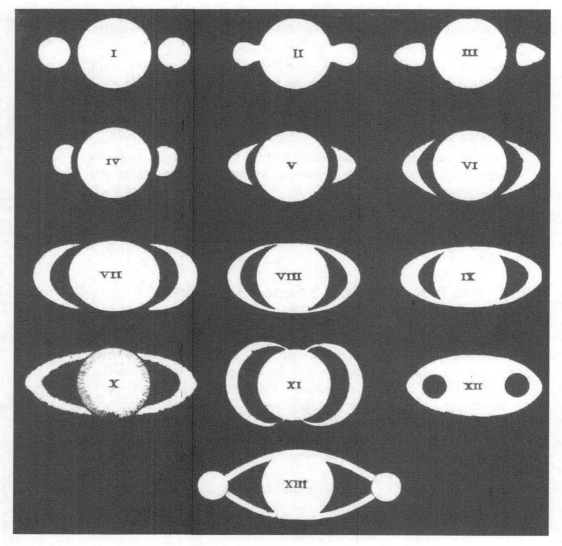

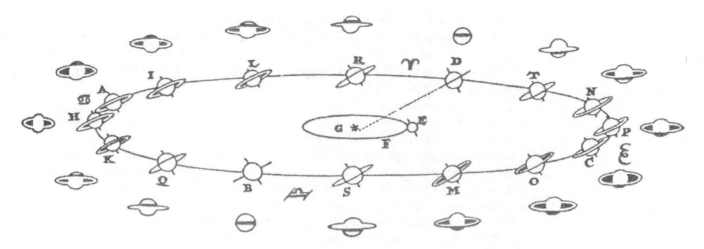

Figure 16.12

Huygens diagram of Saturn's rings, orbit, and appearance in Earth-based telescopes, as presented in *Systema Saturnium*, (1659).

Show your students Figure 16.11 and ask them to guess what the images represent. Students can record their thoughts in their notebooks using Notebook Assignment 16.4. When I've done this for my students, I've received a wide variety of responses, but seldom do students correctly guess that these images represent the earliest telescopic views of the planet Saturn. Galileo as well as other astronomers who observed Saturn were not making errors in their observations; they simply did not have the frame of reference to interpret what they saw. Thus, their experiences with the confusing data about the planet Saturn were much like what you and your students experienced in trying to make sense of the ambiguous figures or text presented in activities 1–3. Keep in mind that the idea of rings around a planet was completely new; astronomers had no prior experience to support this concept (Sheehan, 1988). Making sense of what they were observing required an interpretive framework that was lacking at the time.

Finally, Christiaan Huygens achieved a breakthrough in perception when he concluded that Saturn is surrounded by a "thin, flat ring, nowhere touching" the planet. Huygens' perceptual lead did not result from better data than that of his peers or predecessors, nor did he possess a substantially better telescope. The theory he presented in *Systema Saturnium* (published in 1659) was the product of his creative intuition—a model of Saturn with rings inclined at an angle of 28° to the Earth (Figure 16.12). His model explained the different appearances of the planet as viewed from Earth and served as an interpretive framework that helped astronomers make sense of the disparate data they had collected over the years. From then on, everyone who observed Saturn saw the rings (just as you will always see a Dalmatian and cow when you look back at Figures 16.2 and 16.4).

LESSON WRAP-UP

Christiaan Huygens' model of the orbits of the Earth and the planet Saturn explained the various views of Saturn that astronomers had accumulated over the years, but also provided a framework to interpret all future observations. And that's one of the things that makes models and theories so powerful—they help scientists interpret their observations by providing the big picture and by helping them decide which details to pay attention to and which to ignore. This makes theories among the most important ideas in science and should serve as a reminder that saying, "It's *just* a theory," is never appropriate in science.

While I've chosen to use Huygens' model of the orbits of the Earth and the planet Saturn as an example of the power of interpretive frameworks in science, it is by no means the only example available to you. The seemingly disparate data of sea-floor spreading, the proliferation of volcanic activity and earthquakes along specific boundaries, and the incidence of similar fossils on facing edges of different continents all make sense when viewed from the perspective of plate tectonics theory. Likewise, the diversity of life on Earth, the occurrence of a disproportionate number of flightless birds on remote islands, and the patterns of genetic similarity among organisms all make more sense in light of evolutionary theory. In fact, one of the founders of modern evolutionary theory goes so far as to state, "Nothing in biology makes sense except in the light of evolution." (Dobzhansky, 1973). According to Theodosius Dobzhansky, without evolution, biology "becomes a pile of sundry facts some of them interesting or curious but making no meaningful picture as a whole."

Figure 16.13 provides an overview of the connections among the knowledge, processes, and nature of science addressed for the perception activities presented in this chapter.

Figure 16.13
Connection among the three aspects of science for the "Perception and Conception" activities.

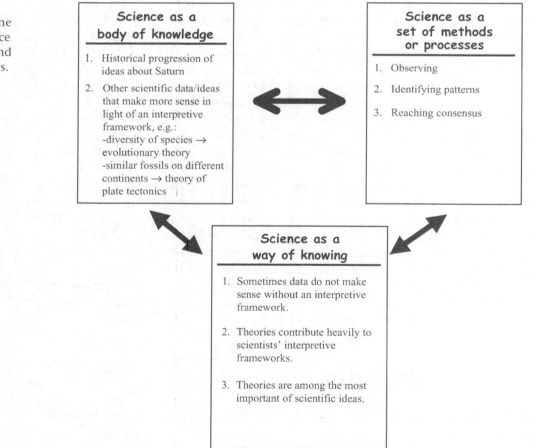

Science as a body of knowledge

1. Historical progression of ideas about Saturn
2. Other scientific data/ideas that make more sense in light of an interpretive framework, e.g.:
   -diversity of species → evolutionary theory
   -similar fossils on different continents → theory of plate tectonics

Science as a set of methods or processes

1. Observing
2. Identifying patterns
3. Reaching consensus

Science as a way of knowing

1. Sometimes data do not make sense without an interpretive framework.
2. Theories contribute heavily to scientists' interpretive frameworks.
3. Theories are among the most important of scientific ideas.

ASSESSMENT

The objective of this chapter is to help you teach your students the importance of perceptual frameworks in data interpretation. The Notebook Assignments are designed to help guide your students through each of the perceptual framework activities described in this chapter and to encourage them to reflect on the role of perceptual frameworks in science.

Name: _____ Date: _____

1. List your observations about each of the images you are shown.

Figure 1.

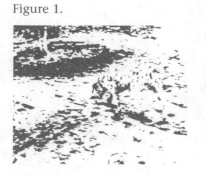

Observations

_____
_____
_____
_____
_____
_____

What do you think this image shows?

Figure 2.

Observations

_____
_____
_____
_____
_____
_____

What do you think this image shows?

Figure 3.

Observations

_____
_____
_____
_____
_____
_____

What do you think this image shows?

2. Why is it so much easier to identify the image after your teacher gives you a hint?

_____

_____

_____

_____

_____

_____

_____

3. In what ways does your making sense of these images relate to how scientists make sense of data?

_____

_____

_____

_____

_____

_____

_____

_____

_____

_____

NOTEBOOK ASSIGNMENT 16.2

Reading is Fundamental

Name: _____ Date: _____

1. Why does the text passage (or passages) read by your teacher make more sense after you are given a hint about its context, *even though the words are the same*?

   Circle one. Picture: 1   2   3   4   5   6   7   8

   _____
   _____
   _____

2. Describe some examples of factors that scientists rely on to make sense of data in their investigations.

   Circle one. Picture: 1   2   3   4   5   6   7   8

   _____
   _____
   _____

3. In what ways does your making sense of the text passage (or passages) relate to how scientists make sense of data?

   _____
   _____
   _____

The Morphing Man

Name: _____ Date: _____

1. When did you first recognize that the image of the man had morphed into something new the first time your teacher showed you the images? Picture:

2. When did you notice the new image the second time you saw the series of pictures? Picture:

3. Why were you able to see the new image sooner the second time?

   _____

   _____

   _____

4. How does seeing the new image sooner the second time relate to scientists' need for an interpretive framework when doing science?

   _____

   _____

   _____

   _____

   _____

   _____

Seeing Saturn

Name: _____ Date: _____

1. Here are the early images of the planet Saturn that your teacher showed you.

2. Why did the early observers of Saturn see the planet so differently?

_____

_____

_____

3. How did Christiaan Huygens' explanation of Saturn as a ringed planet impact what other astronomers saw when they observed the planet?

_____

_____

_____

17

Of Mice, Men, and Scientists

n this activity, students learn that observations can be influenced by the context in which they are made. Students in separate classes are asked to observe one of two series of line drawings and then are asked to identify a final, somewhat ambiguous image that could be seen as a man or a mouse. Students will find that the makeup of the initial images can strongly influence their perceptions of the final image. This effect is known among psychologists as "perceptual set" and refers to the predisposition to perceive a thing in relation to prior perceptual experiences. When broadly applied to science, students learn that scientists' educational background, training, and prior experience can influence their observations and interpretations of the results of investigations.

LAYING THE GROUNDWORK

The setting was my home office the night before I was to give a unit test on chemical reactions to my ninth-grade physical science class. I had hoped to complete final revisions to the test on the previous evening, but our two daughters (8-month-old Adri and 3-year-old Jessi) had required all my attention. So the evening before the test found me working diligently to get all the necessary changes completed and the master copy prepared.

While my attention was focused on my work, Jessi came bouncing into the room (as only a 3-year-old can) and asked in her sweet little voice, "Daddy, can I turn your world around?"

I was overwhelmed by the implications of her question. Lynn and I had waited several years after marrying to start our family, and no two daughters were ever born to parents with greater anticipation and love than our little Adri and Jessi. Like all parents, however, we had underestimated the impact our daughters would have on our home and relationship. Gone were the spontaneous hikes after work and romantic evenings alone. Weeknights were spent taking care of the girls, and weekends were spent catching up on work. There were diapers to wash, late night feedings, more diapers to wash, reading bedtime stories, still more diapers to wash, taking care of boo-boos, and of course, diapers to wash. Even with all of the added responsibilities and work, we would not have dreamed of going back to the days of Lynn and me alone. Our two daughters occupied a place in our hearts that could be filled by no other person or means.

These were the thoughts flashing through my mind when Jessi asked her poignant question, "Daddy, can I turn your world around?" With a knowing smile I responded, "You already have!" With an exasperated look on her face, Jessi clarified her request, "No, Daddy, I want to play with *that*!" Following her pointing finger to the top of the bookshelf on the far wall, I saw my globe of the Earth and immediately realized that I had interpreted her words in a completely different way than she had meant them. Upon this realization, I fetched the globe from its lofty perch and spent the next 20 minutes contemplating the meaning of life, love, and the words of toddlers as I sat on the floor with my daughter, the two of us happily turning each other's worlds around.

Competing Frameworks

The previous chapter demonstrated the importance of interpretive frameworks in making sense of both everyday and scientific observations—much of what we "see" does not make sense unless we have a framework with which to interpret it. But what happens when there is more than one plausible interpretive framework? Does what we "see" actually change with different frameworks (and thus reflect subjectivity) or do our observations remain constant across competing frameworks (demonstrating objectivity)?

In 1961, psychologists B.R. Bugelski and D.A. Alampay conducted an investigation to find out. The researchers showed two groups of observers an ambiguous line drawing that could be seen either as a mouse or as a bald man wearing spectacles. Prior to seeing this image, the two groups were shown either a series of drawings of human faces or drawings of various animals (see Figure 17.1, Image sets a and b).

a. Image Set 1

b. Image Set 2

Figure 17.1
Bugelski and Alampay's perceptual set images.
Source: Copyright ©1961, Canadian Psychological Association. Used by permission.

The Global Climate Change Controversy

Though global climate change is an accepted aspect of our climate history, and there have been cycles of climatic heating and cooling throughout the history of the Earth, recent discussions have used the term "global climate change" to mean "global warming". Global warming theory has attracted attention from scientists and nonscientists alike. The theory is generally stated as such: The average temperature of the Earth's atmosphere has been increasing over the past half century because humans are releasing increased amounts of carbon dioxide (CO_2) through the burning of fossil fuels and other activities. Evidence has been collected from a variety of sources to support this claim, but people tend to view the evidence in different ways and come to different conclusions.

The Vostok Ice Core Data indicate that for more than 400,000 years CO_2 levels in the atmosphere have risen and fallen with the temperature (Stauffer, 1999). Additionally, levels of CO_2 in our atmosphere have recently risen to the highest concentration in 650,000 years, according to a study by the European Project for Ice Coring (Brook, 2005). We know that the CO_2 in our atmosphere has the ability to trap heat. We also know that over the past 60 years we have been recording the Earth's average surface temperature and the measurements are rising. The average surface temperature has increased by $0.6 \pm 0.2°$ C during the twentieth century, as indicated by three independent data sets (National Assessment Synthesis Team, 2003).

However, correlation and causation are two different things. Some scientists are arguing that CO_2 levels do not cause surface temperatures to change, that it may be the other way around. Could changing temperatures affect CO_2 levels? Some atmospheric samples from ice cores indicate that, in the distant past, rises in CO_2 levels have lagged behind rises in temperature by thousands of years (Barnola, Raynaud, Lorius, & Barkov, 2003; Idso & Idso, 2006). Just because there's a correlation, there is not necessarily causation. The Earth's average surface temperature may be on the rise, but that could be due to the fact that we have more large cities that create "urban heat islands." Cities can be 2° to 6°C warmer than the surrounding countryside due to all the concrete, asphalt, and buildings. The same data can be interpreted by different scientists in entirely different ways when they have different perceptual frameworks.

Other scientists argue that CO_2 is only one greenhouse gas, and understanding the effect of other greenhouse gases is critical to decisions about limiting emissions. Methane (CH_4), much of which comes from rice paddies and animals such as African termites and South American beef cattle, is another major greenhouse gas, yet limiting our intake of hamburgers has not yet emerged as a recommendation. Few discussions about global warming consider water vapor, the gas that contributes the greatest amount of heat to our Earth. Many climatologists argue that certain feedback mechanisms that involve water vapor, such as cloud formation, will mitigate global warming and bring balance to atmospheric temperature. Thus, different scientists not only can interpret the same data differently, but may also consider different data. What makes this issue so extraordinarily controversial is that it is politically charged. The impact of CO_2 reduction has economic implications. Perhaps, eventually, enough data will be collected that some consensus will be reached by scientists, politicians, citizens, and business people around the globe.

The more pictures of animals the researchers showed to the "animal" group, the more likely they were to see a mouse rather than a man (100% saw the mouse when showed four prior images of animals). Conversely, more than 70% of the participants in the group shown the series of faces saw a man rather than a mouse. Psychologists refer to this phenomenon as "perceptual set": a predisposition to perceive something in relation to prior experiences. Psychologists have found that perceptual set may involve either long-term prior experiences (e.g., educational or cultural) or, as in this case, short-term or situational factors (Murch, 1973, pp. 300–301).

Perceptual frameworks play an important role in scientific observations as well. In science, just as in everyday experience, what we know and what we expect can influence the observations we make. Often scientific theories provide the perceptual frameworks guiding scientists' work. We have already seen in Chapter 10 how scientific theories provide frameworks that help scientists decide which questions are worth pursuing, what data they should collect, and ultimately, how to interpret this data. Although perceptual frameworks influence all science, they are especially evident in "cutting edge" science, where the data are not conclusive and multiple theories are competing for acceptance (see Sidebars 17.1 and 17.2). Sometimes, enough data are eventually collected that the question is decided and one perceptual framework gains acceptance by a majority of scientists. But it's important to realize that this favorable outcome is not guaranteed—in some cases we may never know enough to decide between competing theories.

The activity in this chapter presents a modified version of Bugelski and Alampay's psychological test. It will provide your students with an engaging introduction to the concept that observations can depend on many factors, not just what is observed.

SIDEBAR 17.2

Theories of the Universe

Philosophical theories about the universe have existed for thousands of years, but scientifically based ones are more recent. What we call the Big Bang Theory was proposed in 1927 by the priest/scientist Father Georges-Henri Lemaître. Calling his theory "the hypothesis of the primeval atom," he stated that the universe emerged from a small state and that it has been expanding ever since. Lemaître based his theory on observations that spiral *nebulae* (actually galaxies outside our own) were receding from us. In 1929, Edwin Hubble observed that the spectrum from the light from these receding galaxies was shifted towards the red end of the spectrum, adding further evidence to the theory. British astronomer Fred Hoyle, however, disagreed. With a different perceptual framework, he argued that the universe was in a steady state and that matter was constantly being created in-between galaxies to take the place of the galaxies moving away. Ironically, Hoyle was the one who coined the term, "Big Bang" in order to mock the opposing theory! Then, in 1965, cosmic microwave background radiation was discovered by scientists at Bell Labs: Arno Penzias and Robert Woodrow Wilson. Predicted years earlier by physicist George Gamow and others, this discovery helped convince the scientific community of the expanding universe, the Big Bang Theory.

THE ACTIVITY: BUGELSKI AND ALAMPAY IMAGES

LESSON AT A GLANCE

1. Students view one of two sets of images.
2. Students identify and record the images in the set, including a fifth, ambiguous image.
3. Students record the number of classmates who saw the ambiguous image as a mouse vs. a man.
4. Students discuss results.
5. Conclusions:
   - Different perceptual frameworks result in different interpretations.
   - Scientists' backgrounds, training, and theoretical commitments can lead them to different interpretations of the same data.
   - There is not always one right answer in science.
   - The phrase "anything goes" does not apply to science. Scientific ideas must be supported by evidence and sound reasoning.

Is Seeing Really Believing?

To introduce the lesson, place the following phrase on the board:

> Seeing is believing.

Ask students to describe what the phrase means and how it applies to everyday life and how it applies to science. Typically, the ensuing discussion will converge on the idea that observing is the most sure and convincing way to collect information about our surroundings. Thus, scientists base their investigations on what they observe, because they want to be certain that their conclusions are correct. Tell your students that while you agree that observations are very important to the work of scientists, there may be more to observation than meets the eye. The purpose of this lesson is to explore observation and its role in science from a different perspective.

If you have more than one class of science students or you can partner with another teacher, you may conduct the two-day version of the activity, as described in the alternative activity box.

Viewing the Images

Hand out the two different sets of images to the same class: Worksheet 17.1 to half the class and Worksheet 17.2 to the other half. Both groups of students should then identify and record the images in each set on their respective data sheets. It's best not to let students know that some are receiving different images. It also helps to remind them before beginning that they are not to discuss their responses with other students or answer out loud.

Table 17.1
Class data for the
ambiguous image.

	Mouse	Old Man
Number of students	12	10

Once students have identified the five images, quickly review each to see what students saw. Then take a class poll (by show of hands) of how many students saw the final image as a mouse and how many saw it as an old man. For both image sets there should be consensus on each of the first four images, and there should be some variation in answers for the fifth (ambiguous). Record the class data on the board, using a table something like the one in Table 17.1. Students should also record the data in their notebook (see Notebook Assignment 17.1).

Comparing Results

You are now ready to discuss the results, but first show students the fifth (ambiguous) image (Figure 17.2) and confirm with the class that this is what they all saw as the last image in the series of images they viewed. Ask, "If everyone had the same drawing, why did you see different images?" This question should generate quite a bit of discussion, as students try to figure out why their classmates saw the image differently. Guide students to come up with an explanation based upon two primary observations.

1. The fifth image is unclear.
2. This unclear image is preceded by different sets of images.

These observations, in turn, lead to the following inference/explanation:

The way we view the unclear image depends on the set of images coming before it.

Before exploring how this conclusion relates to science, you'll want to qualify it a bit. Project a transparency of Image Set 3 (Figure 17.3) for the class to consider. Ask the class how many now see the ambiguous image as a plant? It's unlikely that any will, because the ambiguous image doesn't much resemble a plant. Not just *any* set of images can have a significant impact on what we see. There must be a fairly

Figure 17.2
Fifth image for transparency.

Figure 17.3
Image Set 3.

close relationship between the images that come first and the ambiguous image for the effect to work. In light of this qualification, the class might want to modify its conclusion to something like this:

> The way we view the unclear image depends, in part, on the set of images coming before it.

Table 17.2

Example table showing percentage of students in each class who saw a mouse vs. those who saw a man.

Groups	Mouse	Old Man
Class 1 (animal image set)	90%	10%
Class 2 (people image set)	25%	75%

STRATEGY 17.1

Alternative Version of Activity

This version of the activity requires multiple classes and takes an extra day, but offers the advantage of giving students more data on which to base their conclusions.

On day 1, Image Set 1 should be revealed to one classroom of students (by handing out Worksheet 17.1 to each student). Image Set 2 (Worksheet 17.2) should be revealed to a second set of students. You may, of course, add other groups of students to this data set if they are available.

In order to compare results across classes, students in each class should calculate the percentage of students who saw the fifth image as a mouse vs. the percentage who saw a man. They should divide the number of those who identified the image as a mouse by the total number of students in the class, then multiply the answer by 100. For example, if 18 out of 22 students saw the fifth image as a mouse, then the percentage would be calculated as $(18 \div 22) \times 100 = 82\%$. They can then do the same for those who saw the image as a man.

Collect data from each class so that on the second day you can have students record (Worksheets 17.1 and 17.2) and discuss the data from all of the classes. These data will be a combination of those who saw Image Set 1 (animal images) and those who saw Image Set 2 (people images). You may want to have students construct a table showing the results from each class as in Table 17.2.

Finally, inform the class that you will discuss the activity again during their next class period, after you have collected data from your other classes (or from another teacher's class).

Now proceed with the discussion of the responses as in the original version of this activity.

LESSON WRAP-UP

So how does all of this relate to science? That is a great question to ask your students as a closure to the activity. If you've already introduced them to some of the activities in Chapter 16, then they should quickly see that this lesson involves perceptual frameworks as well. As in the image of the Dalmatian and cow (Chapter 16), the mouse/old man image is difficult to discern without a perceptual framework. Once again we see that data often do not make sense without some framework with which to interpret them. This is a good time to remind your students that the same is true in science, in which scientists' training, experience, and theories contribute to the perceptual framework through which they interpret data.

The mouse/old man image differs from those of the previous chapter in that we have not one but two possible frameworks (the images of the animals or people that precede the ambiguous image). The two competing frameworks lead your students to "see" the ambiguous image as two very different images. Not only does this result emphasize the power of perceptual frameworks, but it gives you an opportunity to discuss the issue of competing interpretations in science.

It is not at all uncommon for there to be different "camps" of scientists who disagree about which explanation best fits the available data. Even though both groups of scientists are looking at the same data, they reach different conclusions. This is especially true in areas where the data are incomplete or unclear (just like with our ambiguous mouse/old man image). Global climate change, the benefits of vitamin supplements, the reason the dinosaurs went extinct, and whether Pluto should be classified as a planet (see Sidebar 13.1, page 170) are all examples of phenomena on which scientists disagreed at the time this book was written.

It's important to emphasize that your students should not see competing interpretations in science as an indication that something is wrong. The scientists don't necessarily disagree because some are doing their work improperly and the others are doing it correctly (although this is sometimes the case). Often, there are simply not enough of the right kinds of data to settle the issue at the present time. And when the data are ambiguous (as with our mouse/old man image), scientists' background, training, and commitment to particular theories can lead them to differing interpretations.

Rather than a weakness, the presence of competing explanations and interpretations can be seen as a strength of the scientific process. Competing explanations and controversies in science are a source of new ideas and provide incentives for scientists to reconsider how the old ideas stack up against the evidence. Science is not a good-ole'-boys network where you must know the right people and have the right background to be heard. In science, new ideas are welcomed and encouraged, provided they are based on sound evidence and reasoning.

Be sure that your students understand this last point—that to compete in the scientific arena, ideas must be based on sound evidence and reasoning. It's not at all true that "anything goes" when it comes to science. This is the point behind projecting the final set of images of plants preceding the mouse/old man image. No matter how many plants you see before the ambiguous image, you're not likely to see it as a plant. It just doesn't fit. And in the real world of science, "fitting" means that an idea is based on solid evidence and sound reasoning.

When ideas fit in science (even competing ideas), they have the potential to make a huge difference in how we view the world. Sometimes, in fact, they can go so far as to turn our world around (just as little Jessi has turned my world around). The big ideas in science that we now take for granted started out as controversial ideas.

- The Big Bang
- All matter is made up of atoms.
- The Sun (not the Earth) is the center of our solar system.
- Plate Tectonics
- The Earth is a sphere.
- Big and small objects fall at the same rate (ignoring air resistance).

I could go on, but you get the picture. So the next time that you read about scientists disagreeing or reaching contradictory conclusions, don't despair or give

Figure 17.4

Connection among the three aspects of science for the "Bugelski and Alampay images" activity.

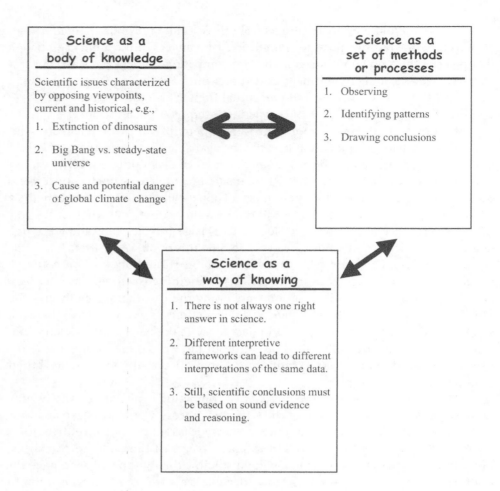

Science as a body of knowledge

Scientific issues characterized by opposing viewpoints, current and historical, e.g.,

1. Extinction of dinosaurs

2. Big Bang vs. steady-state universe

3. Cause and potential danger of global climate change

Science as a set of methods or processes

1. Observing

2. Identifying patterns

3. Drawing conclusions

Science as a way of knowing

1. There is not always one right answer in science.

2. Different interpretive frameworks can lead to different interpretations of the same data.

3. Still, scientific conclusions must be based on sound evidence and reasoning.

up on science. Just remember that controversy is natural in science and can be traced back to alternative ways that scientists view and approach the data. In the end, controversy is just scientists doing what scientists do, and it's an early step in developing new understandings that can turn our worlds around.

Figure 17.4 provides an overview of the connections among the knowledge, processes, and nature of science addressed for the perception activities presented in this chapter.

ASSESSMENT

The objective of this chapter is to help you teach the advantages and disadvantages that perceptual frameworks bring to science. Worksheets 17.1 and 17.2 provide your students with the necessary images for the activity. The worksheets are followed by Notebook Assignment 17.1, which encourages your students to reflect on the value and limitations of perceptual frameworks in science.

Name: _____ Date: _____

Here are five images drawn by an aspiring artist. Use your powers of observation to identify each image in the space below the image (e.g., dog, bunny, etc.).

1._____   2._____   3._____

4._____   5._____

Name: _____ Date: _____

Here are five images drawn by an aspiring artist. Use your powers of observation to identify each image in the space below the image (e.g., boy, woman, etc.).

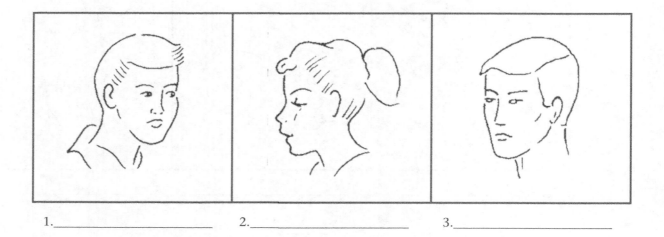

1._____   2._____   3._____

4._____   5._____

Mouse or Man—What Did You See?

Name: _____ Date: _____

Data Table

Construct a data table for your class results in the space below.

If the fifth drawing everyone saw was the same, why did some students see different images?

_____
_____
_____
_____
_____
_____
_____
_____
_____
_____
_____
_____
_____

Science as a Way of Knowing

S tudents continue to explore the meaning of science by taking a closer look at what is meant by "science as a way of knowing." Additionally, they compare science to other ways of understanding reality and the human condition. In completing the activity, students learn that we all view the world through a variety of perspectives and that each perspective contributes something unique to our perception of reality. Thus, while science has proven to be one of the most powerful ways we have of understanding the world and learning to manipulate the world for our own purposes, it is not the only lens available for making sense of reality. In fact, there are many critical questions in life that science alone cannot address.

LAYING THE GROUNDWORK

In Chapter 1, we explored various definitions and descriptions of science and learned that one useful way to view science is as a multifaceted endeavor consisting of three interrelated aspects. The first of these is the body of knowledge, which comprises the facts, concepts, theories, and laws that people typically think of when they think of science. The body of knowledge of science includes the kind of information you typically find in science textbooks. The second aspect refers to science as method and process and includes the various approaches scientists use to produce the body of knowledge. These methods and processes are related to the process skills we teach in science classrooms and include (but are not limited to) such activities as observing, measuring, classifying, and designing experiments. Science as a way of knowing constitutes the third aspect of science. It is by far the least familiar of the three aspects of science. Yet, as this book shows, it can be among the most exciting and engaging aspects of science to teach.

In previous chapters, you have learned that interpretive frameworks are a necessary and powerful aspect of the nature of science. Interpretive frameworks include the educational background, training, and experiences that scientists bring to an investigation, as well as the theories to which they subscribe. These factors guide scientists' work, in that they help scientists decide which questions are worth asking, what data to collect, and how to make sense of the data.

But the idea of interpretive frameworks does not begin and end with a particular science investigation. In fact, you can look at the scientific enterprise itself as an interpretive framework. From this perspective, science is one way among many of making sense of what we experience. As the chapter title indicates, this view of the nature of science is sometimes referred to as "science as a way of knowing." My goal for this chapter is to help you and your students view science itself as a powerful interpretive framework, but not the only framework, for making sense of the human experience. I have included quite a bit of background information before getting to the activity, so hang in there with me! You will find this background information useful as you discuss "science as a way of knowing" with your students.

General Ways of Knowing

To begin our quest to understand science as a way of knowing, consider how we know things in general. In everyday life, people commonly use four different approaches to determine the truth of an idea or statement.

1. Authority
2. Personal experience
3. Intuition
4. Reasoning

The first approach involves believing something is true because we trust the source of the information (knowing by **authority**). Sources we commonly trust by authority include parents (unless you're a teenager), textbooks, and religious literature.

To explore this idea a bit further, think of something that you have been told about, but have not experienced firsthand. For instance, when I was a child my father warned me not to insert anything into an electrical outlet, because I could receive a nasty shock or even be killed by the electricity. Now that was one piece of information for which I was happy to take his word.

A couple of decades later, I received a painful shock with 3,000 volts of electricity while teaching a high school physics demonstration. (All it took was a momentary lack of attention while handling a poorly designed electrical device.) Now I know about high-voltage electrical shock from the perspective of a different way of knowing—personal experience. I no longer have to take my dad's word for it. Personal experience can be a powerful (and painful) way of knowing. Hence, the commonly quoted phrase: "Experience is the best teacher."

Alternatively, I could use insight or personal inspiration to determine the truth of my dad's statement. Sometimes, using "gut feeling" alone is enough to cause you to believe or question a claim!

Finally, I could use reasoning to determine the truth of the statement by carefully considering its logic. For example, by considering the relationship between electric power, voltage, and amperage I could calculate the amount of electrical power available in an outlet and determine whether it is enough to do serious damage (it is). The following activity is designed to help your students reflect on everyday ways of knowing.

A little reflection on your part will verify that each of us employs these general ways of knowing in our everyday experience. Reflection will also reveal that each of these general ways of knowing is potentially flawed. We may learn something from an otherwise credible source that turns out to be wrong. Just think of all the pregnant women around the world prescribed thalidomide in the 1950s and 60s for morning sickness. Their doctors, credible sources for health information, were unaware of the teratogenic properties of this drug. Nearly 12,000 babies were born with devastating birth defects because of it.

Our personal experience may turn out to be a special instance that goes against the norm. Recall the oft-told fable from ancient India: Six blind men went to examine an elephant in order to satisfy their curiosity, with each declaring from personal experience what the elephant was like. One thought the elephant was like a tree, another like a rope, a third declared it to be like a fan. Personal experience is an important way of knowing, but it is subjective, as this popular story illustrates.

Intuition is a valuable tool too, but may well prove to be misleading. Take Princeton professor and Nobel laureate Daniel Kahneman's little math test and see if your intuition will lead you astray.

> If a ball and bat cost $1.10 altogether and the bat costs $1 more than the ball, what does the ball cost?
>
> Quoted by writer Eric Jaffe in *Observer*, May 2004, Vol. 17(5) "What was I thinking? Kahneman explains how intuition leads us astray" http://www.psychologicalscience.org/observer/getArticle.cfm?id=1572.

If you're like half of the Princeton undergraduates he surveyed, you'll answer intuitively that the ball costs 10 cents. But if you get a pencil and actually scribble out the math, you'll discover that your intuition was wrong (see Figure 18.1).

Even reason has its limitations—how often do you hear that experts offer different explanations for the same set of data or that religious leaders interpret the same passages of religious text differently?

In the end, while each of us regularly uses these four general ways of knowing and finds them useful, we also know that they do not offer absolute truth (truth with a capital "T"). Instead, they provide us with a useful approximation of truth (truth with a lowercase "t") that works often enough to suit everyday experience. The question remains: Is this all there is to knowing?

Figure 18.1
Ball and bat problem calculation.

You can set the ball and bat problem up as an algebraic equation, where x = the cost of the ball, and (x + $1.00) = cost of the bat. Therefore,

$$x + (x + \$1.00) = \$1.10$$
$$2x = \$1.10 - \$1.00$$
$$x = 0.10/2$$
$$x = 0.05 \text{ (or 5 cents)}$$

THE ACTIVITIES: WAYS OF KNOWING

Activity 1: The Four General Ways of Knowing

LESSON AT A GLANCE

1. Teacher leads a discussion about how we know what we know.
2. Class develops a list of four everyday ways of knowing.
   - Authority
   - Personal Experience
   - Intuition
   - Reasoning
3. Students write out examples from their own lives that reflect each of these ways of knowing.
4. Teacher leads a class discussion on the strengths and limitations of each way of knowing.

What does all this mean for your science class, and how can you convey these ideas to your students? For starters, you could lead a discussion on the four general ways of knowing and their limitations. On its surface, this is a straightforward activity. You will simply lead students in a discussion about how we know things. At a deeper level, though, you are leading your students in a metacognitive exercise that will likely be the first time they have ever considered how we know what we know in a formal way. Thinking about thinking is not an exercise students pursue often, and in my experience students enjoy the intellectual challenge such critical thinking has to offer. Start by posing the question:

What are the ways we know what we think we know?

In the ensuing discussion, lead students to the conception of the four general ways of knowing. You might spark the conversation by stating some familiar, generally accepted idea, much as I did in my discussion about electricity earlier in this chapter. Then lead your students through a series of examples of the four different ways of knowing, challenging them to define these terms (see Notebook Assignment 18.1) as you go.

Once your students understand that knowing generally comes through authority, personal experience, intuition, and reason, ask them to explain why the question ends with, "what we *think* we know" as opposed to just, "what we know." The goal of discussing this question is to help students understand that each of these general ways of knowing has very real limitations. Therefore, any knowledge stemming from a general way of knowing carries with it some degree of doubt. That doesn't mean the knowledge is useless, only that it cannot be viewed as absolute.

To carry this idea a bit further, you may want to have students explore the limitations of each of the general ways of knowing in more detail. I like to divide the class into groups, assigning each one of the four ways of knowing. I have each group provide examples of how the way of knowing is commonly used and describe its limitations and pitfalls.

Figure 18.2
Four ways of knowing.

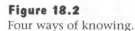

Four Ways of Knowing

	what we think we know	limitations
Authority		
Personal Experience		
Intuition		
Logic and Reason		

After a few minutes of group work, a spokesperson is chosen from each group to present the group's conclusions, which are written on the board for the rest of the class to consider (Figure 18.2). The result of the activity is a complete description of the four ways of knowing, with examples and limitations listed for each one. In this way, you will have prepared your students to understand the need for more formal ways of knowing, as discussed in the next activity.

Activity 2: Formal Ways of Knowing

LESSON AT A GLANCE

1. Students explore the idea that formal disciplines such as science, mathematics, religion, and art are distinct, yet complementary ways of knowing.

2. Students consider science as only one of many formal ways of knowing by completing a table comparing several different aspects of mathematics, science, religion, and art.

3. Students discuss their responses and think about which formal way of knowing answers the questions most important to them.

4. Teacher leads class in a discussion about how all four of the formal ways of knowing enrich our lives because they each give us different perspectives.

Since there are limitations to relying on authority, personal experience, intuition, and reason, other—more formal—systems of knowing have evolved over time. Today, we commonly think of these systems of knowing as disciplines, or schools of thought, and include in them such school subjects as mathematics, history, and of course, science. In a very general sense, science can be thought of as a blend of personal experience and reason. That is not to say that scientists never appeal to authority or that intuition and inspiration have no role in the development of scientific knowledge. However, at its heart, scientific knowledge rests on evidence, which if related back to the four general ways of knowing, can be seen as a special kind of experience. As Richard Feynman succinctly put it:

> It doesn't matter how beautiful your theory is, it doesn't matter how smart you are. If it doesn't agree with the experiment, it's wrong.

So in science if your idea doesn't correspond with reality, if it isn't backed by evidence, then it doesn't go very far.

Although scientific evidence can be seen as a type of experience, it is important not to confuse science with personal experience in the everyday sense. There is no doubt that scientists' personal experiences contribute to the development of new ideas; however, the rigors of the scientific community actually demand much more. For one thing, scientific ideas must conform to reason and make sense in light of currently accepted theories and ideas.

Every scientist dreams of discovering a "breakthrough" that will forever change the way her colleagues view their discipline. The fact of the matter is, however, that colleagues are particularly skeptical of ideas that fall outside of established norms. In fact, to be accepted as scientific, ideas must undergo rigorous public scrutiny by experts. This can be a humbling experience, at best, and a humiliating experience, at worst. As Carl Sagan (1997) put it,

> Again, the reason science works so well is partly that built-in, error-correcting machinery. There are no forbidden questions in science, no matters too sensitive or delicate to be probed, no sacred truths. That openness to new ideas, combined with the most rigorous, skeptical scrutiny of all ideas, sifts the wheat from the chaff. It makes no difference how smart, august, or beloved you are. You must prove your case in the face of determined, expert criticism. Diversity and debate are valued. Opinions are encouraged to contend—substantively and in depth. . . . Why do we put up with it? Do we like to be criticized? No, no scientist enjoys it. Every scientist feels a proprietary affection for his or her ideas and findings. Even so, you don't reply to critics, "Wait a minute; this is a really good idea; I'm very fond of it; it's done you no harm; please leave it alone." Instead, the hard but just rule is that if the ideas don't work, you must throw them away. Don't waste neurons on what doesn't work. Devote those neurons to new ideas that better explain the data (pp. 31–32).

In summary, science can be seen as a way of knowing that recognizes the fallibility of human beings and so differs in key aspects from the four general ways of knowing discussed earlier in the chapter. In science, appeals to authority do not carry much weight. While science makes use of experience, reason, and intuition, it requires more formal application of these processes than is afforded in our everyday experiences. One of the principal hallmarks of science is its self-correcting nature. Even the most cherished scientific ideas may be challenged, with the greatest accolades going to those who successfully dispute established beliefs.

The following activity is designed to facilitate discussion about more formal ways of knowing. Through this activity students will come to understand that science is just one of many ways of trying to make sense of the world around us. Just as is the case with the four general ways of knowing, each formal way of knowing has its own strengths and limitations. I have found this activity to be especially powerful in terms of helping students understand some of the differences between science and religion, as well as helping them understand that science and religion can be complementary—one can value each way of knowing for what it has to offer.

Begin this lesson by writing the following terms on the board:

Mathematics   Science

Religion   Art

Try to engage students by asking them what the terms have in common. Students will have various responses, but guide them into focusing on the idea that these are some of the disciplines of knowledge that they might experience in school and everyday life. These disciplines represent various formal ways of knowing that were mentioned in the previous activity. These ways of knowing may be seen as different approaches to describing and understanding the reality of both our day-to-day experiences and the universe at large. The question for this activity is, "What are the similarities and differences between these formal ways of knowing? Are they compatible, complimentary, or contradictory?"

The activity can proceed either by having students work individually or in small groups to fill in the blanks of a partially competed table or by leading a classroom discussion in which the goal is to complete a table like the one in Figure 18.3. Either way, students should complete their own copies of the table by the end of the lesson. The goal is for students to compare and contrast the strengths and weaknesses of four different formal ways of knowing. There is nothing special about the formal ways of knowing I've selected, other than the fact that they include science

Figure 18.3
Sample table for describing some formal ways of knowing.

	Mathematics	Science	Religion	Art
Practitioners				
Goal				
Paths to Truth				
Appropriate Questions				

and provide a bit of diversity. Feel free to add to or subtract from the list as you deem necessary.

It would be a useful exercise for you to complete the table yourself as I describe the activity. Therefore, consider yourself the student as I describe how the lesson proceeds.

Let's start off with an easy one. The goal is to complete the first row of the table by answering the question, "Who practices _____?" By practice, I mean who is it that develops knowledge for each of the different ways of knowing in the table? For mathematics, you could place "mathematicians" in the cell. (I told you this was going to be easy.) For science, you would fill in "scientists." You might also add "some doctors" and "some engineers." Although these disciplines are primarily concerned with using what we already know to benefit society, they sometimes involve producing new knowledge.

You might also argue that we shouldn't leave out the many people who pursue science for the love of the discipline, rather than as a profession. I certainly agree with this point and would add that we call these people *amateurs* (from the Latin word *amator*, or lover). In fact, I've been an amateur astronomer for years. So, if you'd like to add "amateur scientist" to your table, that's fine with me. Come to think of it, I'm sure that there are amateur mathematicians as well—think of all those folks who do Sudoku puzzles.

Continuing with this process, you should complete the row with various types of religious leaders under the "Religion" column, followed by "Artists." Thus, the knowledge for each of the different ways of knowing in the table is produced by people practicing very different kinds of professions.

Now, let's tackle the second row of the table. The question here is what is the primary goal of each of the formal ways of knowing? Think about the connection between the discipline and "reality" (or Truth with a capital "T") as you formulate responses. Let's start with mathematics. You may not have considered this before, but whether you are creating a number line, solving an equation, or writing a formula, mathematics is about relationships and patterns between numbers. Therefore, you could say that at its heart mathematics attempts to represent and explain reality through exploring patterns and relationships.

Now, let's come up with a statement for the overall goal of science. Like our statement for the goal of mathematics, we want to focus on how the discipline of science attempts to describe and explain reality. Go ahead and try to write a statement for science before reading any further.

My students' first responses typically focus on describing scientific activities (such as observing, inferring, and experimenting) with the goal of answering all questions. Despite their initial reactions, it is not the goal of science to answer *all* questions. The goal of science is to answer only those questions that pertain to perceived reality. Worded more formally, science attempts to describe and explain reality (as we perceive it) through the investigation of nature.

Now, go ahead and try to compose similar statements for the other two ways of knowing in the table. You might say that the goal of religion is to understand reality through spirituality. Art on the other hand, is not so much about understanding reality, but about conveying perceptions of reality and the human condition. Thus, the goals of each of the ways of knowing listed in the table are very different.

Now consider what I refer to as "paths to truth" on the table. In other words, what are the primary methods and evidence that each different way of knowing employs to make sense of what we experience in the world around us? Go ahead and try filling out this row before reading on.

As with the other rows, you probably found it more difficult to provide the requested information for some of the columns than others. Nevertheless, I trust you were able to provide some information about the goals for each of the four formal ways of knowing in the table.

Let's start once again with mathematics. In trying to reach the goal of understanding reality through exploring patterns and relationships, mathematicians use many different approaches. For my completed table, I include such things as logic, creative thought, consistency, and reason. At the heart of all mathematical approaches is the reasoned, demonstrative argument (i.e., proof), which "proves" to the audience that the postulate in question is consistent with what we know.

Scientists value many approaches and methodologies in their quests for understanding. Many of these approaches are familiar to you and have been discussed throughout this book. For my table, I've included many of the process skills we teach in science classes, including observation, inference, measuring, predicting, hypothesizing, and classification. In addition to these process skills, I've included experimenting, creativity, reason, and logic, as all of these play important roles in the development of scientific knowledge. You could add other aspects of science as well, such as peer review, consistency, parsimony, etc. Perhaps the heart of matter, though, lies in the data. Although creative thought, theoretical musings, and other aspects of human element can play a role in the development of scientific knowledge, in the end scientific ideas must pass muster against the data.

Paths to truth in religion include a variety of approaches, as well, but with more of a focus on individual experience and reliance on authority. To understand reality through spiritual means, one typically is encouraged to read scripture, meditate, pray, and participate in ritualistic acts. Additionally, religious knowledge and understanding typically rely heavily on listening to spiritual leaders and reading and interpreting scripture.

As we have seen earlier, art is not so much about understanding the universe as it is about expressing thoughts and feelings about being human in the universe. The methods of art include such familiar activities as painting, sculpting, writing, and composing. It's through these methods that artists of all kinds attempt to convey the human condition and what life is all about.

Look at the final row in the table: "What types of questions are appropriate for each formal way of knowing?" As before, go ahead and try to complete the row on your own before reading my thoughts about it.

What kinds of questions do mathematicians pose about the world? They ask about how to represent reality with numbers. They try and determine the relationships between concepts. They seek to find patterns and commonalities in different situations. What key questions do scientists ask? They want to find out how the universe behaves to explain why it behaves as it does. They ask how the living and non-living aspects of our universe interact. They want to find out what the building blocks of nature are.

People asking religious or spiritual questions may not ever find answers with evidence. They ask questions like, "What happens to me when I die?" or "What is the meaning of life?" or "How should I best lead my life?"

See an example of a completed table in Figure 18.4.

	Mathematics	Science	Religion	Art
Developers of Knowledge in the Discipline	Mathematicians Amateur mathematicians Scientists	Scientists Amateur scientists Mathematicians	Rabbis Theologians Prophets Clerics Clergymen	Artists Actors Musicians Poets
Goal	Understand reality through exploring and generalizing patterns and relationships	Understand reality through investigation of natural phenomena	Understand reality through spirituality	Convey perceptions of reality, and create the concrete from ideas
Paths to Truth	Logic Consistency Creativity Proofs (inductive and deductive) Algorithms Generalization Abstraction	Observation Inference Measuring Predicting Hypothesizing Classification Data Experimenting Creativity Reason Logic	Revelation Tradition Ritual Scripture Meditation Interpretation	Creativity Expressiveness Interpretation Inspiration Personal experience
Appropriate Questions	• How do objects, ideas, and numbers relate to each other? • How can I represent ideas with numbers or visual graphics and figures? • What is the pattern in this particular situation? • How can I represent my idea algebraically?	• What happened? • When did it happen? • How does it happen? • What makes things behave as they do? • What goes on inside that which we cannot see? (ex: the atom) • What goes on outside of that which we can see? (ex: the known universe)	• Why am I here? • Where did evil come from? • What's the meaning of life? • What is good? • What is most important in life? • Why do bad things happen to good people? • Is this life all there is?	• What is beauty? • How can I express what I know and feel? • How can I best convey my creative works to others so that they can learn from them?

Figure 18.4
Sample of a completed "formal ways of knowing" table.

LESSON WRAP-UP

Take a look at the images in Figures 18.5–18.8 and answer this question, "What do these images have in common?"

You may recognize these images as ways to represent or describe stars. Vincent Van Gogh did this artistically in 1889 with oil paints. Ejnar Hertzsprung and Henry

Figure 18.5
Vincent Van Gogh's *Starry Night*.
Source: Digital Image. © The Museum of Modern Art Licenced by SCALA/ART Resource, NY.

Figure 18.6
The Hertzsprung-Russell diagram.

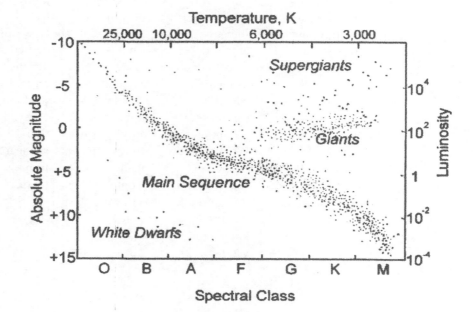

Figure 18.7
Psalm 8:3–4, New International Version of the Bible.

3 When I consider your heavens,
   the work of your fingers,
   the moon and the stars,
   which you have set in place,

4 What is man that you are mindful of him,
   the son of man that you care for him?

$$(m - M) = 5\log\left(\frac{DISTANCE}{10\ PARSEC}\right)$$

Figure 18.8
Distance modulus—a mathematical way to represent the distance to stars.

Norris Russell did this scientifically in 1910 by representing the relationship between luminosity and distance of stars. Three thousand years ago King David did this through his poetic pondering of man's place amongst the stars, and the distance modulus does this mathematically through the formula depicted. The point is that each of these representations has something to offer. It's not that one is more "right" than the others; together they offer different perspectives that provide a richer understanding of the reality of the universe.

As you look over this small sampling of questions that each way of knowing is equipped to address, consider one last question: Which of these sets of questions is most relevant and important to you? Now, you might suppose that because this is a book on the nature of science that the expected answer is *science*. That's certainly what my students expect when we do this activity. However, when encouraged to answer honestly, every one of my students has responded that the questions addressed by religion or philosophy have the most meaning for their lives.

Although science can provide many answers about the wonders of the world, it is the questions of religion and philosophy that give meaning to our lives. In my experience, acknowledging this truth early in my science courses has helped students realize that my goal is not to change what they value, but simply to teach them science. In fact, I encourage my students to pursue these other ways of knowing in other classes and outside of school. But at the same time, I remind them that in my class they are here to learn about what the formal way of knowing called *science* has to offer. And as they will come to see, the scientific perspective can enrich our lives in ways that they cannot even imagine.

It's not the scientific perspective alone that makes our lives worth living, however. Perhaps the richest way to come to understand reality is by viewing the world through multiple perspectives. Part of the beauty of human existence is the myriad ways in which we can seek to know more about the experiences of our lives. Reflecting on religion, philosophy, art, mathematics, and science, as we have done in this lesson, is a great way to begin to develop these multiple perspectives.

ASSESSMENT

You can use this chapter's Notebook Assignments as writing prompts or stand-alone worksheets. The first assignment is designed to help students reflect on the four general ways of knowing (and their limitations), as discussed in the early part of this chapter. The second assignment is designed to help students follow along and reflect upon the discussion comparing the different formal ways of knowing.

General Ways of Knowing

Name: _____ Date: _____

1. Define the following general ways of knowing
   - Authority

   _____
   _____
   _____
   _____
   _____

   - Personal experience

   _____
   _____
   _____
   _____
   _____

   - Intuition

   _____
   _____
   _____
   _____
   _____

   - Reasoning

   _____
   _____
   _____
   _____
   _____

2. Now compare the different general ways of knowing by listing some everyday examples in column 1 and limitations of each of the general ways of knowing in column 2 of the following table. For example, in the first row of column 1, you might write "Fruits and vegetables are good for you." In the second column you might list that "Even reliable sources can be wrong."

	Examples of what we know from each of these ways of knowing	What are some limitations of each of these ways of knowing?
Authority		
Personal Experience		
Intuition		
Logic and Reason		

Formal Ways of Knowing

Name: _____ Date: _____

1. What are the similarities and differences between these formal ways of knowing? Complete the following chart as you think about this question.

	Mathematics	Science	Religion	Art
Practitioners				
Goal				
Paths to Truth				
Appropriate Questions				

2. Do you think these four formal ways of knowing are compatible with each other?

_____

_____

3. Do you think they contradict each other?

_____

_____

4. Which formal way of knowing is most important to you?

_____

_____

19

Assessment and the Nature of Science

This chapter describes several approaches to assessing student understandings of the nature of science, including formative, summative, informal, and formal. Traditional multiple-choice tests, open-ended questionnaires, and alternative assessments are also addressed. The chapter provides a wide variety of examples of previously developed nature of science assessments to serve as guides for developing your own assessment tools specifically tailored to the needs of your students.

LAYING THE GROUNDWORK

As we enter into this penultimate chapter, I want you to think about the answer to an interesting question: "Have you really taught the nature of science if you never assess what your students' know?" Before answering, you might consider that the question is analogous to the familiar: "If a tree falls in the forest with no one around to hear it, does it make a sound?" My answer to both questions is that if no one is there to hear the tree fall—or bothers to assess what his/her students know—the answer is moot. Either way, we don't know what happened. And one thing for sure is that not knowing what your students have learned puts you on shaky ground in regard to improving your instruction and their knowledge.

One of the things my colleagues and I have found in our research into how teachers address the nature of science in their instruction is that most find it a difficult topic to assess. In fact, few of the teachers participating in our studies had made any attempt at all to assess their students' understandings of the nature of science (Abd-El-Khalick, Bell, & Lederman, 1998; Bell, Lederman, & Abd-El-Khalick, 2000). For the majority of these teachers, the biggest obstacle to nature of science assessment was the lack of example tests and questions to guide them in developing their own assessments. That's where this chapter comes in.

My goal is not to provide you with complete ready-to-use assessments, because the range of student ages and abilities addressed in this book is too wide to make that practical. No matter what I presented, you'd find the need to modify it for your own teaching style and your students' needs. So instead, I'll discuss some issues surrounding nature of science assessment and provide you with example questions in a variety of formats. You can take what you find here to inform your own assessments.

FORMATIVE NATURE OF SCIENCE ASSESSMENTS

Formative assessment is just a fancy term for ongoing measures of student performance while they are learning a topic. Formative assessment has two purposes: (a) to provide feedback to students on their learning progress, and (b) to give the teacher an indication of what students have mastered about the topic and areas with which they are having trouble. As such, formative assessments provide an ongoing measure of the effectiveness of instruction. They can be graded or not, depending on the teacher's goals and philosophy.

The key idea about formative assessment is that it is designed for improvement. Used regularly, formative assessment can help you modify and tailor your science instruction on the fly. It will also help your students monitor and improve their learning. Formative assessment is especially important for nature of science instruction, because the topic is so unfamiliar and abstract for many students. Without formative assessment, it is all too easy for you to "forge ahead" and leave your students behind in regard to their understanding.

Informal Formative Assessment

Many times, formative assessment is informal. Such assessment includes asking your students questions about what they've learned about the nature of science at the end of a lesson. An example of the informal variety of formative assessment is as follows: Why were the results in a measurement activity so varied, despite the fact that you all measured the same object? If you then ask students to consider how their experiences with measurement compare to that of scientists, you have moved the informal assessment into the realm of the nature of science. Informal formative assessment can also take the form of simply talking to students one on one to get a feel for what they're thinking and learning about science. As the name implies, this is an informal, nonthreatening way to gauge your students' understandings.

Formal Formative Assessment

Formative assessment can also be more formal than asking questions at the end of a lesson. Generally speaking, *formal* means that students turn something in to you to assess and possibly grade. Notebooking assignments, worksheets, and projects all fall into the category of formal formative assessment. The Notebook Assignments at the end of the chapters of this book are good examples of the more formal kind of formative assessment and can serve as guides for developing your assignments. Just remember to include questions or tasks related to specific aspects of the nature of science when designing your assessments, just as I have done throughout this book.

SUMMATIVE NATURE OF SCIENCE ASSESSMENTS

Summative assessment is the two-dollar term for measures of learning that come at the end of a unit of instruction or course. Like its formative cousin, summative assessment has two primary goals. The first is to assess student learning and guide the assignment of appropriate grades. The second, and less familiar, goal is to determine the success of the instruction. For our purposes, the second goal of summative assessment is to answer the question: To what extent did the instructional approach I used achieve its goal of teaching a more accurate view of the nature of science?

Summative assessment is not limited to, but typically takes the form of, tests and quizzes. Having students complete a concept map of their views of the nature of science or participating in an oral exam could serve as alternative forms of summative assessment.

You may be surprised to learn that the past five decades have seen the development of more than 30 assessment tools for finding out what students know about the nature of science. The majority of these assessments were developed before the 1980s as summative assessments for research purposes and typically focused on easily graded, multiple-choice approaches to assessment. It was not unusual for some of these tests to include upwards of a hundred questions, and many were written at reading levels beyond that of elementary and middle school students. Even so, these assessments can still be useful—key questions on a particular researcher's test can serve as models as you develop your own questions to better meet the needs of your students.

Table 19.1 presents a timeline of a few of the nature of science assessment tools developed over the past five decades, with emphasis on key tests and ones that are likely to be most useful to you as an elementary or middle school teacher. Next, I'll summarize some of these tools and highlight questions that seem especially useful for our purposes.

True/False: The Myths of Science Quiz

The November 2004 issue of the National Science Teachers Association journal, *The Science Teacher*, is devoted entirely to teaching about the nature of science. The capstone feature article is concerned with assessing student myths about science, in particular, their misconceptions about the nature of science. In the article, authors Chiappetta and Koballa (2004) discuss several common myths about scientific knowledge and present a true/false quiz designed to assess your students' views about the nature of science (Figure 19.1).

Although this quiz paints a quick and easy picture of your students' understandings of some of the key aspects of the nature of science presented in this book, it is too short and simple to provide an in-depth assessment of your students' views. Still, it can be useful during a unit as a quiz or as a source of true/false questions for a larger test. You could also increase the utility of the quiz by having students explain in a short paragraph the reason why they answered each question as they did. You may want to take the quiz yourself to see how well you do (quite well, I hope, now that you've read this book). See Chiappetta and Koballa (2004) for a description of the common myths of science that the quiz addresses.

Multiple-Choice Questions: Test on Understanding Science (TOUS)

The Test on Understanding Science (TOUS), published by the Educational Testing Service, was developed in 1961 by William Cooley and Leopold Klopfer. This assessment measures students' understandings about three related domains:

Table 19.1
A timeline of key nature
of science assessments.

Date	Test Name	Developer(s)	Question Format	Number of Questions
1957	Image of the Scientist	Mead and Metraux	Short essay	1
1961	Test on Understanding Science (TOUS)	Cooley & Klopfer	Multiple choice	60
1968	Nature of Science Scale (NOSS)	Kimball	Agree/disagree	29
1975	Nature of Science Test (NOST)	Billeh & Hasan	Multiple choice	60
1978	Nature of Scientific Knowledge Scale (NSKS)	Rubba & Anderson	Agree/disagree	48
1983	Draw-A-Scientist Test (DAST)	Chambers	Drawing	1
1987	Views on Science-Technology-Society (VOSTS)	Aikenhead, Fleming, & Ryan	Empirically derived multiple choice	113
1992	Modified Nature of Scientific Knowledge Scale (MNSKS)	Meichtry	Agree/disagree	32
1998	Views of Nature of Science B (VNOS B)	Abd-El-Khalick, Bell, & Lederman	Short essay	6
2002	Views of Nature of Science D (VNOS D)	Lederman & Khishfe	Short essay	7
2004	"Myths of Science" quiz	Chiappetta & Koballa	True/false	12

Figure 19.1

The Myths of Science Quiz.

Source: By Eugene Chiappetta and Thomas Koballa. Copyright ©2004 the National Science Teachers Association. Used by permission.

Myths of Science Quiz (Answer key is below.)

Directions Each statement below is about science. Some statements are true and some are false. On the line in front of each statement, write a "T" if it is true and an "F" if false.

_____ 1. Science is a system of beliefs.

_____ 2. Most scientists are men because males are better at scientific thinking.

_____ 3. Scientists rely heavily on imagination to carry out their work.

_____ 4. Scientists are totally objective in their work.

_____ 5. The scientific method is the accepted guide for conducting research.

_____ 6. Experiments are carried out to prove cause-and-effect relationships.

_____ 7. All scientific ideas are discovered and tested by controlled experiments.

_____ 8. A hypothesis is an educated guess.

_____ 9. When a theory has been supported by a great deal of scientific evidence, it becomes a law.

_____ 10. Scientific ideas are tentative and can be modified or disproved, but never proved.

_____ 11. Technology preceded science in the history of civilization.

_____ 12. In time, science can solve most of society's problems.

1. The scientific enterprise
2. Scientists
3. The methods and aims of science

It was originally developed with 60 multiple-choice items. The topics of the third domain overlap most closely (but not completely) with the topic of this book and include questions on the following topics:

- Scientific methods
- Tactics and strategies of doing science
- Theories and models
- Aims of science
- Accumulation and falsification
- Controversies in science
- Science and technology
- Unity and interdependence of the sciences

This assessment was one of the most widely used early assessments of students' understandings of the nature of science. It is not used much in educational research today for a variety of reasons, but the structure and content of some of its questions can still provide a model for writing your own multiple-choice questions. Figure 19.2 contains some sample questions from the original TOUS.

Empirically Derived Multiple-Choice Questions: Views on Science-Technology-Society

Aikenhead, Ryan, and Fleming (1989) developed the Views on Science-Technology-Society (VOSTS) (see Table 19.2) instrument to assess secondary students' understanding

Answer Key: 1-F, 2-F, 3-T, 4-F, 5-F, 6-F, 7-F, 8-F, 9-F, 10-T, 11-T, 12-F

Figure 19.2
Sample questions from the TOUS.

12. The principal aim of science is to
   a. verify what has already been discovered about the physical world.
   b. explain natural phenomena in terms of principles and theories.
   c. discover, collect and classify facts about animate and inanimate nature.
   d. provide the people of 'the world' with the means for leading better lives.

16. Which one of the following statements best describes the most important contribution scientists make to our society?
   a. Scientists provide knowledge about natural events.
   b. Scientists make improved products for better living.
   c. Scientists provide skilled services or advice to others.
   d. Scientists show us what we should strive for.

30. An example of a scientific model is: "The atom is like a miniature solar system composed of electrons in orbits, and, in the center, a nucleus containing protons and neutrons." Which one of the following statements about scientific models is NOT correct?
   a. They are man-made constructs and may not represent reality.
   b. They consist of a relatively small number of assumptions.
   c. They represent what scientists could see with very powerful instruments.
   d. They are tentative and may be modified or discarded.

43. Which of the following is the best description of a scientific law?
   a. It is an exact report of the observations of scientists.
   b. It is a generalized statement of relationships among natural phenomena.
   c. It is a theoretical explanation of a natural phenomenon.
   d. It is enforced by nature and cannot be violated.

45. When some of the facts in a certain area of science are not explained by an existing theory, scientists
   a. may revise the unexplained facts so that they will fit into the theory.
   b. may modify the theory so that more of the facts will be explained.
   c. should discard the theory and formulate a new one immediately.
   d. should show the theory to be in error in all cases.

50. Ralph said: "Scientists do experiments to ask questions of nature." The best interpretation of Ralph's statement is that experiments and tests are used in science to
   a. prove the regularity of nature.
   b. learn by trial and error.
   c. check predictions made from scientists' observations and ideas.
   d. inquire into the mystery of creation.

of the nature of science and technology and their interactions with society. The test consists of a "pool" of 113 multiple-choice questions developed from written statements and interview responses from more than 10,000 students in the eleventh and twelfth grades. The 113 questions are divided among eight categories of knowledge about science and technology and their interactions with society (Table 19.2). The entire VOSTS is available for download from Glen Aikenhead's Web page at the University of Saskatchewan Web site: http://www.usask.ca/education/people/aikenhead/vosts.pdf.

Don't let the size of the test discourage you from using it—the developers did not expect you to use all 113 questions. Of particular interest to our purposes are the 22 questions in category 9: Nature of Scientific Knowledge, a more manageable number for a unit or end-of-year assessment. A close examination of the topics assessed

Table 19.2
Structure of the Views on Science-Technology-Society (VOSTS) Test.

Category	Number of Questions
1. Science and Technology	7
2. Influence of Society on Science/Technology	13
3. (not used)	0
4. Influence of Science/Technology on Society	28
5. Influence of School Science on Society	4
6. Characteristics of Scientists	16
7. Social Construction of Scientific Knowledge	15
8. Social Construction of Technology	8
9. Nature of Scientific Knowledge	22

in this category reveals a strong correlation to the concepts and topics presented in this book (Table 19.3).

A fundamental assumption underlying the development of the VOSTS is that students do not necessarily understand test questions in the same way that the teacher intended. Thus, assessments based on typical multiple-choice and true/false questions may be suspect, because it's likely that as many as a quarter of the students didn't really understand many of the questions, especially with questions related to abstract concepts like the nature of science (Aikenhead, 1979). Aikenhead, Ryan, and Fleming's solution to this problem was to make the possible responses to VOSTS

Table 19.3
VOSTS "Nature of Scientific Knowledge" Questions.

Concept/Topic	Number of Questions	VOSTS Question ID Numbers
Nature of observations	1	90111
Nature of scientific models	1	90211
Nature of classification schemes	1	90311
Tentativeness of scientific knowledge	1	90411
Hypotheses, theories and laws	4	90511, 90521, 90531, 90541
Scientific approach to investigations (e.g., no single scientific method)	5	90611, 90621, 90631, 90641, 90651
Precision and uncertainty in scientific/technological knowledge	2	90711, 90721,
Logical reasoning	1	90811
Fundamental assumptions for all science	1	90921
Status of scientific knowledge (e.g., perception vs. reality).	3	91011, 91012, 91013
Paradigms vs. coherence of concepts across disciplines	2	91111, 91121

Figure 19.3

Example of a VOSTS question about the nature of observations.

90111 Scientific observations made by competent scientists will usually be different if the scientists believe different theories.

Your position, basically:

(Please read from A to H, and then choose one.)

A. Yes, because scientists will **experiment** in different ways and will notice different things.

B. Yes, because scientists will **think** differently and this will **alter their observations.**

C. Scientific observations will **not differ** very much even though scientists believe different theories. If the scientists are indeed **competent** their observations will be similar.

D. No, because observations are as exact as possible. This is how science has been able to advance.

E. No, observations are exactly what we see and nothing more; they are the facts.

F. I don't understand.

G. I don't know enough about this subject to make a choice.

H. None of these choices fits my basic viewpoint.

questions come from what students actually think about the topic, rather than what the test-developer or teacher thinks students think. This required extensive analysis of students' written responses and interviews (more than 10,000 students were involved), but resulted in a more valid approach to nature of science assessment.

On the VOSTS, students choose from a number of choices (sometimes up to 10 different views) to respond to a statement or situation based on a science/technology concept or issue (Figure 19.3). Included as a choice in every question is the statement, "I don't understand," or "I don't know enough about this subject to make a choice." This serves to eliminate a weakness of most multiple-choice and true/false tests, that is, forcing students to choose an answer for a question they do not understand or that does not match their own views.

Should you choose to use questions from the VOSTS to assess your students' views of the nature of science, you'll need to make a few modifications. First, you will likely choose not to use most of the 113 questions, since many assess concepts that fall outside the realm of the nature of science. All 22 questions in section 9 that address the nature of science may not suit your needs, so feel free to pick and choose those that best fit what you've taught.

Also, be aware that VOSTS questions were written for high school-aged students and are not appropriate for younger elementary students. Even upper elementary and middle school teachers will want to modify most questions to better match the reading level of their students.

Finally, keep in mind that since the VOSTS was designed as an assessment for research purposes, there is no single "best" answer for each question, and it does not provide numerical scores based on the number of "correct" responses. Rather, it provides a profile of your students' views, which should still prove valuable in informing your instruction to best suit the needs of your students. A typical way of analyzing VOSTS responses is to calculate the percent of students who selected each possible answer. Thus, if most of your students selected answers on the more absolute side, you would know that more instruction about the tentative nature of science is in order.

Figure 19.4
A modified multiple-
choice version of
question 90111 from the
VOSTS.

Can scientific observations made by competent scientists be different if the scientists believe different theories?

A. No, scientific observations will not differ very much even though scientists believe different theories. If the scientists are competent, their observations will be similar.
B. Yes, because scientists will think differently and this may cause their observations and conclusions to differ.
C. No, observations are exactly what we see and nothing more; they are the facts.
D. Yes, because different theories give scientists different answers. It's impossible to determine which answers are correct.

Of course, VOSTS questions could easily be modified to include only a single correct answer. All you would need to do is select one of the answers most in agreement with the views of science presented in this book as your "correct" response. Figure 19.4 presents a modified version of the same VOSTS question in Figure 19.3. Note that I have revised the wording of the question and several of the answer choices to provide a single correct answer (in this case, B). Also, I have eliminated three choices: "I don't understand," "I don't know enough about this subject to make a choice," and "None of these choices fits my basic viewpoint." These modifications bring the question into alignment with typical multiple-choice questions, and make scoring responses to the question more straightforward. However, be aware that making such changes raises the same concerns about multiple-choice assessments that Aikenhead, Ryan, and Fleming were trying to avoid with the VOSTS. Still, if you want to create multiple-choice assessments for the nature of science, modified VOSTS questions are a reasonable place to start.

Essay Questions: Views of the Nature of Science

Norman Lederman, Molly O'Malley, and a team of graduate students worked together over a period of 12 years to develop a series of questionnaires designed to assess a wide range of student understandings of the nature of science (Table 19.4).

Table 19.4
The versions of the Views of the Nature of Science Questionnaire.

Version and Reference	Appropriate Grade Levels	Number of Questions
VNOS-A Lederman & O'Malley (1990).	High School/College	7
VNOS-B Bell, Lederman, & Abd-El-Khalick (2000).	High School/College	6
VNOS-C Abd-El-Khalick & Lederman (2000).	High School/College	10
VNOS-D Lederman & Khishfe (2002).	Elementary/Middle School	7
VNOS-E Lederman & Lederman (2004).	Elementary	7

1. After scientists have developed a theory (e.g., atomic theory), does the theory ever change? If you believe that theories do change, explain why we bother to teach scientific theories. Defend your answer with examples.

2. What does an atom look like? How certain are scientists about the structure of the atom? What specific evidence do you think scientists used to determine what an atom looks like?

3. Is there a difference between a scientific theory and a scientific law? Give an example to illustrate your answer.

4. How are science and art similar? How are they different?

5. Some astronomers believe that the universe is expanding while others believe that it is shrinking; still others believe that the universe is in a static state without any expansion or shrinkage. How are these different conclusions possible if all of these scientists are looking at the same experiments and data?

Figure 19.5
Sample questions from the VNOS-B.

All five versions of the Views of the Nature of Science (VNOS) questionnaire (with answer keys) are available for download from the Project ICAN Web site: http://www.projectican.com/assessment.html.

Each version of the VNOS questionnaire consists of a series of open-ended questions designed to elicit students' views about the nature of science in an indirect manner (Figure 19.5). For example, rather than asking students directly about the roles of indirect evidence and inference in the development of scientific knowledge, a VNOS question might ask how scientists know about the internal structure of atoms. A student who (incorrectly) responds that scientists use high-powered microscopes to directly view atomic structure would be assessed with a more naïve view of science than one who (correctly) explains that scientists observe how atoms react and what particles they emit to infer what's inside.

The VNOS's use of open-ended questions avoids some of the problems associated with multiple-choice and true/false questions. For example, when you have to use your own words to explain your answer, there is no opportunity to get a question correct by guessing. Also, it is immediately evident if students do not understand a question by the substance (or lack of substance) of their answers. In the best cases, students' answers to open-ended questions can be quite complete and reveal much more about their thinking than typical forced-choice questions. On the other hand, the open-ended questions of the VNOS can be frustrating for students with poor writing skills, and it's not uncommon for students to answer the questions incompletely due to lack of time or motivation, giving the perception that they know less than they actually do.

When using the VNOS for research purposes, researchers get around these limitations by interviewing students. By asking students to explain and elaborate upon their VNOS responses and by asking probing questions, researchers are able to get an accurate picture of what students understand about the nature of science. Interviewing your students would be a good way for you to assess their understandings as well, although time limitations often prevent formal interviews from being used as assessment tools in today's classrooms. Still, the various versions of the VNOS are excellent sources of essay questions for tests, especially VNOS-D and VNOS-E, which were written specifically for elementary and middle school students.

Alternative Assessment: Draw-A-Scientist Test

How do your students envision scientists and the work that they do? To what degree are your students influenced by the common stereotypes depicted in popular media? Movies, books, and comic books are wrought with images of scientists as Caucasian men in white lab coats sporting eyeglasses and beards. At their worst, scientists are depicted as diabolical madmen or as clumsy eccentrics with poor social skills (i.e., nerds) who prefer working alone in dark laboratories to pursuing any kind of social life. Does this describe your students' views of a scientist? If so, it's hardly surprising that many of your students may not aspire to a career in science, or even hold in high regard the knowledge that such scientists produce.

David W. Chambers (1983) developed the Draw-A-Scientist Test (DAST) as an alternative assessment tool designed to illuminate students' views of scientists and the work that they do. The original assessment is simple in structure, consisting of a single prompt, "Draw a scientist," with no further instructions.

Concerns that students may not be drawing their own views, but rather, their perceptions of what the public thinks about scientists led Symington and Spulring (1990) to revise the prompt slightly to, "Do a drawing which tells what you know about scientists and their work." Symington and Spulring's research indicated that their version of the prompt elicits more valid responses from students—something you should consider should you choose to assess your students with the DAST. Students' responses to the prompt amazed Chambers (and the many other researchers who have subsequently used the DAST) with their consistency in depicting stereotypical images of scientists (Figure 19.6).

To analyze student drawings, Finson, Beaver, and Cramond (1995) created a checklist in which a maximum of one mark per blank is placed on the checklist and then tallied at the end (see Figure 19.7). Often, the DAST is given at the beginning of the school year as a pretest, and then again at the end of the year as a posttest. Pretest scores can then be compared to posttest scores to see if students' views of scientists and their work have changed over the course of the year.

The fact that the DAST requires students to draw instead of write is both a strength and weakness of the assessment. Certainly, it is easier for many students (especially younger ones) to depict their ideas in a drawing than it is for them to

Figure 19.6

Three examples of student responses to the Draw-A-Scientist Test (DAST).

DRAW-A-SCIENTIST CHECKLIST

1. Lab Coat (usually but not necessarily white) _____
2. Eyeglasses _____
3. Facial Growth of Hair (beards, mustaches, abnormally long sideburns) _____
4. Symbols of Research (scientific instruments, lab equipment of any kind) _____
    a. Size of Scientific Instruments/Equipment in Relation to Scientist:[a]
        1. Small _____
        2. Normal _____
        3. Large _____
    b. Types of Scientific Instruments/Equipment:
5. Symbols of Knowledge (principally books, filing cabinets, clipboards, pens in pockets, etc.) _____
6. Technology (the "products" of science) _____
    a. Types of Technology (TV, telephone, missiles, computers, etc.):
7. Relevant Captions (formulae, taxonomic, classification, the "eureka!" syndrome) _____

ALTERNATIVE IMAGES:
8. Male Gender _____
9. Caucasian _____
10. Indications of Danger _____
11. Presence of Light Bulbs _____
12. Mythic Stereotypes (Frankenstein creatures, Jekyll/Hyde figures, "Mad/Crazed") _____
13. Indications of Secrecy (signs or warnings of "Private," "Keep Out," "Do Not Enter," "Go Away," "Top Secret," etc.) _____
14. Scientist Doing Work Indoors _____
15. Middle Aged or Elderly Scientist _____

NOTE: Several indicators of the same type in a single drawing count as ONE indicator (e.g., Two scientists each with eyeglasses counts as one, not two).

16. Open Comments (dress items, neckties/necklaces, hair style/grooming, smile or frown, stoic expression, bubbling liquids, smoke/steam, type of scientist—chemist, physicist, etc.):

UPPER SCORE: _____   LOWER SCORE: _____   TOTAL SCORE: _____

[a] Blanks for "size" are not counted in the checklist score.

Figure 19.7
Draw-a-Scientist checklist.
Source: Copyright ©1990 by Kevin D. Finson, John. B. Beaver, & Bonnie L. Cramond. Used by permission.

express them in writing. Indeed, Chambers originally developed the DAST for elementary students for just that reason. On the other hand, it is not always possible to tell exactly what a student intends to convey with a particular image, so caution must be exercised not to infer too much. Finally, the biggest concern for our purposes is that the DAST was not really intended to assess views of the nature of science: Even though its purpose includes depicting "scientists and their work," a quick look at the elements listed in Table 19.2 indicates that the DAST is much more about views of scientists than it is about the nature of scientific knowledge as presented in this book.

Still, the DAST provides an easy and fun method for your students to convey their views of scientists, and there's little doubt that these views are related to how they understand and accept the knowledge produced by scientists. It might also be useful to employ the DAST to determine whether your students' views of scientists change over the course of the year, particularly if you are incorporating lots of nature of science activities in your instruction. It's reasonable to expect that your students' views of scientists will include fewer negative stereotypes providing that you are effectively teaching about the nature of science and how scientific knowledge is developed.

LESSON WRAP-UP

Teaching does not occur in the absence of learning, so if you are not assessing your students' understandings, then you really don't know whether you are teaching the nature of science. Effective assessment involves both informal and formal approaches, as well as formative (ongoing) and summative (concluding) measures of student learning. In all cases, assessment serves a dual purpose: to measure what your students have learned and, just as importantly, to assess the effectiveness of your instruction.

Used appropriately, formative and summative assessment will help you avoid making false assumptions about your students' understandings and will make you a better teacher over time. This knowledge is especially important when it comes to the nature of science, a topic that is often as unfamiliar for you to teach as it is for your students to learn. My hope is that you find the formative and summative assessments provided in this book to be useful guides in developing your own approaches to finding out what your students understand about the nature of science.

20

Conclusion

This chapter summarizes what the activities described in this book teach about process skills and the nature of science and discusses a variety of strategies for addressing process skills and the nature of science throughout the school year. It concludes with two cautionary notes. The first concerns the developmental appropriateness of teaching abstract ideas to school-aged children, and the second deals with the consequences of choosing to avoid instruction about the nature of science.

THIS VIEW OF SCIENCE

As depicted in the activities described in this book, the nature of science is a multi-faceted concept that defies simple definition. In fact, you've probably noticed by now that I have avoided providing a specific definition or complete description of the nature of science. Instead, it's been my hope that your view of the nature of science would unfold and develop as you read through the chapters and shared the activities with your students.

You'll remember from the discussion in Chapter 2 that national standards documents (and some state standard documents) challenge science teachers to address the three domains of science (Figure 20.1), and that the nature of science is by far the most abstract and least familiar of the three. Yet, I hope the activities and discussions of this book have helped you see that these abstract ideas can be made concrete for your students, and lessons about the nature of science can be thought provoking and engaging for students of all ages. Certainly, many of my former students have told me that what they remember most about my science classes were the nature of science lessons.

Now that you've read through the book, it's an appropriate time to recap and formalize our view of the nature of science and the goals for nature of science instruction. Essentially, the concepts discussed here constitute the overall vision of the nature of science that I hope you've gained from the book and will, in turn, teach to your students. In essence, the ideas summarized in the Key Concepts box on page 265 constitute the heart of the ideas that students should learn about the nature of science.

Figure 20.1
Three domains of science.

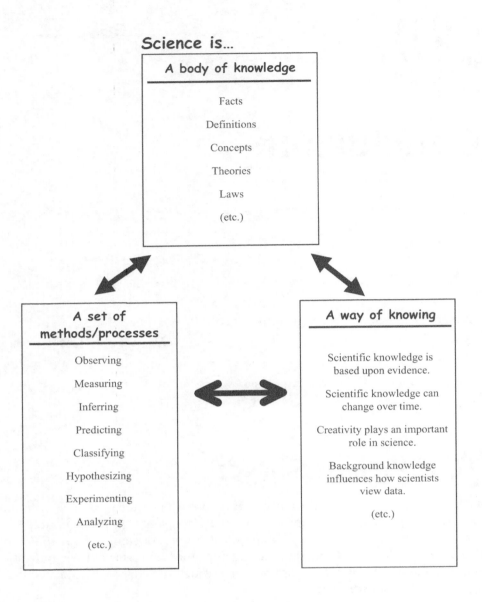

Science is...

A body of knowledge

Facts

Definitions

Concepts

Theories

Laws

(etc.)

A set of methods/processes

Observing

Measuring

Inferring

Predicting

Classifying

Hypothesizing

Experimenting

Analyzing

(etc.)

A way of knowing

Scientific knowledge is based upon evidence.

Scientific knowledge can change over time.

Creativity plays an important role in science.

Background knowledge influences how scientists view data.

(etc.)

These concepts may seem disconnected at first—eight separate ideas about science and scientific knowledge that have little in common. Look a little closer and I think you will agree that they all fall under the umbrella of tentativeness: There are no ideas in science so cherished or privileged as to be outside the possibility of revision, or even rejection, in light of new evidence. In fact, one way to look at Key Concepts 2 through 8 is that together they provide the rationale for *why* scientific knowledge is tentative.

Empirical Evidence

For example, the second factor emphasizes the seminal role of evidence in the construction and validation of scientific knowledge. This empirical base has the necessary implication that as we gather additional data about a particular phenomenon there is always the chance that we will learn something new that adds to or contradicts some previously developed concept or principal.

Key Concepts About the Nature of Science

1. *Tentativeness.* All scientific knowledge is subject to change—even scientific laws change in light of new evidence and new ways of thinking. New ideas in science are often received with a degree of skepticism, especially if they are contrary to well-established scientific concepts. On the other hand, scientific knowledge, once generally accepted, can be robust and durable. Many ideas in science have survived repeated challenges, and have remained largely unchanged for hundreds of years.

2. *Empirical evidence.* Scientific knowledge is based upon empirical evidence. Empirical refers to data, whether quantitative or qualitative. Although some scientific concepts may be considered theoretical in that they are derived primarily from logic and reasoning, in the end, all scientific ideas must conform to observational or experimental data to be considered valid.

3. *Observation and inference.* Scientific knowledge is derived from both observation and inference. Observation involves using the five senses to gather information. It is common for scientists to enhance their observations with technology. An inference is a logical interpretation based on observations and prior knowledge.

4. *Hypotheses, laws, and theories.* In science, a hypothesis is typically used as a proposed explanation or answer to a research question. Scientific laws are succinct descriptions of consistent relationships or patterns in nature. A scientific theory is a well-supported explanation of natural phenomena and associated laws. Theories and laws are two distinct types of knowledge. They both have substantial supporting evidence and are widely accepted by scientists. Either can change in light of new evidence.

5. *Scientific methods.* There is no single universal scientific method. Scientists apply many methods to their research.

6. *Creativity.* Creativity is a source of innovation and inspiration in science. Scientists use imagination, evidence, reason, and prior knowledge to generate new scientific ideas.

7. *Objectivity and subjectivity.* Scientists tend to be skeptical and apply mechanisms such as peer review and crosschecking with existing data to improve objectivity. On the other hand, values, intuition, personal beliefs, perceptual frameworks, and creativity all play significant roles in the development of scientific knowledge. The result is an inherent degree of subjectivity that is reflected in scientific observations, inferences, and interpretations.

8. *A way of knowing.* Science cannot answer all questions. Science is a way of knowing, but not the only way of knowing. There are limits to the kinds of questions that can be asked of science, as well as to the answers science can give.

Observation and Inference

Scientific knowledge is the product of both observation and inference. Observations constitute the empirical basis of scientific knowledge and are descriptions of natural phenomena that may be directly perceived by the senses (or instrumental extensions of the senses). For example, the statement, "This star is brighter than that one," represents an observation. Inferences, on the other hand, are conjectures that go beyond what is directly accessible to the senses. The statement, "This star is brighter than that one *because* it is significantly closer to earth," represents an inference. The distances to stars cannot be directly measured. Rather, our estimates of stellar distances are inferences based upon interpretations of geocentric parallax and other indirect evidence.

Obviously, since inferences are conjectures beyond observable data, any claims based upon inferences are inherently tentative. Additionally, errors in measurement and perceptual illusions give rise to uncertainty in observational data.

Furthermore, because no one can ever be certain of having observed all instances of a phenomenon, scientific claims based upon observation are also tentative. In Karl Popper's (1963) well-known argument of this point, he used the analogy of swans. You may have seen hundreds of white swans and come to the conclusion that all swans are white. Yet you haven't proven that all swans are white until you've seen every single one. One the other hand, all it takes is one black swan to disprove your assertion.

Hypotheses, Laws, and Theories

The distinction between observation and inference in science is significant because these two types of scientific knowledge give rise to different kinds of scientific claims. Scientific laws are based primarily on observation, while theories have a greater inferential component. For example, scientists are sometimes able to recognize generalized patterns and relationships within large sets of observations. Once established and recognized by scientists, these patterns and relationships may become known as scientific laws. For example, Newton's first law of motion describes a concept called inertia, often expressed in the following manner.

> Objects in motion tend to stay in motion,
> and objects at rest tend to stay at rest
> unless acted on by an unbalanced force.

Essentially, this law indicates a generalized pattern that objects tend to remain in the state they are in (moving or resting) unless an unbalanced force is applied. The law expresses *what* happens, but offers no explanation for *why* it happens. (In fact, currently, there is no widely accepted explanation for why inertia exists.)

Theories, on the other hand, like the Kinetic Molecular Theory, seek to explain what we observe and experience in the natural world. These explanations always involve inferences—one inference in the case of the Kinetic Molecular Theory is that all matter is made up of tiny particles in constant motion. The particles are too tiny to be seen directly, hence, their inferential nature. These inferential explanations, when well supported by evidence and accepted by scientists, can become known as scientific theories. For example, the Kinetic Molecular Theory explains why a gas expands when heated and contracts when cooled, expressed in terms of the speed of motion of the molecules that make up gases.

Because scientific laws and theories serve different purposes, the common notion that when theories are proven they become laws is misguided. Theories and laws are different kinds of knowledge and play different roles in science. As such, one can never become the other. Additionally, because both laws and theories are based on evidence, which always has the potential to change with new observations and experiments, neither is absolute. Laws are no more proven than theories—both are subject to change.

Scientific Methods

There is no single, universal method that all scientists follow. You'll never find a poster of the "Scientific Method" posted on the wall of a research lab, just as you'll never find research scientists methodically ticking off the steps in their notebooks as they conduct investigations. In fact, you'll find the steps of the scientific method listed only in school classrooms. The Scientific Method is an overly idealized description of *one* method scientists use (experiments), but there are many others, including observation studies, correlation studies, and just plain intuition and serendipitous discovery. Much science comes from unguided observation and following where curiosity leads, rather than from proposing hypotheses or even from conducting experiments.

One consequence of the lack of a single, universal scientific method is that there is not a magic method scientists use to produce absolute truth or to prove their postulates for all time. Rather, scientists follow where their curiosity leads, and in the process they use both formal and informal methods to answer their questions. The knowledge they produce may be strongly confirmed, but never proven in any absolute sense.

Creativity

Creativity and imagination also contribute to the tentativeness of scientific knowledge. Science is not simply the product of logic and rationality. As we have seen, scientists use a wide variety of creative methods and procedures to answer their research questions, bound only by the limitation that they must be able to justify their approaches to the satisfaction of their peers. Within the limits of peer review, creativity abounds in the ways that scientists design their investigations and in how they analyze and interpret their results.

Many of the most celebrated scientific discoveries have stemmed from intuition and creative approaches, as much as from steady, methodical adherence to a research program. Darwin's synthesis of the theory of natural selection to explain evolution required the creative work of pulling together data and ideas from several diverse sources, including observations and samples from his tenure on the *H.M.S. Beagle*, the geologic principles of Lyell, and Malthus' theory of populations.

Although he is known as a careful and methodical observer, Darwin's recognized genius stems from his ability to synthesize a powerful scientific explanation from a variety of sources and clues.

Objectivity and Subjectivity

Understanding the roles of creativity and imagination in science leads to the understanding of subjectivity in science. On the one hand, a principal goal of science is to seek understandings and knowledge that are objective (i.e., independent of the biases of the observer). Despite our best efforts, however, we can never divorce ourselves from all bias, nor would we necessarily want to. It is often the uniqueness of an individual's perspective that leads to scientific discovery.

As we saw in Chapter 16, sometimes data do not even make sense without a perceptual framework with which they can be interpreted. Theories, educational background, personal experiences, and intuition combine to form these perceptual frameworks. Sometimes, there exists more than one potential perceptual framework. This is especially true early in a particular research program when the data are too few and ambiguous. Choosing among these frameworks becomes a matter of choice, and the choice made ultimately influences how the data are interpreted.

A Way of Knowing

One of the principal messages of this book is that tentativeness is a pervasive characteristic of science and the knowledge it produces. But the absence of absolutes in science should not be seen as a weakness. Instead, the tentative nature of science is actually one of its greatest strengths—for progress toward truth and away from error would never be possible without the skepticism and scrutiny of new and existing claims, along with the possibility of revising or rejecting those that fall short. In fact, it is the ability of science to readily respond to new evidence and new perspectives on existing evidence that makes it a unique way of knowing. Change, then, is at the heart of science as a way of knowing and is one of the key characteristics distinguishing it from other ways of knowing.

Change in science is not arbitrary, as can be true of everyday changes your students' experience, such as the fashion they prefer, the music they listen to, and the TV shows they like to watch. When scientific knowledge is revised, it does so as a result of further inquiry and observational or experimental evidence. Thus, changes in science move our understandings toward truths about the universe, at least as we currently experience them. Although these truths cannot be viewed as definitive or final, they are among the most reliable that we have. One need only look at the advances in such diverse fields as medicine, agriculture, engineering, and transportation (all fields that make extensive use of the body of knowledge produced by science) for verification that science works.

TEACHING THIS VIEW OF SCIENCE

I hope that by now you agree with the national and state standards that teaching this tentative view of science and scientific knowledge should be an important component of your science instruction. However, simply telling students these rather esoteric ideas is not likely to change what they think about science. You'll need more concrete and creative approaches that illustrate the nature of science, and of course, that is what the activities of this book are designed to provide.

One theme emphasized throughout the book is that nature of science activities should not be taught in isolation. The nature of science is closely interconnected with the knowledge and processes of science (Figure 20.1, page 264) and is best taught in the context of these domains. The approach advocated in this book has been to link nature of science instruction to the process skills you already teach (Figure 20.2). Thus, any science process skills lesson is a potential lesson about the nature of science, provided you highlight the connection between the two.

Process Skill	Nature of Science Tenet
Observing	Scientific knowledge is based upon evidence. Scientific knowledge changes as new evidence becomes available. Scientific laws are generalizations that summarize vast amounts of observational data.
Inferring	Scientific conclusions involve observation and inference (not just observation alone). Scientific theories are based partly on things that cannot be observed directly, and hence are inferential.
Classifying	There is often no single "right" answer in science.
Predicting/ hypothesizing	Scientific theories provide the foundation on which predictions and hypotheses are built.
Designing experiments	There are many ways to do good science. There is no single scientific method that all scientists follow.
Concluding	Scientific conclusions can be influenced by scientists' background knowledge. Theories provide frameworks for data interpretation.

Figure 20.2
Linking process skills instruction to the nature of science.

All of the activities in this book provide explicit examples of how to connect characteristics of the nature of science to such process skills as observing, inferring, measuring, and classifying. Armed with these examples, you will no doubt be able to find and develop your own lessons that provide explicit connections between process skills and the nature of science.

When to teach about the nature of science is another important question to consider as you plan your instruction. If you teach a couple of lessons on the nature of science in September as an introduction to science and then never mention these concepts again during the school year, your students are not likely to understand the tentative nature of science.

Although including a nature of science unit at the beginning of the year is appropriate, you will be much more effective if you periodically include nature of science lessons throughout the school year. Many of the activities in this book lend themselves to warm-up lessons to start the day or filler activities when an assembly or another activity interrupts your normal schedule. Even better, you might consider including one nature of science lesson for each science unit you teach, progressing, as this book does, from the more concrete ideas in the earlier chapters to the more abstract ideas in the later ones.

Since many of the activities described in this book involve surprise endings or discrepant events, some teachers have wondered how nature of science instruction can be implemented across grade levels or by more than one teacher in a school. For most of the nature of science concepts described in this book, multiple activities are provided for teaching them.

Also, you will find that a little coordination goes a long way in helping you avoid overlapping your colleagues' lessons, or worse, contradicting each other in your nature of science instruction. Thus, teachers in an elementary school might decide on a schedule of nature of science instruction that looks something like that presented in Table 20.1.

Table 20.1

An example schedule for nature of science instruction in an elementary school.

Grade Level	Concept & Activities	Chapter(s)
3	**Observation and Nature of Science**	
	-Jelly Belly Tasting Game	2
	-Smelly Cans	2
	-Grasshopper Gazing	2
	Inference and Nature of Science	
	-Crazy Ketchup	3
	-Goodnight Moon	4
	-What Do You Do with a Tail Like This?	4
	-Mystery Cookies	5
4	**Observation, Inference, and Nature of Science**	
	-Magnifying Water Droplets	2
	-One of a Collection	2
	-When Is a Worm not a Worm?	2
	-The Burning Candle	3
	-Fossil Tracks	6
	-Fossil Fragments	7
	Science Is Pattern Seeking	
	-Inquiry Cubes	11
	Classification and Nature of Science	
	-Creative Constellations	12
5	**Observation, Inference, and Nature of Science**	
	-Blind Meet-a-Tree	2
	-Fascinating Feathers	2
	-Comic Strip Observation and Inference	4
	-How do we know . . . ?	4
	-Mystery Shapes Game	8
	Classification and Nature of Science	
	-Petals Around the Rose	11
	-Classifying Everyday Objects	13
	Scientific Theories and Laws	
	-Book Stacking	9
	-Mystery Tube	10
	Science as a Way of Knowing	
	-Ways of Knowing	18

This particular schedule emphasizes observation and inference at each grade level, avoids repeating activities, and builds on the complexity of the implications of observation and inference as the students mature. Students progressing through this series would participate in at least 25 nature of science lessons by the time they reach middle school. Not only would they have begun to develop a more accurate view of science, but they would have been extensively challenged to develop and apply critical thinking skills.

A FINAL WORD

Before closing, it is worth reiterating the point that the tentative nature of science should be taught as a strength, not a weakness. Some worry that teaching the nature of science, as presented in this book, to school-aged children might create more problems than it solves. They worry that students may throw out the good with the bad when their absolute views of science are challenged (Winchester, 1993). There isn't much educational research to support this view. Recent studies into students' understandings of the nature of science have demonstrated that students are able to handle abstract ideas at an earlier age than researchers had once thought possible (Metz, 1995). For example, investigations into the beliefs of elementary school children have shown that even six-year-olds can recognize inference as a source of knowledge (Sodian & Wimmer, 1987) and that one's background knowledge can influence interpretation of images (Taylor, 1988; Taylor, Cartwright, & Bowden, 1991).

Still, concerns about the developmental appropriateness of introducing abstract concepts are well founded and should be carefully considered by all teachers who strive to represent science more accurately in their instruction. Before adopting the most pessimistic viewpoint, however, one must consider the alternative.

By choosing not to challenge students' absolute views about science, we leave them with the overly simplistic view of science as a superhuman endeavor, able to wholly compensate for human flaws and biases and with diligent application, able to produce absolute truth. This view, which ignores the history and philosophy of science, is a distortion of the scientific enterprise.

Further, it is unlikely to serve students well as they mature into adult decision-makers who will be confronted with controversies that emerge from science as it really is, not the absolute way we might want it to be.

Considered in this manner, the question becomes do we leave our students with a "safe" caricature of science or do we strive to help them gain a more realistic, if less comforting, understanding of science as a human endeavor? For me—and you too now that you've read this book—the answer is obvious.

SUGGESTED READINGS

American Association for the Advancement of Science. (1989). *Science for All Americans.* Oxford, England: Oxford University Press.

This book outlines what the average person needs to know about science in order to be scientifically literate. There are sections on the nature of science and mathematics, chapters on basic science concepts, sections on the history of science and technology, and suggestions for educational reforms.

Bauer, H.H. (1992). *Scientific literacy and the myth of the scientific method.* Urbana, IL: University of Illinois Press.

Henry Bauer, a chemistry professor at Virginia Tech, demystifies science by explaining why science literacy is important, how science is actually done in the real world, and what misconceptions the public generally has about science. He discusses the differences between the textbook science taught in schools and the exciting frontier science done in laboratories around the globe.

Beard, J., Nelson, C.E., Nickels, M. (n.d.). *Evolution and the nature of science institutes.* Retrieved July 8, 2006, from http://www.indiana.edu/~ensiweb/.

This Web site contains a collection of science lessons to help teachers more effectively teach about evolution, with a special emphasis on the nature of science. The lessons were developed and tested by biology teachers across the country.

Bell, R.L., Smetana, L., & Binns, I. (2005). Simplifying inquiry instruction: Assessing the inquiry level of classroom activities. *The Science Teacher, 72*(7), 30–33.

The authors present a simple explanation of inquiry and include guidelines to help teachers determine whether a given activity supports inquiry and if it does, to assess the level of inquiry it supports. The article also describes how teachers can scaffold and revise the inquiry level of activities they teach.

Ben-Ari, M. (2005). *Just a theory: Exploring the nature of science.* Amherst, MA: Prometheus Books.

This book provides an overview of the nature of science with an introduction into the philosophy, history, and sociology of science as well. Ben-Ari provides many examples for students and teachers alike to identify. The book contains biographical vignettes of famous scientists and essays such as "Science and Religion," "Statistics," "Logic and Mathematics," and "The Future of Science."

Bronowski, J. (1956). *Science and human values.* New York: Harper & Row.

The three essays in this book were lectures that Jacob Bronowski delivered at MIT while he was a visiting professor there. This classic book was reprinted in 1990 and has been read by generations of people seeking to understand the very human and very creative endeavor of science. He argues that art and science are not so separate because both are driven by human creativity.

Bronowski, J. (1958). *The common sense of science.* Cambridge, MA: Harvard University Press.

Written a half-century ago, this timeless book has recently been republished in paperback form. Bronowski examines how science and scientific thinking have developed as a union of logic and observation, as an investigation of cause and effect, and as a quest to understand the uncertain.

Campbell, V., Lofstrom, J., & Jerome, B. (1997). *Decisions based on science.* Arlington, VA: National Science Teachers Association.

One of the goals of nature of science instruction is to improve science literacy and decision-making on socio-scientific issues. This book contains information and activities designed to teach decision-making skills for students and to apply these skills to decisions about scientific issues. From issues of xenotransplants to ozone depletion, this book will help you teach your students to be more scientifically literate decision makers.

Chalmers, A.F. (1999). *What is this thing called science?* (3rd ed.). Indianapolis, IN: Hackett Publishing.

An introduction to modern views on the nature of science, Chalmers' book is in its third edition since its initial publication in 1976. Translated into 15 languages, this book has been widely read, and some call it the best introductory text on the philosophy of science. Rather than answer the question in the title of the book, Chalmers describes various sciences at stages in the development of this thing called *science.*

Collins, F. (2006). *The language of God: A scientist presents evidence for belief.* New York: Free Press.

This compelling book combines a personal account of Collins' faith and experiences as the head of the Human Genome Project with discussions about science and religion, especially centering on the concept of evolution. Collins' position as scientist and believer provides a powerful perspective on science and religion as complementary ways of knowing.

Collins, H. & Pinch, T. (2000). *The golem: What you should know about science* (2nd ed.). Cambridge: Cambridge University Press.

This engaging book contains a series of stories about important scientific discoveries. However, these discoveries didn't exactly take place the way the newspapers (and textbooks) reported. Through the story of the "discovery" of cold fusion, the study of relativity, Pasteur's investigations into the origins of life, and other fascinating accounts, Collins and Pinch reveal that the path to scientific discovery is much more complicated and subjective than we typically think. Science isn't a straightforward march of discovery, but an ongoing creature (golem) of our own human art and craft.

Cromer, A. (1993.). *Uncommon sense: The heretical nature of science.* New York: Oxford University Press.

What is the origin of modern science? Are its roots in ancient Greece, ancient Babylonia, or in our very nature? This is an age of spectacular discovery and insight, but for the vast majority of human history, science did not play a role. Cromer argues that it did not play a role in the development of our civilization, and that it is not a particularly natural human endeavor. In this book, he supports the claim that science is a unique invention that began at a specific time and place in history: Greece, 2,700 years ago.

Dotlich, R.K. (2006). *What is science?* New York: Henry Holt.

This read-aloud book for children 4 and older is written as a poem and emphasizes that science is about curiosity, asking questions and the fun of trying to find answers.

Dobzhansky, T. (1973). Nothing in biology makes sense except in the light of evolution. *The American Biology Teacher,* 35:125–129. Also available online at: http://www.pbs.org/wgbh/evolution/library/10/2/l_102_01.html.

In this short essay, evolutionary theorist Theodosius Dobzhansky describes evolution as the cornerstone of biology and explains how evolutionary theory provides an interpretive framework that supports and unifies the many fields within biology.

Driver, R., Leach, J., Millar, R., & Scott, P. (1996). *Young people's images of science.* Buckingham, UK: Open University Press.

This book describes the results of a major research study of school students in the UK, aged 9 to 16. The study suggests that the school science curriculum is limited in helping children understand the nature of scientific knowledge and its role in society. It brings to light what young people of different ages are thinking about science and the implications of their thinking for reforms in science teaching.

Dunbar, R. (1995). *The trouble with science.* Cambridge, MA: Harvard University Press.

Dunbar, a British psychologist, explains in this book what science is, what its history is, what its roots are in human society, and why we have difficulty with it at times. The book may be too philosophical for some tastes, but it's a compelling read.

Gilovich, T. (1991). *How we know what isn't so.* New York: Simon & Schuster.

This fascinating book provides examples of faulty reasoning in everyday life, including how our expectations influence perception (e.g., faith healing, ESP), finding patterns where none exist, (e.g., as in clouds and gamblers' streaks), and failure to record negative outcomes (how many times do you *not* have an old friend call after thinking about her for the first time in years?). In addition to the examples, the book addresses the root causes of these and other forms of faulty reasoning.

Gould, S.J. (1994). Evolution as fact and theory. In *Hen's teeth and horse's toes* (pp. 253–262). New York: W.W. Norton & Company. (Originally published in *Discover Magazine*, 1981.)

A classic article by the famous paleontologist on the nature of facts and theories in science.

Kuhn, T.S. (1996). *The structure of scientific revolutions* (3rd ed.). Chicago, IL: University of Chicago Press.

This book is a classic that anyone interested in science philosophy should read. First published over 40 years ago, it sparked its own revolution in the way people examined the history and nature of science. It's a philosophical and challenging read, but an excellent look into the twisted and interrupted path of science "progression." Thomas Kuhn coined the phrase, "paradigm shift" in this book, describing how scientific revolutions occur when scientists re-evaluate and revise their interpretive frameworks.

Mannoia, V.J. (1980). *What is science? An introduction to the structure and methodology of science.* Lanham, MD: University Press of America.

An introductory text on the philosophy of science, this short (just over 100 pages) and humorously illustrated book is an easy read on topics from scientific methods to scientific ideas.

McComas, W.F. (1996). Ten myths of science: Re-examining what we think we know about the nature of science. *School Science and Mathematics, 96* 10–16.

This article focuses on ten misconceptions students commonly hold regarding the nature of science and the more appropriate views of science that teachers should address in their instruction.

McComas, W.F. (1998). *The nature of science in science education: Rationales and strategies.* Dordrecht, Netherlands: Kluwer Academic Publishers.

This book addresses a wide variety of issues related to nature of science, including research summaries, activities, and assessment ideas. It is a bit pricey and written for an academic audience, but still provides a wealth of information for the classroom teacher.

Medawar, P. (1984). *The limits of science.* Oxford, England: Oxford University Press.

In this small book of essays, Nobel laureate, Sir Peter Medawar defines what science is and what it is not. Using a familiar and engaging voice, he addresses some of the big questions about science, revealing its true nature to the learned scientist and the novice alike.

Metz, S. (Ed.). (2004). The history and nature of science. *The Science Teacher, 71*(9).

This is a special issue of the NSTA journal, *The Science Teacher,* devoted entirely to the history and nature of science. The articles address the main tenets of the nature of science, ways to include the history and nature of science in your instruction, and how to assess student understandings of the nature of science.

Murphy E., & Bell, R.L. (2005). How far are the stars? *The Science Teacher, 72*(2), 38–43.

This article provides a detailed account of the roles that observation and inference play when astronomers determine the distance to stars. As such, it can serve as an excellent background for a "How do we know what we know?" lesson in Chapter 4.

National Academy of Sciences. (1998). *Teaching about evolution and the nature of science.* Washington, DC: National Academy Press.

This beautiful book is a must-read for any teacher of the life sciences. Additionally, it provides a succinct introduction to the nature of science. It's written with the school teacher in mind, with activities and worksheets related to teaching about evolution and the nature of science. The book is also available free online at http://www.nap.edu/readingroom/books/evolution98/.

Sagan, C. (1997). *The demon-haunted world: Science as a candle in the dark.* New York: Ballantine Books.

Astronomer and best-selling author Carl Sagan debunks the paranormal and offers skepticism and scientific literacy as answers to the proliferation of unsubstantiated claims in the dawning of the information age. Sagan's earnest, but nonthreatening style provides a gentle introduction to the nature of science and its potential to influence what we believe and how we act in our daily lives.

Shermer, M. (2002). *Why people believe weird things: Pseudoscience, superstition, and other confusions of our time.* New York: Henry Holt and Company.

In this engaging book, Michael Shermer describes the erroneous thinking that leads people to truly believe in such unsubstantiated claims as alien abduction, psychic power, and recovered memories of satanic ritual. He gently explains the fallacy of such beliefs and offers a rationale for skeptical thinking and its role in science.

Wolpert, L. (1992). *The unnatural nature of science.* Cambridge, MA: Harvard University Press.

Science is not common sense. Many of the ideas of science are based on abstract and mathematical foundations, requiring a certain type of thinking. In order to understand science, Wolpert explains, we must break out of the natural thinking called "common sense." In this very readable book, Wolpert describes the differences between science and technology and dispels many of the common myths and misconceptions regarding scientific progress.

Youngston, R. (1998). *Scientific blunders: A brief history of how wrong scientists can sometimes be.* New York: Carrol & Graf.

From Empedocles's idea that everything is made up of four elements to Lamarck's ideas on evolution, science history is full of important "discoveries" that were later refuted. Rather than just laugh at these goofs of science, Youngston leads us through blunder upon blunder in order to describe how human nature is connected to the nature of science.

REFERENCES

Abd-El-Khalick, F., Bell, R.L., & Lederman, N.G. (1998). The nature of science and instructional practice: Making the unnatural natural. *Science Education, 82*, 417–436.

Abd-El-Khalick, F., & Lederman, N.G. (2000). The influence of history of science courses on students' views of nature of science. *Journal of Research in Science Teaching, 37*(10), 1057–1095.

Aikenhead, G.S. (1979). Using qualitative data in formative evaluation. *Alberta Journal of Educational Research, 25*. 117–129.

Aikenhead, G., Ryan, A.G., & Fleming, R.W. (1989). Retrieved July 30, 2006, from the University of Saskatchawan Web site: http://www.usask.ca/education/people/aikenhead/vosts.pdf

American Association for the Advancement of Science. (1993). *Benchmarks for science literacy: A Project 2061 report.* New York: Oxford University Press.

Bell, R., Blair, L., Crawford, B., & Lederman, N.G. (2003). Just do it? The impact of a science apprenticeship program on high school students' understandings of the nature of science and scientific inquiry. *Journal of Research in Science Teaching, 40*, 487–509.

Bell, R., & Lederman, N.G. (2003). Understandings of the nature of science and decision making on science and technology based issues. *Science Education, 87*, 352–377.

Bell, R.L., Lederman, N.G., & Abd-El-Khalick, F. (2000). Developing and acting upon one's conception of the nature of science: A follow-up study. *Journal of Research in Science Teaching, 37*, 563–581.

Bell, R.L., Smetana, L., & Binns, I. (2005). Simplifying inquiry instruction. *The Science Teacher, 72*(7), 30–35.

Billeh, V.Y., & Hasan, O. (1975). Factors affecting teachers' gain in understanding the nature of science. *Journal of Research in Science Teaching, 12*, 209–219.

Bransford, J.D., & Johnson, M.K. (1972). Contextual prerequisites for understanding: Some investigations of comprehension and recall. *Journal of Verbal Learning and Verbal Behavior, 11*, 717–726.

Brook, E.J. (2005). Tiny bubbles tell all. *Science, 310*(5752), 1285–1287.

Bugelski, B.R., & Alampay, D.A. (1961). The role of frequency in developing perceptual sets. *Canadian Journal of Psychology, 15*(4), 201–211.

Campbell, B., & Fulton, L. (2003). *Science Notebooks: Writing about Inquiry.* Portsmouth, NH: Heinemann.

Carey, S., & Smith, C. (1993). On understanding the nature of scientific knowledge. *Educational Psychologist, 28*, 235–251.

Chambers, D.W. (1983). Stereotypic images of the scientist: The Draw-A-Scientist Test. *Science Education 67*, 255–265.

Chiappetta, E.L., & Koballa, T. (2004, November). Quizzing students on the myths of science. *The Science Teacher, 71*(9), 58–61.

Collins, H.M. & Pinch, T. (1998) *The golem: What you should know about science.* (2nd ed.). Cambridge, MA: Cambridge University Press.

Cooley, W.W., & Klopfer, L.E. (1961). *Test on understanding science: Form W.* Princeton, NJ: Educational Testing Service.

Dallenbach, K.M. (1951). A picture-puzzle with a new principle of concealment. *American Journal of Psychology, 64*(3), 431–433.

Dobzhansky, T. (1973). Nothing in biology makes sense except in the light of evolution. *The American Biology Teacher, 35*, 125–129.

Driver, R., Leach, J., Millar, R., & Scott, P. (1996). *Young people's images of science.* Philadelphia: Open University Press.

Duschl, R.A. (1987). Abandoning the scientific legacy of science education. *Science Education, 72*, 51–62.

Feynman, R. (1968). What is science? *The Physics Teacher, 7*(6), 313–320.

Finson, K.D., Beaver, J.B., & Cramond, B.L. (1995). Development of and field-test of a checklist for the Draw-a-Scientist Test. *School Science and Mathematics, 95*(4), 195–205.

Hodson, D. (1988). Experiments in science and science teaching. *Educational Philosophy and Theory, 20*, 53–66.

Huygens, C. (1659). *Systema Saturnium: Sive de causis mirandorum Saturni phaenomenon, et comite ejus planeta novo.*

Kimball, M.E. (1968). Understanding the nature of science: A comparison of scientists and science teachers. *Journal of Research in Science Teaching, 5,* 110–120.

Lederman, J.S., & Khishfe, R. (2002). *Views of nature of science, Form D.* Retrieved July 26, 2006, from http://www.projectican.com/

Lederman, J.S., & Lederman, N.G. (2004). *Views of nature of science, Form E.* Retrieved July 26, 2006, from http://www.projectican.com/

Lederman, N.G. (1992). Students' and teachers' conceptions of the nature of science: A review of the research. *Journal of Research in Science Teaching, 29,* 331–359.

Lederman, N.G. (1999). Teachers' understanding of the nature of science and classroom practice: Factors that facilitate or impede the relationship. *Journal of Research in Science Teaching, 36,* 916–929.

Lederman, N., & O'Malley, M. (1990). Students' perception of tentativeness in science: Development, use, and sources of change. *Science Education, 74,* 225–239.

Marr, D. (1982). *Vision.* San Francisco: W.H. Freeman and Company.

Matthews, M.R. (1994). *Science teaching: The role of history and philosophy of science.* Routledge Press, New York.

McComas, W.F., Clough, M.P., & Almzroa, H. (1998). The role and character of the nature of science in science education. In W. McComas (Ed.), *The nature of science in science education: Rationales and strategies* (pp. 3–39). The Netherlands: Kluwer Academic Publishers.

Mead, M., & Metraux, R. (1957). Image of the scientist among high school students: A pilot study. *Science, 126,* 384–390.

Meichtry, Y.J. (1992). Influencing student understanding of the nature of science: Data from a case of curriculum development. *Journal of Research in Science Teaching, 29,* 389–407.

Metz, K. (1995). Reassessment of developmental constraints on children's science instruction. *Review of Educational Research, 65,* 93–127.

Meyling, H. (1997). How to change students' conceptions of the epistemology of science. *Science and Education, 6,* 397–416.

National Assessment Synthesis Team. (2003). *Looking at America's climate.* Retrieved July 15, 2006, from http://www.usgcrp.gov/usgcrp/Library/nationalassessment/overviewlooking.htm

National Research Council. (1996). *National science education standards.* Washington, DC: National Academic Press.

Popper, K.R. (1963). *Conjectures and refutations: The growth of scientific knowledge.* London: Routledge.

Rubba, P., & Anderson, H. (1978). Development of an instrument to assess secondary school students' understanding of the nature of scientific knowledge. *Science Education, 62,* 449–458.

Sagan, C. (1997). *The demon-haunted world: Science as a candle in the dark.* New York: Ballantine Books.

Shamos, M.H. (1995). *The myth of scientific literacy.* New Brunswick, NJ: Rutgers University Press.

Sheehan, W. (1988). *Planets & perception.* Tuscon, AZ: The University of Arizona Press.

Sodian, N.B., & Wimmer, H. (1987). Children's understanding of inference as a source of knowledge. *Child Development, 58,* 424–433.

Songer, N., & Linn, M. (1991). How do students' views of science influence knowledge integration? *Journal of Research in Science Teaching, 28,* 761–784.

Stauffer, G. (1999). Cornucopia of ice core results. *Nature, 399*(6735), 412–413.

Taylor, M. (1988). Conceptual perspective-taking: Children's ability to distinguish what they know from what they see. *Child Development, 59,* 703–718.

Taylor, M., Cartwright, B., & Bowden, T. (1991). Perspective taking and theory of mind: Do children predict interpretive diversity as a function of differences in observers' knowledge? *Child Development, 62,* 1334–1351.

Tobias, S. (1990). *They're not dumb, they're different: Stalking the second tier.* Tucson, AZ: The Research Corporation.

Wilson, E.O. (1992). *The diversity of life.* Cambridge, MA: Harvard University Press.

Winchester, I. (1993). "Science is dead. We have killed it, you and I"—How attacking the presuppositional structures of our scientific age can doom the interrogation of nature. *Interchange, 24,* 191–198.

Zupo, S. (1993). Constructing dichotomous keys. In L.R. Sanders (Ed.), *Favorite labs from outstanding teachers* (Vol. 2; pp. 8–9). Reston, VA: National Association of Biology Teachers.

INDEX

A

Alampay, D. A. 222, 224–225
Analyze (analyzing, analysis) 4, 7, 20, 48, 58, 85, 92, 181, 185, 194, 267
Aristotle 23, 167, 171

B

Bassi, Agostino 54
Bias(es) 16–17, 267, 271
Body of knowledge 14, 15, 18, 19, 20, 21, 33, 42, 43, 59, 69, 94 110,
    135, 150, 162, 175, 185, 194, 214, 230, 234, 264, 268
Brahe, Tycho 24
Brown, Michael 170
Bugelski, B. R. 222, 224–225

C

Cavendish, Henry 189
Celsius, Anders 188, 189
Chadwick, James 104, 105, 106, 107, 108
Classify (classifying, classification, classifications) 11, 20, 142, 161, 166,
    167, 169, 171, 172, 173, 174, 175, 176, 178, 166–179, 234,
    242–243, 264, 269–270
Conclude (concluding, conclusions) 3, 6, 7, 11, 22, 32, 33, 34, 41, 64,
    68, 73, 74, 83, 84, 85, 92, 99, 103, 106, 108, 110, 119, 127, 154,
    184, 187, 192, 194, 211, 214, 226–227, 229–230, 269
Consensus 64, 66–67, 85, 89, 108, 214
Controlled 55, 57–58, 84, 92–93
Courtillot, Vincent 90
Crick, Francis 56

D

Dalton, John 100–101, 106
Darwin, Charles 126, 128, 267
De Roberval, Gilles 212
Democritus 100, 106
Dependent variable 84, 93, 182, 184, 185, 186, 187
Descriptive 93
Dobzhansky, Theodosius 214

E

Einstein, Albert 16, 108
Experiment (experiments) 83, 85, 92, 130, 180, 181, 182, 184, 185, 187,
    189, 267, 269
Experiment, definition 182
Experimental 7, 15, 23, 93, 183, 185
Experimentation (experimenting) 4, 8, 11, 14, 18, 20, 55, 83, 84, 93,
    130, 180, 234, 239, 241–243, 264, 267, 269

F

Fabri, Honoré 212
Facts, definition 126
Fahrenheit, Daniel Gabriel 188, 193

Feynman, Richard 15, 16, 17, 19, 21
Framework(s) 7, 11, 18, 33, 204, 213, 222, 229, 268–269
Framework, interpretive 202, 204, 207, 211, 213–214, 222, 224, 230,
    234–235
Framework, perceptual 206, 215, 224, 225, 228–230, 265, 268
Franklin, Rosalind 56

G

Galilei, Galileo 211, 213
Gamow, George 224
Global climate change 223, 229
Goodall, Jane 25, 30
Gould, Stephen J. 126

H

Hero of Alexandria 136
Hertzsprung, Ejnar 244
Hoyle, Fred 224
Hubble, Edwin 224
Huygens, Christiaan 213–214
Hypothesis (hypotheses, hypothesized, hypothesizing) 2, 4, 6, 7, 10, 20,
    82, 83, 84, 85, 92, 93, 104, 182, 183, 184, 185, 186, 242, 243,
    267–267, 269
Hypothesis, definition 182, 183

I

Independent variable 84, 182–187
Indirect (indirectly) 99–100, 103–104, 106, 107, 109
Inference, activities 47–59, 64–68, 73–78, 84–93, 106–109, 119–121,
    127–134, 136–137
Inference, definition 6–7, 40–41, 48, 64–65
Inquiry 180–185, 195
Interpret (interpreted, interpreting, interpretation, interpretations) 6, 11,
    48, 74–75, 83, 89–91, 107–109, 204, 206, 209, 213, 221–223, 225,
    228–229, 235, 243, 265, 267, 268–269, 271
Intuition 235–239, 247–248, 265, 267–268
Ivory-billed woodpecker 17

K

Kahneman, Daniel 236

L

Lavoisier, Antoine 115, 118
Law (laws) 7–9, 11, 14, 20, 36, 113–14, 116, 119, 121, 124, 126, 132,
    150–151
Law, Boyle's 115, 118
Law, Charles' 115, 118
Law, Ideal Gas 114–115, 118
Law, in everyday use 2, 117, 119, 121, 126
Law of Conservation of Mass and Energy 118
Law of Conservation of Matter 115–116, 118
Law of Independent Assortment 115, 118
Law of motion, Newton's First 114, 118, 131, 266

Law of Motion, Newton's Second 131, 132
Law of Segregation 115, 118
Law of Superposition 113, 115–119, 121, 123
Law of Tube Strings 124, 130, 131, 140
Law of Universal Gravitation 189
Law, Ohm's 115, 118
Law, scientific, definition 113, 123, 126; 131
Law, scientific, examples of 115
Laws, Mendel's 115, 118
Laws of Motion 6, 115, 118
Laws of physics 121
Lemaître, Georges Henri 224
Lyell, Charley 267

M

Malthus, Thomas Robert 267
Measure (measuring, measurements) 18, 20, 23, 25, 31, 109, 183, 184,
    189, 190–200, 234, 242–243, 251, 265

N

Nature of science, definition 234–235, 263–268
Nature of science, how to teach 10–11, 93, 268–271
Nature of science, key concepts of
    Based on empirical evidence 4–6, 9, 11, 16–17, 19, 20, 22, 24, 36, 41,
        94, 122, 264, 269
    Influenced by Culture 5, 9, 156–157, 161
    Nature of Theories and Laws 7, 9, 11, 119, 121–122, 127–128,
        134–135, 202, 214, 225, 228–229, 265–267, 269
    Role of Background Knowledge 81, 89–91, 94, 108, 109, 221,
        264–265, 267–269, 271
    Role of creativity 7, 9, 19–20, 81, 85, 88–89, 93–94, 100, 106–109,
        176, 178, 195, 243, 265, 267
    Role of observation/inference 4, 6–7, 11, 22, 24, 33–34, 36–44, 45–62,
        69, 84, 106, 108–110, 122, 135, 203, 205, 225, 256, 265–266, 269
    Role of Perceptual Frameworks 7, 9, 23, 222–225, 228–230, 234–235,
        264, 268–269
    Subject to change see Nature of science, tentative
    Subjective 7, 9, 85, 154, 162, 171, 174–176, 178, 188, 190, 194, 198,
        201, 222, 225, 229, 236, 265, 267
    Tentative 4–6, 8, 10, 19–20, 24, 69, 84, 100, 106, 110, 121–122, 171, 175,
        185, 190, 193–194, 198, 201, 203, 225, 230, 256, 264–265, 267–271
Nature of science, students' conceptions of 1–2, 13, 14
Nature of science, why teach 1–3, 8–9, 14, 268, 271
Newton, Isaac 266

O

Observation, activities 26–33, 37–42, 47–59, 61–62, 64, 64–68, 70–71,
    73–78, 84–93, 106–109, 119–121, 127–134, 136–137
Observation, definition 22–26
Observational studies 7, 181–183, 267

P

Pattern (patterns) 6, 7, 11, 25, 114, 122, 142, 143, 144, 145, 146, 147,
    148, 149, 150, 151, 152, 153, 154, 160, 162, 166, 175, 214, 242, 266
Penzias, Arno 224
Perceptual set 221, 223
Pickering, William 170
Pluto 170, 229
Popper, Karl 148, 182
Predict (predicting, prediction, predictions) 3–7, 11, 18, 20, 83, 119, 127,
    130, 143, 150, 183, 242–243, 264, 269
Pseudoscience (pseudoscientific) 8, 24, 82

R

Raup, David 90
Reason (reasoning) 225, 229–230, 235, 237–239, 242, 247–248, 265
Russell, Henry Norris 244–245
Rutherford, Ernest 102–104, 106–108

S

Sagan, Carl 17, 91, 239
Scientific method 1, 7–8, 11, 13, 81–85, 88, 92–95, 265, 267, 269
Set of methods/processes 18–21, 33, 42–43, 59, 69, 94, 110, 135, 150,
    162, 175, 185, 194, 214, 230, 234, 265
Shermer, Michael 24
Skeptical, (skepticism) 7, 9, 239, 265, 268
Snow, John 54
Stedl, Todd 106
Steno, Nicholas 115–118, 121

T

Thomson, J. J. 101–103, 106–108
Theory (theories) 2, 4–5, 7–9, 11, 20, 25, 36, 54, 68, 113–114, 124, 127,
    136, 150–151, 171, 174, 211, 214, 224, 228, 234, 239, 254, 264,
    266–268
Theory, Asteroid Impact 90
Theory, Atomic 100–101, 128
Theory, Big Bang 224, 229
Theory, Germ, of Disease 54–55, 128
Theory, Global Climate Change 223
Theory, in everyday use 2, 124–126
Theory, Heliocentric 25
Theory, Kinetic Molecular 114, 126, 128, 266
Theory, Miasma, of Disease 55
Theory of Evolution 171, 174, 214
Theory of Gravity 16
Theory of Natural Selection 93, 126, 128, 267
Theory of Plate Tectonics 128, 150, 214, 229
Theory of Population 267
Theory of Relativity 16, 118, 132
Theory, scientific definition 126–127, 134
Theory, scientific, examples of 128
Theory, Tube String 124

U

Urban heat islands 223

V

Van Gogh, Vincent 244
Viète, Francois 189

W

Watson, James 56
Way of knowing 18–21, 33, 42–43, 59, 69, 94, 110, 135, 150, 162, 175,
    185, 194, 214, 230–246, 264–265, 268
Wegner, Alfred 128
Whitaker, R. H. 179
Wilson, Edward O. 166
Wilson, Robert Woodrow 224
Woese, C. R. 179